China's
New Role
in Africa

China's New Role in Africa

Ian Taylor

LYNNE
RIENNER
PUBLISHERS

BOULDER
LONDON

Paperback edition published in the United States of America in 2010 by
Lynne Rienner Publishers, Inc.
1800 30th Street, Boulder, Colorado 80301
www.rienner.com

and in the United Kingdom by
Lynne Rienner Publishers, Inc.
3 Henrietta Street, Covent Garden, London WC2E 8LU

Hardcover edition published in 2009 by Lynne Rienner Publishers, Inc.

ISBN 978-1-58826-736-8 (paperback : alk. paper)
LC 2008021841

Printed and bound in the United States of America

The paper used in this publication meets the requirements
of the American National Standard for Permanence of
Paper for Printed Library Materials Z39.48-1992.

5 4 3 2 1

Contents

Tables

Acknowledgments

This study is based on fieldwork, interviews, and archival research I conducted in Botswana, Cape Verde, Eritrea, Ethiopia, The Gambia, Mauritius, Namibia, Nigeria, Senegal, Sierra Leone, South Africa, Uganda, Zambia, Zimbabwe, China (Beijing and Hong Kong), London, and Washington, DC. I would like to thank the British Academy, the Carnegie Trust for the Universities of Scotland, the Chiang Ching-kuo Foundation for International Scholarly Exchange, the Russell Trust, and the Taiwan Foundation for Democracy for their generous support of my work.

Marc Lanteigne, my colleague at the University of St. Andrews, has been extremely supportive, and his insightful reading of early drafts of this study was valuable. Padraig Carmody of Trinity College, Dublin; Barry Sautman of the Hong Kong University of Science and Technology; Lucy Corkin and Sanusha Naidu of the University of Stellenbosch; and Zha Daojiong of Peking University have also been very encouraging. In addition, both Pang Zhongying of Nankai University and He Wenping of the Chinese Academy of Social Science were helpful in explaining various facets of Sino-African ties. Not least, I am also very grateful to Shu Zhan, the Chinese ambassador to Eritrea, who gave up a substantial amount of his time to talk to me frankly about the politics of China's African ties.

My thanks go as well to all those who helped me with my research at the UK Foreign and Commonwealth Office and Department for International Development and at the US State Department. My brother's facilitating access to various British diplomatic posts around Africa was particularly helpful. Thanks, Eric.

Back in 1994, when I began studying Sino-African relations at the University of Hong Kong, the literature on the subject was sparse. I would like to acknowledge Deborah Brautigam and Philip Snow for bringing the topic to light before it was fashionable to do so. No doubt they had to endure the same question I did: why bother studying China's ties with Africa? I hope the answer is now apparent.

In the course of my research I have had the privilege of visiting a number of institutions. In particular, I would like to acknowledge the assistance provided by staff members of libraries at the University of Botswana, the University of Cape Town, the Centre of Asian Studies at the University of Hong Kong, the University of Mauritius, the Mbarara University of Science and Technology, the University of Namibia, Fourah Bay College at the University of Sierra Leone, the University of Stellenbosch, the University of the Witwatersrand, the University of Zambia and the National Archives of Zambia, and the University of Zimbabwe and the National Archives of Zimbabwe. I would also like to acknowledge access to the libraries at the School of Oriental and African Studies in London, the University of Edinburgh, and the University of St. Andrews.

I first aired the ideas in this book during seminars at the University of Nottingham, Goodenough College, the University of Glasgow, the University of Plymouth, Queen's University in Belfast, the University of Warwick, the US State Department, Johns Hopkins University, Centro di Alti Studi sulla Cina Contemporanea, Università degli Studi di Napoli L'Orientale, the Mbarara University of Science and Technology, the University of Stellenbosch, and the Hong Kong University of Science and Technology. I am grateful to the participants for their advice. Any errors remain my own.

I would especially like to thank my wife, Joanne, and my two children, Blythe and Archibald (the Wee Archie), for their love and inspiration. I dedicate this book to them.

—*Ian Taylor*

China's Africa Policy in Context

The increase in China's economic and political involvement in Africa is arguably the most momentous development on the continent since the end of the Cold War.[1] The People's Republic of China (PRC) is now Africa's second most important trading partner; though behind the United States, it is ahead of the United Kingdom, with Sino-African trade hitting US$55.5 billion in 2006 (*People's Daily,* January 30, 2007) and approximately US$74 billion in 2007 (Fundira, 2008). Comparing those figures to the estimate for 1997, when China was doing US$5 billion worth of official trade with Africa, one can appreciate the rapid rise in economic activity, although in fact Sino-African ties are long-standing (Taylor, 2006a). Furthermore, a senior economist at the Chinese Ministry of Commerce predicts that trade between China and Africa will top the US$100 billion mark in the next five years (*China Daily,* January 13, 2006). Apart from the flurry of articles in the popular media "discovering" the topic, the burgeoning relationship has been particularly well illustrated by two events: the summit of the Forum on China-Africa Cooperation (FOCAC) in Beijing in November 2006 and the annual meeting of the African Development Bank (ADB) in Shanghai in May 2007. These followed the early 2006 release of an official White Paper by Beijing, titled *China's Africa Policy,* which lays out in general terms the contours of China's official policies toward Africa.

At both events, the Chinese leadership was enthusiastic in showcasing its country's engagement with Africa and publicizing what it habitually describes as a relationship that "has always been based on mutual benefits and win-win results" (*Xinhua,* May 15, 2007). In contrast, critics have claimed that, for the most part, Africa is exporting oil and other raw materials to China while importing cheap manufactured Chinese goods—an exchange remarkably similar to that of the colonial era.[2] Indeed, the accusation that China is a new colonizing power, exploiting Africa's natural resources and flooding the continent with low-priced manufactured products while turning a blind eye to its autocracies is at the core of most critiques of China's current engagement with Africa (Tull, 2006; Taylor, 2007a). Among the accusers are senior politicians in both the West and Africa. For instance, Karin Kortmann, parliamentary state secretary in the German Development Ministry, has declared, "Our African partners really have to watch out that they will not be facing a new process of colonization" in their relations with China (*Guardian*, November 16, 2006); in December 2006, South Africa's President Thabo Mbeki warned that "the potential danger . . . was of the emergence of an unequal relationship similar to that which existed in the past between African colonies and the colonial powers. China can not only just come here and dig for raw materials [but] then go away and sell us manufactured goods" (*Business Day*, January 6, 2007). Meanwhile, African newspapers talk of whether "Africa might be China's next imperial frontier base" (*East African Standard*, January 8, 2007). In response, Chinese academics such as He Wenping aver that "China's behavior in Africa is no worse and, on balance, probably better than that of the West" (He Wenping, 2007: 29). This book seeks to examine the evidence and arrive at some conclusions regarding the validity of such competing claims.

Chinese engagement with Africa is long-standing (see, for instance, Duyvendak, 1949; Ismael, 1971; Larkin, 1971; Filesi, 1972; Ogunsanwo, 1974; Hutchison, 1975; Bermingham and Clausen, 1981; Gao Jinyuan, 1984; Snow, 1988; Han Nianlong, 1990; Taylor, 2006a; and Sautman and Yan Hairong, 2007). In contrast to the past, Chinese ties with Africa are now generally based on the cool realities of trade and profit in keeping with *Jianshe you Zhongguo tesede shehuizhuyi* or "socialism with Chinese characteristics" (Deng Xiaoping, 1985). Official trade between Africa and China began to accelerate noticeably around 2000 and between 2001 and 2006, when Africa's exports to China rose at an annual rate of over 40 percent, from US$4.8 billion in 2001 to US$28.8 billion in 2006 (Wang Jianye, 2007: 5). Sub-Saharan Africa accounts for the vast majority of Sino-African trade, and it is on sub-Saharan Africa that this book focuses. Most of the expansion in trade is driven by a desire to obtain raw materials and energy sources for China's ongoing economic growth and for new export markets. While of benefit to some African economies and actors, the nature and political repercussions of such trade need to be discussed.

Indeed, as we've already suggested, Chinese expansion into Africa has not been met with universal acclaim. Although the Chinese are agreeable to expanding economic and political relations with poor and frequently volatile African states anxious for foreign direct investment (FDI), their methods are sometimes at odds with official Western policies regarding governance and development.[3] The resulting censure and criticism have had an interesting impact upon Beijing's foreign policies toward Africa, as will be detailed in this volume.

Even though ties between Beijing and sub-Saharan Africa go back decades, the exponential increase in China's trade with sub-Saharan Africa since 2000 means that the solidified Sino-African relationship is still at an early stage.[4] The repercussions of China's sustained, in-depth political and economic involvement toward the end of broad-based development in Africa have yet to be ascertained.[5] As of this publication, the picture appears mixed. There are instances in which China's role in Africa is clearly positive and appreciated (Sautman and Yan Hairong, 2007); conversely, there are instances in which Beijing plays an equivocal role, one that arguably threatens to unravel some of the progress Africa has made on issues of good governance and accountability.[6] As of 2008, Beijing's role in Africa—like that of all other foreign actors—is diverse, and its effect on the continent varies widely, depending on local economic and political circumstances.[7] To reiterate, a balanced appraisal of China's engagement in Africa is the aim of this volume. It is thus particularly important to contextualize and discuss both Beijing's foreign policy and the evolving political economy of the PRC. Relatedly, the diverse nature of both China and sub-Saharan Africa warrants prompt consideration if we are to develop a coherent picture of what is going on.

▒   Which China?

It is commonplace in the literature on Sino-African ties thus far to refer to "China." Although the label may make sense heuristically, it potentially obfuscates which processes are unfolding and why.[8] Ontologically, "China" is increasingly problematic, as it is less and less plausible to speak of the area it ostensibly covers as some sort of monolithic entity (Brown, 2007). For instance, in a globalizing world, China's foreign-economic policies are put into practice by an increasingly diverse set of actors under pressure from a wide variety of interest groups and constituency demands (Zhang Yongjin, 2005). As Shaun Breslin (2007: 61) notes, however, "some non-China specialists still seem somewhat surprised to discover that [China] is not a monolithic political structure with all power emanating from Beijing."

Although we might agree that the nexus between economic growth and national security has gained prominence in China since the mid-1990s (Wang Zhengyi, 2004), the reality of contemporary China and the ways in which power is exercised there complicates the linkage (Wu Guoguang, 2005). If we were to summarize what Chinese foreign policy is, we might connect it to the key domestic concern of the Communist Party of China (CPC), namely "promoting China's economic development while maintaining political and social stability" (Sutter, 2008: 2). This connection reflects a process whereby the CPC has changed from a revolutionary party grounded in class struggle and mass mobilization to a ruling party, with its attendant focus on order and security (Zheng Shiping, 2003: 54).

Domestically, the post-Mao Chinese state has arguably been based on "an unwritten social contract between the party and the people, where[by] the people do not compete with the party for political power as long as the party looks after their economic fortunes" (Breslin, 2005a: 749; see also Meisner, 1999); meanwhile, "foreign policy that sustains an international environment supportive of economic growth and stability in China serves these objectives" (Sutter, 2008: 2; see also Nathan and Ross, 1997). One way this policy is articulated is through the promotion of China as a responsible great power *(fuzeren de daguo),* a state that operates according to international norms and within multilateral institutions.[9] This image is reinforced by the official concept, initially proposed by Zheng Bijian at the 2003 Bo'ao Forum for Asia (Zheng Bijian, 2005), of China's "peaceful rise" or *heping jueqi* (Guo Sujian, 2006; Pan Chengxin, 2008). The expression was promptly endorsed by China's fourth-generation leadership, appearing both in Premier Wen Jiabao's speech at Harvard University in December 2003 and in President Hu Jintao's address at the forum commemorating Mao Zedong's 110th birthday (Zha Daojiong, 2005a). Because some observers have focused on the inevitability of China's "rise" rather than its "peaceful" character (such concern predates the phrase; see Overholt, 1993), the concept was recast as "peaceful development" *(heping fazhan)* as a means to reassure other countries about Beijing's intentions (Glaser and Medeiros, 2007), although the issue of rising nationalist emotions within China continues to cause alarm in some quarters (Wang Fei-ling, 2005; see also Gries, 2005).[10] In fact, Beijing's policymakers seem to be going out of their way not to alarm the world about China's rise, their stated policy now merely to build a "moderately prosperous society in all respects" *(xiaokang shehui)* along technocratic lines, according to the Scientific Outlook on Development or *kexue fazhan guan* (Hu Jintao, 2007).

According to Liu Guoli (2006), China's "deep reform" requires a peaceful international environment whose maintenance is central to Beijing's current diplomacy. This goal fits with the strategy to "go global" *(zouchuqu),* which encourages Chinese corporations to invest overseas and play a role in international capital markets (see Hong Eunsuk and Sun Laixiang, 2006; Gu, 2006). It also reflects the argument that globalization forces countries such as China, which are competing for foreign investment, to maintain peaceful, stable markets (Liu Guoli, 2004). In short, there is a growing awareness regarding the interconnectedness of the international and domestic settings, which is illustrated by the slogan *yu guoji jiegui,* or "linking up with the international track" (Wang Hongying, 2007). However, the situation is not always *heping* or "win-win" *(shuangying)* despite its portrayal by Beijing. As one informant put it, there are obvious limits to "mutual benefit" due to the widely different levels of development between China and Africa as well as within Africa.[11] Additionally, Chinese compliance with international norms depends on the issue and its context (Wang Hongying, 2007). Furthermore, there is an antihegemonic aspect to the promotion of mutualism, one that either helps generate a support constituency (Taylor, 2006a) or serves to undermine the domination of the United States (Breslin, 2007). These are intrinsic parts of the *heping fazhan* hypothesis. Yet the ability to make effective decisions about and—probably more crucial—implement such a policy is complicated by the growing plethora of interests struggling for attention and influence.[12]

Central government ministries as well as provincial and municipal bureaucracies all have input, while state-owned enterprises (SOEs) now have to be sensitive both to general government policies and proclamations and to the profit motive.[13] Although the central government may have a broad Africa policy, it has to be mediated via the economic interests of private corporations and the political motivations and aspirations of local state officials who, with growing autonomy, may not share the enunciated central vision (Pearson, 1999). A form of "fragmented authoritarianism," whereby policy made at the center becomes ever more malleable to the organizational and political goals of the different parochial and regional agencies entrusted with enforcing policy, is a reality in contemporary China (Lampton, 1987; Lieberthal and Oksenberg, 1988; Lieberthal and Lampton, 1992; Lieberthal, 1995). Throw into this mix the facts that commercial organizations in China are ever more centered on profitability (see Naughton, 2007) and that the numbers and types of actors within the fragmented-authoritarianism framework have increased dramatically, and the decreasing willingness of many Chinese actors to perform activities willy-nilly at the behest of Beijing becomes clear.[14]

Meanwhile, a new and still-changing combination of forces has been remaking Chinese foreign policy, a development intimately linked to the reform era (Lampton, 2001). There now exists "a more pluralistic range of Chinese decisionmakers whose diverse interests are reflected in foreign policy and behavior"; they "represent a variety of government, party, and military bureaucracies, government-affiliated and nongovernmental think tanks, and provincial and local governments" (Sutter, 2008: 58). Competition and compromise with respect to policy formulation is now the norm at all levels of government as the policy process has become more open, facilitating greater, more proactive input from various agencies rather than the former reactive version.[15] Although the role of the paramount leader continues to be significant, one informant has asserted that, in general, policy direction is increasingly open to advice from academics and business associations and that China's policies toward Africa are becoming more nuanced as a result.[16] Other academics interviewed in Beijing in September 2007 and February 2008 concurred that there was greater receptivity to policy counsel, although Chinese capacity in African Studies was held to be weak.[17] Consultations using internal reports, conferences, and public policy debates, as well as policy NGOs all now take place (Zhao Quansheng, 2006; Leonard, 2008). As Robert Sutter notes (2008: 60), "Among key administrative actors consulted in . . . decisionmaking are the Ministry of Foreign Affairs, the Commerce Ministry, the *Xinhua* news agency . . . and components of the PLA [People's Liberation Army] dealing with intelligence, military exchanges, and arms transfers." The International Department of the Chinese Communist Party (CCP/ID) has also played a role in some foreign policy matters (Shambaugh, 2007; Zhong Lianyan, 2007).

Interestingly, Chinese think tanks are playing a larger role in policy formulation across a range of issues (Glaser and Saunders, 2002; Tanner, 2002; Leonard, 2008) and foreign policy is no exception, with the China Institutes of Contemporary International Relations (CICIR), China Institute of International Studies (CIIS), China Institute of International Strategic Studies (CIISS), the Chinese Academy of Social Sciences (CASS), and others all serving a function (Shambaugh, 2002a; Zhao Quansheng, 2005; Liao Xuanli, 2006). These organizations are obviously not independent by Western standards, but under Hu Jintao's leadership, pluralism does appear to have increased, as the CPC seeks new ideas and new solutions rather than simply relying on sources that justify already-held beliefs or policies. Although there are clear limits to what can be said within the Chinese political system (Zhao Quansheng, 2005), greater receptivity to new ideas is in evidence.

However, "a weak link" is also in evidence, one that concerns "the problems regarding implementation of policy choices. It is here that the Chinese state reveals itself as a bargainer and negotiator" (Narayanan, 2005: 463). Bates Gill and James Reilly (2007) identify an array of actors supposed to oversee policy, illustrating the complexity of contemporary China's engagements abroad. For instance, the State-owned Assets Supervision and Administration Commission (SASAC) either own or have controlling shares in SOEs. Thus, SASAC "has a clear incentive to maximize value and profit in China's SOEs, even if these companies' pursuit of profits ends up damaging China's broader diplomatic or strategic interests in Africa" (Gill and Reilly, 2007: 42). Alongside SASAC, the Ministry of Commerce and Ministry of Foreign Affairs (MFA) play a role. But it must also be pointed out that the Ministry of Commerce and the SOEs have provincial and city as well as national offices, each with their own often divergent interests (Oi and Walder, 1999). Given that provincial SOEs make up nearly 90 percent of all Chinese companies investing overseas, center-provincial tensions—long a problem within the domestic polity (Goodman and Segal, 1994; Breslin, 1996a; Goodman, 1997)—clearly have the potential to play out abroad, further complicating policy coherence. A 2007 report, however, suggests that the central government is aware of these issues, as "several recent initiatives by SASAC specifically and [the] central government more generally appear aimed at reestablishing central government authority over the crème de la crème of SOEs" (Mattlin, 2007: 44). The development of such initiatives is something to scrutinize in future.

At the same time, some of the pathologies associated with the post-Maoist liberalization regime, such as an inattention to environmental safeguards and workers' rights (see Ogden, 1995; Teather and Yee, 1999; Tubilewicz, 2006; Wang and Wong, 2007), are being replicated abroad as Chinese corporations increasingly operate outside of China, notably in Africa.[18] In China itself, companies habitually dodge environmental and labor regulations liable to impede the profitability of any given venture, either by colluding with local state officials interested in encouraging economic growth or by graft (Sun Yan, 2004). Either way, violations of environmental law and hazardous conditions for workers are the norm in much of China. It can therefore be no surprise that similar circumstances develop overseas.[19] Since the central state cannot control such problems within China, it is doubly unlikely to regulate what myriad Chinese actors do in Africa. In other words, "the interests of Chinese corporations and their supporting bureaucratic agencies [in] the Chinese government may conflict with the interests of other Chinese government bureaucratic actors also engaged in Africa" (Gill and Reilly, 2007: 44).

Even with regard to ostensibly strategic arms of government, policy coherence has its limitations. For instance, Beijing has as of this publication been incapable of enforcing a geographical division of labor on the main national oil companies, namely the China National Petroleum Corporation (CNPC), the China Petroleum and Chemical Corporation (Sinopec), and the China National Offshore Oil Corporation (CNOOC). The result is overlap and competition among China's national oil companies, even though they are all ostensibly central to Beijing's energy-security policies. All three corporations possess subsidiary companies and have independent seats on their executive boards, meaning that various agendas are often pursued (Jiang Wenran, 2005). There is arguably little in the way of a unified strategy to secure an entrée into specific oil and gas fields; in some instances, national oil companies have even bid against one another—as when CNPC and Sinopec vied against each other for a pipeline project in Sudan.[20] Indeed, "the [national oil companies] view one another as rivals, competing not only for oil and gas assets but also for political advantage. The more high-quality assets a company acquires, the more likely it is to obtain diplomatic and financial support from the Chinese government for its subsequent investments. This is especially true for CNOOC, which does not have as much political clout as CNPC and Sinopec" (Downs, 2007: 50). This interfirm competition is normal in the capitalist West but sheds a more unexpected light on "China Inc." (Fishman, 2006) and its presumed oil strategy in Africa. There is in fact growing pressure on Chinese actors abroad to unify their thinking *(tongyi sixiang)* so as to avoid policy incoherence and ensure that "going global" serves China's domestic priorities (Glaser, 2007).

The central state has acted more forcefully with respect to the construction industry, at times compelling Chinese building companies to deliver projects in Africa at a loss as a means to advance wider national interests. Deng Guoping, general manager of the China Road and Bridge Corporation in Ethiopia, has stated that he is "instructed to slice projected profit margins so thin—about 3 [percent]—that losses are inevitable, given perennial cost overruns in Africa.

Western businesses, by contrast, typically paid bids with projected profits of 15 [percent] and more. . . . 'We're a government company and the Chinese government wants us here building things,' he says" (*Sudan Tribune*, March 30, 2005). However, this is not the only story, and a clash of interests often leads to corporate attempts to maneuver around government directives and/or recoup losses by going into businesses not sanctioned by the central government.[21] This can result in "an increasing set of tensions and contradictions between the interests and aims of government principals—the bureaucracies based in Beijing tasked with advancing China's overall national interest—and the aims and interests of ostensible agents—the companies and businesspeople operating on the ground in Africa" (Gill and Reilly, 2007: 38–39). In an environment where corrupt networks have arguably been able to infiltrate and take over some Chinese state institutions (Shieh, 2005), discussing "China's" ability to control piracy, unethical business practices, or even low-level arms sales abroad becomes even more problematic (as Chapters 3 and 5 further attest).

In short, bureaucratic interests, domestic politics, corruption, and other pathologies of China's capitalist development, as well as the increasing diversity in Beijing's foreign-policy procedures, all coalesce to undermine the notion of a unitary Chinese state relentlessly pushing forward a single agenda, in Africa or elsewhere.[22] Domestically, while state capacity to enforce policy continues to erode (Wright, 2007) competition among state agencies, even bureaus within single municipalities, is relentlessly increasing, as detailed case studies have demonstrated (Duckett, 1998; Zhang Jianjun, 2008). In Catherine Boone's estimation,

> the capacity of the center to administer, monitor, and enforce national policy in the provinces and localities—and presumably to overcome local resistance to central directive—remains limited, and arguably even diminished, over the course of the 1990s. Local despotisms, fiefdoms of personal rule, maverick localities, and entrenched interests at the local level compete against each other, and sometimes against central actors, via means both fair and foul. Some of these problems were laid bare during the SARS (severe acute respiratory syndrome) crisis in the spring of 2003, when center-provincial tensions, apparent breakdowns in official chains of command, and perverse incentives that encouraged local officials to cover up local problems were on full display. (2004: 230)

Such difficulties are not restricted to the domestic sphere; they are often—and increasingly—reproduced abroad, as various chapters in this book make clear.

The idea of the strategic use of economic relations by Beijing as a means of achieving power-politics objectives (see, e.g., Kurlantzick, 2007) thus needs to be treated with caution. It is important not to overestimate the degree to which the Chinese state has been able to control and direct the evolution of its international economic relations.[23] Indeed, economic liberalization has made it ever-more complicated for state authorities to identify exactly what Chinese firms and entrepreneurs are doing outside of China.[24] The behavior of the three main national oil companies is one thing—although, as we have noted, they are not as monolithic as perhaps presumed—but the large number of small, often private, traders is something quite different.[25] The notion that their actions are in some way representative of the Chinese state, or an element of some grand Chinese strategy, is far-fetched.[26] Yet despite the ongoing liberalization process and the concomitant diversity of Chinese actors and interests overseas, studies are remarkably likely to refer to a unitary "China" with a single set of interests.[27] Part of this book's aim is to examine how "evidence from Africa suggests that the Chinese government is now struggling to address tensions arising from . . . internal contradictions" (Gill and Reilly, 2007: 45)—and to consider how this struggle plays itself out in Africa.

▓ Which Africa?

When talking of "Africa," we are required to generalize even as we recognize that each state in Africa is different and, as a consequence, that the way in which Chinese engagement with any particular African country will always be contingent on the latter's political economy.[28] In this sense, discussing "Chinese" engagement with "Africa" has its limitations. Having said that, we cannot deny that in a good many African countries, power is a function of patrimonial power and not a representation of the sovereign will of the people. In other words, behind the façade of the modern state, power in many African polities progresses informally between patron and client along lines of political reciprocity; it is intensely personalized and is not exercised on behalf of the public. In being reflexive about which states we are discussing, we arguably avoid the dangers of generalization.

Claude Ake (1991: 316) argues that "we are never going to understand the current crisis in Africa . . . as long as we continue to think of it as an economic crisis." Indeed, one of the fundamental problems in much of postcolonial Africa is that the ruling classes lack hegemony. The early years of nationalism saw an attempt to build a hegemonic project, but it quickly failed, collapsing into autocracy. Moral and political modes that transcend economic-corporate interests are generally absent; the ethicopolitical aspect that, in a hegemonic project, helps build economic configurations but also lends legitimacy, is lacking. As a result, the ruling classes express their domination and their modalities of governance via both the threat and the use of violence as well as the immediate disbursal of material benefits to supporters in neopatrimonial regimes (Bratton and van de Walle, 1994). Without these twin strategies—both inimical to long-term development and stability—the African ruling elites cannot rule: "The struggle for power has become so intense and so absorbing that it has overshadowed everything else, including the pursuit of development" (Ake, 1991: 318). Nonhegemonic rule often leads to despotism and unpredictability—the latter of course being anathema to capitalism. In fact, many African states are trapped in a cycle of underdevelopment, which stimulates societal conflict. As of 2008, it seems apparent that Chinese policymakers seem neither to realize this nor to understand the complexities of African politics, among them the fact that, when developing official state-to-state relations in Africa, they are often dealing with "quasi-states" (Jackson, 1993).

Within much of postcolonial Africa, ruling classes have been forced by their lack of hegemony to take direct charge of the state (Markovitz, 1987: 8). By the ruling classes, we mean political elites and top bureaucrats, the leading members of the liberal professions, the nascent bourgeoisie, and the upper echelons of state security forces. However, African leaders have relied on control and patronage rather than through building effective hegemonies. They control the state, but it is one their own practices often undermine and subvert. This dilemma springs from the reality that bureaucracies inherited from the colonial era have since been "transformed into far larger, patrimonial-type administrations in which staff were less agents of state policy (civil servants) than proprietors, distributors, and even major consumers of the authority and resources of the government" (Jackson and Rosberg, 1994: 300).

The nonhegemonic nature of much of Africa's ruling elites means that the state lacks the sort of autonomy that would allow reforms, make autocracy redundant, and create the soil in which liberal democracy might be nurtured (Carmody, 2007). Indeed, the modern state envisioned by donors and external actors is dependent upon the intrinsically bourgeois-liberal distinction between the public and the private, which in turn allows for the distinction between politics and economics. Yet the very kernel of politics in large parts of Africa is the absolute conflation of the public and the private spheres. Indeed, the state is the main battleground on which both political and economic domination can be not only achieved but exercised with no concern over its effect on the dominated.

Central to this scenario is the fact that, in most parts of Africa, class power is fundamentally dependent upon state power, and capturing the state—or at least being linked favorably to its leaders—is an essential precondition for acquisition and self-enrichment: "The absence of a hegemonic bourgeoisie, grounded in a solid and independent economic base and successfully engaged in a private accumulation of capital, has transformed politics into material struggle. . . . Political instability is . . . rooted in the extreme politicization of the state as an organ to be monopolized for absolute power and accelerated economic advancement" (Fatton, 1988: 34–35). Instead of a stable hegemonic project that binds different levels of society together, what we have in much of Africa is an intrinsically unstable, personalized system of domination. Absolutism reigns and power is maintained through patrimony, by means of the illegal commandeering of state resources. Corruption, not hegemonic rule, is the cement that keeps the system together, yoking the patrons to their predatory ruling class (Fatton, 1988: 36).

Clientelism is central to neopatrimonialism, with widespread networks of clients receiving services and resources in return for support. This fact is well understood and accepted in many African countries. Indeed, the system of personalized exchange, clientelism, and corruption is internalized and constitutes an "essential operating code for politics" in Africa (Bratton and van de Walle, 1997: 63). "Accepted as normal," this behavioral code is "condemned only insofar as it benefits someone else rather than oneself" (Clapham, 1985: 49). Indeed, many African countries possess what Olivier De Sardan (1999: 28) terms "a moral economy of corruption," whereby corruption is so commonplace it is construed as normal. De Sardan goes so far as to assert that it is inaccurate to describe various types of transactions in Africa as corrupt, since they have become a legitimized and routinized part of everyday life. However, he also notes that the forms of corruption that take place at the upper end of the sociopolitical spectrum—the spectacular theft and grand larceny of the Nigerian governors and Kenyan cabinet ministers, for instance—have not become normalized and still draw condemnation from the people.

Still, in general, the personalization of political power depends on the participants' understanding of well-defined roles that are less clearly understood by external actors. This accounts for the distinct naïveté external actors often exhibit in their dealings with large parts of the continent (Taylor, 2004b): "One of the most amazing things about the literature on development in Africa is how readily it assumes that everyone is interested in development and that when [African] leaders proclaim their commitment to development and fashion their impressive development plans and negotiate with international organizations for development assistance, they are ready for development and for getting on with it" (Ake, 1991: 319; see also Taylor, 2006b).

It has been argued that, in China, the party is the government and the government is the state, just as is the case in much of Africa. Thus the concept of politics in China is very similar to that in many African countries, and the Chinese have been accused of personalizing their political engagement with African leaders, hence reifying the extant neopatrimonial regimes.[29] For instance, Chinese officials in Namibia commissioned a Chinese translation of former president Sam Nujoma's hagiographical "autobiography," which was in practical terms a show of support for Nujoma's personality cult.[30] Similarly, China is famed for building presidential palaces and national stadiums across the continent. These gestures inflate the egos of many African leaders, creating in them an affinity for and sense of gratitude toward Beijing.[31] Not everyone, however, sees such investments as a good thing; as one informant put it, "our elites do not see the big picture and are happy to get some infrastructure built by the Chinese, which they can show off to the people as if they themselves have delivered it. However, they have no idea about how development is pursued or in fact have any real interest in this."[32] An official in Sierra Leone commented that "[many] Chinese infrastructure projects in Africa are for demonstration and are often built with little regard for sustainability or even suitability. They are also deliberately high-profile, such as national stadiums, ministry buildings, et cetera. But this is the fault of African governments who accept such things and think the Chinese must be devoted to them, when it is obvious what is going on."[33] In some ways, these sorts of personalized activities are similar to those in which the French, with their own policy of presidentialism and culture of personalization, engage.[34] In short, Beijing has been accused of seeking to exploit the personalization and informalization that are the hallmarks of politics in many African states.[35]

Problematically for the continent's development, resources obtained from the state or the economy are deployed as the means to maintain support and legitimacy in this system, with the concomitant effect that control of the state is equivalent to control of resources, which, in turn, is crucial for maintaining power. Control of the state serves the twin purposes of lubricating the patronage networks and satisfying the selfish desire of elites to enrich themselves, often in quite spectacular fashion. Greed is what lies at the heart of the profound reluctance of most African presidents to hand over power voluntarily and what causes many African regimes to end messily, often in coups. In most cases the democratic option is either absent or is not respected by the loser—the stakes simply are too high. Once one is out of the loop vis-à-vis access to state resources, the continuation of one's status as a Big Man and hence the ability to enrich oneself becomes virtually impossible. Politics in Africa thus tends to be a zero-sum game (Flanary, 1998).

The fact is that a hegemonic project that encompasses national development and a broad-based, productive economy is far less a concern for elites within African neopatrimonial systems (who may in fact oppose such notions) than is continued control over resources for the individual advantage of the ruler and his clientelistic networks. Paradoxically, "intense processes of class formation based on the struggle to the death between contending blocs to capture the state for the establishment of predatory rule and the utter dependence of African societies on external constellations of financial and military power have ultimately contributed to the decay of the African state" (Fatton, 1999: 4). The parts external actors such as Beijing play in this scenario must be carefully considered if they are not merely to reinforce some of the negative trajectories that have defined Africa's postcolonial history.

In simple terms, under a neopatrimonial system, the separation of the public from the private is recognized, at least nominally, and is certainly manifested in the symbols of the rational-bureaucratic state: there are flags, borders, governments, bureaucracies, and so on. These are what China's leaders generally encounter when they invite delegations to Beijing or visit Africa.

However, in practical terms, the private and public spheres are largely attached, and the outward manifestations of statehood are façades hiding the real workings of the system. This may prove a problem for Beijing as it attempts to craft coherent, long-term developmental relationships according to its stated foreign-policy goals in Africa, although short-term commercial exchanges of mutual benefit to African elites and Chinese corporations are evidently possible. In the critique of one informant, China's "Africa" is really an assortment of regimes.[36] This elision is a potential conundrum that we will return to in other chapters. Africa's role in Chinese foreign policy is what we turn to next.

▓ China's Africa Policies

Africa has been important for China since the late 1950s, when Chinese diplomacy began to emerge, in the aftermath of the Korean War, from the shadow of the Soviet Union (for a detailed history of Sino-African relations from 1949 to 2005, see Taylor, 2006a). During the early period of Sino-African interaction, China was ideologically motivated, providing support for national liberation movements as well as direct state-to-state aid, most noticeably for Tanzania (Yu, 1970 and 1975). Indeed, by the mid-1970s, China had a greater number of aid projects in Africa than did the United States.[37] However, as the socialist modernization program picked up under Deng Xiaoping from the late 1970s onwards, Chinese interest in the continent dwindled, although Chinese policymakers have always denied this was the case (see Taylor, 1997).[38] The retreat can in part be explained by the fact that

> Africa's failure to develop its economies efficiently and open up to the international market militated against Chinese policy aims, and the increasing extraneous role the continent played in global (read: superpower) geopolitics resulted in a halt to closer Chinese involvement. Essentially, Beijing not only viewed Africa as largely immaterial in its quest for modernization but also saw that the rationale behind its support for anti-Soviet elements in the continent was no longer valid. (Taylor, 1998a: 443–444)

However, three developments—one in Africa and the others in China— came together to stimulate the close involvement of China in Africa in the postmillennial era. Following the events in and around Tiananmen Square on June 4, 1989, Beijing underwent a major reevaluation of its foreign policy toward the developing world. While Tiananmen Square triggered a crisis, albeit temporary, in China's relations with the West, Africa's reaction was far more muted, if not openly supportive: "It was . . . our African friends who stood by us and extended a helping hand in the difficult times following the political turmoil in Beijing, when Western countries imposed sanctions on China" (Qian Qichen, 2005: 200). Angola's foreign minister, for example, expressed "support for the resolute actions to quell the counterrevolutionary rebellion" (*Xinhua,* August 7, 1989), while Namibia's Sam Nujoma sent a telegram of congratulations to the Chinese army (*Xinhua,* June 21, 1989). According to one commentator, "The events of June 1989 . . . did not affect the PRC's relations with the third world as [they] did with the Western world . . . what changed [was] the PRC's attitude toward the third world countries, which . . . turned from one of benign neglect to one of renewed emphasis" (Gu Weiqun, 1995: 125).

As a result, the developing world became a "cornerstone" of Beijing's foreign policy.[39] After 1989, the 1970s-era depiction of China as an "all-weather friend" (*quan tianhou pengyou*) of Africa was dusted off; in the postmillennium, such rhetoric is still deployed with vigor (Taylor, 2004a). This posture is a reaffirmation of the Five Principles of Peaceful Coexistence, formulated in 1954 to set out the guidelines for Beijing's foreign policy and its relations with other countries.[40] The Five Principles are mutual respect for territorial integrity; nonaggression; reciprocal noninterference in internal affairs; equality and mutual benefit; and peaceful coexistence. Thus Chinese policymakers are reasserting an old theme in Beijing's foreign policy.[41]

Another macroprocess facilitating Sino-African relations involved the increasing momentum of Africa's economic reform programs in the 1990s. Beijing officials began to believe that the macroeconomic situation in Africa was taking a favorable turn, with resultant opportunities for Chinese commerce.[42] This analysis was based on the assumption that African countries had adopted a set of active measures to hasten the pace of privatization, opening up international trade and reform based on bilateral and multilateral agreements. An implicit proposition was that African economies were beginning to copy China in its open-door policy.[43]

Beijing has sought to take advantage of these developments in Africa, officially encouraging joint ventures and economic cooperation at multiple levels. This move couples with the belief held by many Chinese manufacturers and entrepreneurs that the types of goods that they produce and sell (household appliances, garments, and other domestic products) potentially have immense value in Africa, where the economy is less developed than it is in Western nations and where the consumers are thus perceived to be more receptive to such inexpensive products.[44] That the domestic markets of many African countries are relatively small means that there is relatively little competition and hence that market share can be large even from day one of operations.[45] Additionally, both the Chinese government and Chinese companies perceive Africa to be rich in natural resources, particularly in crude oil, nonferrous metals, and fisheries.[46]

The third, related macroprocess is that China's rapidly developing economy in itself propels Sino-African trade. China's growth in recent years has been extraordinary and needs no rehearsing here. However, what is often overlooked in discussions of Sino-African relations is that the significance of China to Africa has to be appreciated in terms of Beijing's own development trajectory.[47] China's real economic growth—on average just under 9 percent annually for the last thirty years—has been grounded in export growth averaging over 17 percent. This figure is based on the fact that Chinese factories process and assemble parts and materials originating from outside of China (see Breslin, 2007). China's leadership depends on the continuation of this high-speed growth as, with the effective abandonment of Marxist ideology (Meisner, 1996; Misra, 1998), the only thing that lends de facto legitimacy to Communist Party rule is economic growth. However, the mounting saturation of China's export markets, combined with a rapid increase in the cost of importing raw materials into China (due in the main to China's own demand, which increases prices), makes Africa more and more important to China's economy.[48] Indeed, as the value of Chinese exports depreciates, Beijing has to maintain the growth of its economy by adding more Chinese "content" to its exports (*Business Day,* February 22, 2007). Getting hold of raw materials is integral to this strategy; Africa, with its natural resources, thus fits squarely into Chinese policy both foreign and domestic. Indeed, it would be difficult to overstate the importance of Africa to China's own development.[49]

Consequently, although maintaining strong links with Washington is also fundamental to Chinese foreign policy, Africa is becoming more and more important.[50] To reiterate, Beijing has often expressed concern about the rise of an unchallenged hegemon, namely the United States, and this concern implicitly shapes its discourse on "peaceful development." Chinese policymakers have maintained the opinion that, in the postmillennial international system, Beijing and the developing world must support each other and work together to prevent the overdomination by this new hegemon. The assertion that mutual respect for and noninterference in domestic affairs should underpin any new international order is fundamental to this stance (see Chapter 4), as is a policy of accommodation and equivocation toward Washington when deemed appropriate (Foot, 2006).

This position feeds into the long-held stance by Beijing that it is the leader of the developing world (formerly known as the third world).[51] On a trip to South Africa in early 2007, Hu Jintao remarked, typically, that although "Africa is the continent with the largest number of developing countries . . . China is the biggest developing country" (*Xinhua,* February 8, 2007). The theme of solidarity is familiar in Sino-African diplomacy, as is the refrain that, "as . . . is known to all, Western powers, not China, colonized Africa and looted resources there in the history" (*People's Daily,* April 26, 2006). Echoes former Chinese foreign minister Qian Qichen, "As developing regions that . . . once suffered the oppression and exploitation of imperialism and colonialism, China and the African countries . . . easily understand [one another's] pursuit of independence and freedom and . . . have a natural feeling of intimacy" (Qian Qichen, 2005:

200). Such sentiments are used to argue that "there is no . . . interest conflicts [*sic*] between China and African countries" (*People's Daily,* April 26, 2006). Whether there are in fact "interest conflicts" and how they manifest themselves are major topics of this book.

Paradoxically, as China's leaders increasingly integrate themselves into the global economy and start, however tentatively, to play by essentially Western rules—as is exemplified by Beijing's membership in the World Trade Organization (see Breslin, 2003)—they have simultaneously sought to strengthen political ties with various African countries, arguably (at least in part) as a defensive mechanism against Westernization if and when it should threaten influential domestic interests. This contradiction reflects the overall tension in Chinese diplomacy between engagement in and distance from the global order (Breslin, 2007; Lanteigne, 2008). This tension, combined with the notion that China seeks to "restore" its "rightful place" in world politics (Mosher, 2000; Scott, 2007) casting itself as a "responsible power" at the forefront of the developing world (Foot, 2001), is seen by many as a key influence on policy (Yong Deng, 2008). Certainly it helps explain the postmillennial developments in Sino-African diplomacy so graphically illustrated by the Sino-African forums held in 2000, 2003, and 2006.

▨ Forum on China-Africa Cooperation Ministerial Conference

The first forum met in October 2000 in Beijing and was attended by nearly eighty ministers from forty-four African countries. The second ministerial conference was held in Addis Ababa, Ethiopia, in December 2003, when the Addis Ababa Action Plan (2004–2006) was passed. The FOCAC summit and the third ministerial conference were held in Beijing in November 2006; the next ministerial-level FOCAC meeting will be held in Cairo, Egypt, in late 2009.

The initial meeting had three main objectives. One reflected Beijing's overall foreign-policy strategy, namely its declared aim of overhauling the global order and opposing perceived hegemony (Blum, 2003). Critics within China view this attempt at domination, dressed up as "globalization" *(qianqiuhua),* as detrimental to the autonomy and sovereignty of China, arguing that it needs careful management (Breslin, 2006). By extension, this perceived hegemony of the United States applies to the developing world. As then Chinese premier Zhu Rongji said at the forum, Sino-African ties would help "build up our capacity against possible risks, which will put us in a better position to participate in economic globalization and safeguard our economic interests and economic security." They would also "improve the standing of the developing countries in North-South dialogue so as to facilitate the establishment of a fair and rational new international political and economic order" (Embassy of the People's Republic of China in the Republic of Zimbabwe, 2000a).

Such a position is based on the belief that—as then minister of foreign trade and economic cooperation[52] Shi Guangsheng put it at the time—"when the new international economic order has not been established and countries differ considerably in economic development, the benefits of economic globalization are not enjoyed in a balanced way." Consequently, "developed countries are benefiting most from economic globalization; but the large number of developing countries are facing more risks and challenges, and some countries are even endangered by marginalization." Thus the global community should "give more considerations to the will and demands of developing countries" (Embassy of the People's Republic of China in the Republic of Zimbabwe, 2000a).

It's crucial to note that China's leadership is intensely suspicious of the West's promotion of human rights, regarding it as a Trojan horse by which the West might undermine Beijing.[53] Importantly, the perceived Western strategy of "peaceful evolution" (*heping yanbian*) being exercised on Beijing's political security has been cast—not unreasonably—as being analogous to regime change (Ong, 2007). This sees Western powers surreptitiously working to undermine CPC rule by advancing liberal capitalism and its attendant values system. The Chinese have long responded by depicting liberal conceptions of democracy and human rights (and, occasionally, of the environment) as the tools of neoimperialists advancing on both China and the developing world. This falls on many receptive ears in Africa at the elite level, a fact of which China's policymakers are not unaware, as we will see in Chapter 4. Indeed, Beijing has long managed to rely on the developing world's strength in numbers to evade international condemnation.[54] FOCAC likewise serves as a means by which Beijing can advance a position of moral relativism regarding human rights to a mostly sympathetic audience, consolidating its standing within African elite circles. The assertion made in the *People's Daily* (October 12, 2000) at the time of the first FOCAC that China and Africa "should . . . enhance their cooperation and consultation in multilateral . . . organizations in order to safeguard the interests of both" is a reflection of this concern. Hence the Beijing Declaration of the Forum on China-Africa Cooperation, released at the end of the meeting, stated that "countries that vary from one another in social system, stages of development, historical and cultural background, and values, have the right to choose their own approaches and models in promoting and protecting human rights in their own countries" (Embassy of the People's Republic of China in the Republic of Zimbabwe, 2000b). The declaration further claimed that "the politicization of human rights and the imposition of human-rights conditionalities" themselves "constitute a violation of human rights" and that the inclusion of good governance and respect for human rights as requirements for development assistance "should be vigorously opposed." Such statements were no doubt music to the ears of many of the African leaders who sat in the hall in Beijing, and all were arguably meant to promote an "alternative" global order.

The outcomes of FOCAC reflect the increased priority China's leadership places on Africa. The summit in late 2006 approved a three-year action plan to forge a "new type of strategic partnership," which included a pledge that China would double aid to Africa by 2009 (to reach about US$1 billion); set up a US$5 billion China-Africa development fund to encourage Chinese companies to invest in Africa; provide US$3 billion in preferential loans and US$2 billion in preferential buyer's credits to African countries; cancel all debt stemming from interest-free government loans that, by the end of 2005, had matured for thirty-one of the least developed countries (LDCs) most indebted to China (an amount estimated at around US$1.4 billion); further open China's markets to exports from African LDCs by increasing from 190 to 440 the number of products receiving zero-tariff treatment; train 15,000 African professionals and double the number of Chinese government scholarships given annually to Africans to 4,000; send 100 senior agricultural experts and 300 youth volunteers to Africa; and build thirty hospitals, thirty malaria treatment centers and 100 rural schools there (*Africa Renewal,* January 19, 2007). Bilateral loans are presumably separate. Whether any of the above will materialize remains to be seen.

Indeed, the capacity of the state to compel Chinese companies to invest in Africa or even open up its markets to Africa is limited by the threat of undermining domestic economic and political interests. Delaying transport once products reach China, warehousing them interminably, or even "losing" them are all curious possibilities for potential sabotage.[55] Having said that, symbolic diplomacy achieved with rhetorical flourish and backed by some actual headline-grabbing initiatives is, as with all other countries' foreign policies, integral to Chinese engagement with Africa. But what is especially important when discussing FOCAC is recognizing the growing economic imperatives that underpin Sino-African relations, a subject to which we will briefly turn.

▓ Sino-African Economic Interaction

As we have claimed, the legitimacy of the CPC's political system is based on its ability to sustain economic growth in the postmillennial era—one that is hampered by a long-term decline in domestic oil production (Taylor, 2006c). Chapters 2 and 3 discuss these issues in greater depth. As Chapter 2 demonstrates, China's policymakers are aggressively pursuing oil and other natural resources in Africa. China is currently the world's second-largest oil importer and the second-largest consumer of African resources. Indeed, the abundance of natural resources in Africa has led Beijing to seek long-term deals with

African governments that ensure continued access to all its raw materials and sources of energy. As China's national oil companies are excluded from the majority of Middle Eastern oil supplies, Beijing—determined to limit its vulnerability to the international oil market—encourages investment in Africa, courting states that the West has overlooked. This approach to securing access to African resources is what David Zweig and Bi Jianhai have dubbed a resource-based foreign policy, which by its very nature has "little room for morality" (2005: 31). Chapter 2 discusses some of the potential repercussions such policy may have for China's reputation on the continent.

China's interest in ensuring resource security and economic growth via involvement in Africa is by no means restricted to oil; it encompasses all natural resources. From copper investments in Zambia and platinum interests in Zimbabwe to fishing ventures in Gabon and Namibia, Chinese corporations have vigorously pursued the political and business elite in Africa, often sweetening the deals they make with incentives provided by the central government. One of the benefits of Chinese interest in African resources is that it has dramatically increased demand, revitalizing such commercial sectors as Zambia's copper industry.[56] However, the influx of capital into weak and authoritarian governments may also have adverse long-term consequences for Africa, as leaders may be tempted by their newly perceived economic security to neglect necessary reforms. Yet, as this book makes clear, such problems cannot be specifically associated with Chinese engagement with Africa; they are intimately linked to the state of the continent in general. Indeed, there is a real danger that "China" is being constructed as some sort of scapegoat for concerns that have very little to do with Beijing. As a source from within the African Union admitted in 2007, "Totalitarian regimes in Africa are the problem. If China was engaging with serious governments the relationship would be very different—and better."[57] One purpose of this book is to point out this reality and move the debate about Chinese involvement in Africa forward, beyond some of the more simplistic analyses offered thus far.

Granted, we must note that, with the exception of oil exports into China, Sino-African trade is generally lopsided in favor of Chinese exporters who are penetrating African markets with cheap household products. Critics charge such trade is doing little to encourage indigenous African manufacturing.[58] That said, it is the failure of African economies to industrialize and develop postindependence that has made them a natural target for Chinese exporters.[59] Referring specifically to one industry in Nigeria, one informant made a point that could apply to all industries across the continent: "The government is uninterested in investing in the petrochemicals industry, and so Nigeria has to import products from China and India [that] we could easily make ourselves."[60] These serious and complex issues are discussed in depth in Chapter 3.

At any rate, Chinese estimates of trade with Africa need to be treated with caution. The part played by Hong Kong as a transit point for Chinese imports and exports makes the official bilateral figures very dubious. A huge proportion of Chinese exports are routed through Hong Kong; whether they are counted as Chinese re-exports has an enormous bearing on trade statistics.[61] In addition, foreign-invested firms account for just over half of all Chinese trade, which means that much of Chinese trade is not actually "Chinese" at all, especially if we take into account domestic Chinese companies that produce under contract for export using foreign components. In fact, the majority of Chinese exports are produced by foreign-funded enterprises; many are joint ventures, but an increasing number are wholly foreign owned. In addition, "as Chinese producers can claim a 15 percent VAT [value-added tax] rebate for exports, there is an incentive for producers to overstate the value of exports or even to totally fabricate exports and sell them at home instead" (Breslin, 2007: 107). That any visitor to an African market these days will observe huge amounts of Chinese-made products on sale is not in dispute. The specific (and colossal) figures provided by Beijing regarding Sino-African trade, however, do need to be taken under caution.

■ China's Developmental Assistance

Another core, long-standing element of Beijing's strategy in Africa is development assistance (Brautigam, 1998). The 2006 governmental White Paper states that "the Chinese government encourages and supports competent Chinese enterprises to cooperate with African nations . . . on the principle of mutual benefit and common development" (*China's Africa Policy*, 2006: 5). Whether it has the capacity to do so is questionable; as of 2008, Chinese development assistance primarily consists of aid packages and investment by SOEs. Tremendous debt and low levels of FDI across Africa mean that Chinese investment and aid are both welcomed and needed in many countries. Yet they have had decidedly mixed effects.[62]

It is clear that, in distributing aid, China favors countries that are rich in resources, to the point of apparent disregard for potential political repercussions. It would be a "big mistake," in one informant's words, "to rely on China as the 'savior of Africa.' If a country is resource rich, China is useful, but otherwise, [it] cannot be counted upon, even for aid."[63] This assessment is probably unfair, but the US$2 billion in aid that China gave Angola in 2005 does illustrate how resource-driven policies elicit such condemnation.[64] After three decades of civil war, Angolan government officials were on the verge of accepting a loan package from the International Monetary Fund (IMF) that stipulated strict monitoring of the domestic situation of what was after all one of the most corrupt nations on the continent. However, in the face of an almost unconditional aid package from Beijing worth US$2 billion, the Angolan government rejected the IMF's offer in favor of China's, of which one of the few stipulations was the right to 10,000 barrels of oil per day. This arguably undercut the IMF's efforts at increasing transparency, although we should point out that in 2004, Standard Chartered, backed by a consortium of European banks that included Barclays and Royal Bank of Scotland, disbursed a loan of US$2.35 billion to Angola's state oil company, Sonangol. Repayments over five years were guaranteed based on future oil production (*Guardian,* June 1, 2005). In other words, the Chinese are not the only ones financing the corrupt regime in Luanda.[65]

However, the situation in Angola is by no means unique and thus it underscores concerns that Beijing is at times undermining opportunities to promote good governance. Supporting unlawful or despotic regimes has potential consequences not only for the African people but also for China's own legacy on the continent, for if these regimes are toppled, Beijing runs the risk of being branded as their ally and losing its access to the resources it had tried to secure (see Chapters 2 and 5). The continuation of bad governance is to both Beijing's and Africa's long-term disadvantage, as it sabotages the long-term possibilities of Sino-African economic links. There are, however, signs of evolution in Chinese thinking in this regard, as will be detailed in the following chapters.

In terms of FDI, Chinese corporations, unlike other (primarily Western) companies operating in Africa, are generally undeterred by risk, as they are state owned and therefore not accountable to investors, serving political interests instead.[66] However, as Chinese business dealings progress on the continent, their long-term effects are being questioned. Although the arrival of new actors on the continent who are eager to invest is largely positive, the possible downside is that the leaders of some African states may, in the quest for economic growth, dodge the political and economic reforms necessary to revitalize the continent.[67] And although China has forgiven billions in debt to African countries, further loan packages negotiated at unfavorable rates jeopardize both the strongest growth rates on the continent since independence and the benefits of the original debt cancellation.[68]

Meanwhile, China has made much of opening up its markets to Africa and places no tariffs on the twenty-five poorest African states. However, the huge supply of inexpensive Chinese goods pushes domestic goods out of the African market, as Chapter 3 shows. According to Sanusha Naidu and Martyn Davies (2006: 79), "African producers have been marginalized and displaced from the market because of the influx of cheap Chinese goods . . . their livelihoods will have been eroded by competition from cheap Chinese goods." And of course, despite Chinese claims that the opening of its markets to African goods is to the continent's economic benefit, the inescapable fact remains that, natural resources aside, Africa would have very few products of value to China's consumers even if it were able to export them in sufficient numbers, efficiently, and with the guarantee of satisfactory quality.[69]

An arguably positive aspect of Chinese investment for ordinary Africans is its focus on building infrastructure, a need that has largely been ignored by Western donors in recent years. This has considerable potential for good, according to one Western diplomat, as "China is able to build a railway before the World Bank would get round to doing a cost-benefit analysis."[70] This willingness to construct or repair infrastructure has to be appreciated. However, one of the criticisms leveled against Chinese investment in and loan packages to African states is that they often stipulate that contracts be awarded to Chinese companies.[71] Since Chinese aid often comes in the form of loans, not grants, leverage to insist on such provisions are robust. For example, the terms of the previously mentioned US$2 billion loan to Angola were that, in addition to the aforementioned oil rights, 70 percent of contracts must go to Chinese corporations. Chinese corporations are further accused of using cheap contract labor from China rather than employing Africans. These criticisms will be discussed in other chapters.

As of 2008, most Chinese aid is conditional, connected to the purchase of Chinese goods and services; around 69 percent of Beijing's aid funds are spent on Chinese equipment. That said, virtually all donors practice tied aid. For instance, about 60–75 percent of Canadian aid is tied, while the United States, Germany, Japan, and France still insist that a major portion of their money be used to buy products originating from their respective countries, according to a UN Economic and Social Council (ECOSOC) report (*Inter Press Service,* July 6, 2007). In countries with underdeveloped economies, Chinese engagement at least provides the capital and skills necessary for infrastructure building while supplying affordable products to the markets—actions that many Western donors could be accused of shirking.[72] And given that Africa desperately needs its infrastructure built, refurbished, and/or replaced, Beijing's construction companies are playing at least a partly positive role in Africa. Indeed, their investment of large amounts of money in infrastructure is arguably laying a solid foundation for Africa's future development—if managed properly by its leaders.[73] The World Bank has estimated that loans from the China Export-Import Bank to sub-Saharan Africa in the infrastructure sector alone amounted to over US$12.5 billion by the middle of 2006 (*China Daily,* July 17, 2007). (Since the mid-1990s, Chinese companies have been securing about 20 percent of all construction contracts in Africa under the aegis of the World Bank.)

Chinese companies with aid experience in Africa have an important advantage in securing contracts over other engineering companies in that they are prepared to undertake projects at very low tenders as a means to ensure future contracts. Once in country, these companies keep hold of equipment such as bulldozers and other apparatus, which greatly increases the competitive costing for postaid, commercial construction contracts.[74] Indeed, Chinese construction teams typically stay on in African countries once an aid project is completed in order to set up a branch office of their home companies.[75] The teams then go into business alone or launch joint ventures with local partners.[76] In short, many Chinese aid teams are spurred on by potential future profits.[77] Ministries, provinces, counties, and SOEs have all reorganized their foreign-aid offices to reap the benefits afforded by an upsurge in Sino-African relations and the projects it has engendered (even at the arguable expense of policy coherence from the macro perspective of the Chinese state).

▓ China as a Model for Africa?

Politically as well as economically, China has provided an alternate development model for African states in the eyes of many of their leaders.[78] According to Naidu and Davies (2006: 80), China poses "a refreshing alternative to the traditional engagement models of the West. . . . African governments see China's engagement as a point of departure from Western neocolonialism and political conditions." Concurs one Nigerian analyst:

> For some among Africa's contemporary rulers, China is living proof of "successful" alternatives to Western political and economic models. . . . For many of Africa's ruled, who are physically and intellectually exhausted by two decades of economic "reform" supposedly adopted by African governments but driven by Western governments, donors and the IFIs [international financial institutions], China represents the hope that another world is possible, in which bread comes before the freedom to vote. (Obiorah, 2007: 38)

Countering the West's promotion of neoliberal reforms in Africa, Chinese sources have argued that the imposition of an essentially Western ideology on African states is a form of neoimperialism.[79] In what has been termed the post-Washington consensus era (ostensibly a move away from hardcore neoliberalism toward sustainable and egalitarian growth) the search for a new developmental path is understandable (Fine, Lapavitsas, and Pincus, 2001), and China's model of development provides an appealing alternative for some. Joshua Cooper Ramo (2004) has called this pro-China perspective the "Beijing Consensus," consisting of three key parts: a commitment to innovation and constant experimentation instead of to one-size-fits-all neoliberal projects; a rejection of per capita gross domestic product (GDP) as the be-all and end-all in favor of equal concern for sustainability and equality in policymaking; and self-determination and opposition to international hierarchies. This model still reflects the neoliberal paradigm but possesses idiosyncratic facets. Although Chinese diplomats deny that they seek to export any model to Africa or elsewhere,[80] it is a fact that Ramo's ideas have been promoted within China, approvingly cited in *Xinhua* and elsewhere, and that Chinese academics see soft power as intrinsic to building Sino-African ties (see, e.g., Liu Yong, 2007).

Meanwhile, the Chinese leadership has been very politically dexterous in the way they court African leaders. This is notwithstanding a general disdain for Africans on the part of the Chinese, which has historically caused problems for Sino-African relations but which is now a taboo subject (Dikötter, 1992; Sautman, 1994). By holding political and business summits such as the various Sino-African forums and arranging state visits by high-ranking Chinese political officials, Beijing symbolically accords Africa equal diplomatic status with the dominant world powers. For instance, it has become a tradition that the first overseas visit that China's foreign minister undertakes each year is to Africa. For their part, African elites are deeply appreciative of being given the red carpet treatment whenever they turn up in Beijing. On a research trip to Beijing in September 2007 that coincided with a visit by Chad's president, I was impressed by the way the diplomatic occasion was covered in the media, where it received top billing, and by how the Chadian flag was prominently displayed around Tiananmen Square.

In contrast, when African leaders visit London or Washington, unless they are from South Africa, Egypt, or one of the few other states deemed important, they are barely afforded a few minutes and even then they are more likely to be admonished for their chronic failures in governance than they are to be toasted as dear friends or, more important, credible statesmen.[81] China's leadership realizes this and thus expends energy on massaging the egos of Africa's leaders. And it pays off. Beijing has been successful in gaining African support at institutions such as the United Nations (UN), where the vote of the African block has allowed China to block resolutions on domestic human-rights abuses (see Chapter 4). African support also helped Beijing in its campaign to host the 2008 Olympics; explained an official in Sierra Leone's ministry of foreign affairs, "In Africa we look after our friends and help them."[82]

Symbolic diplomacy, defined as the promotion of national representation abroad, has become an increasingly important component of Chinese foreign policy in Africa and elsewhere (see Kurlantzick, 2007). Thanks to the experiences of their own developing nation, Beijing's policymakers are very much aware of the importance of prestige projects in asserting the power of state leaders and thus have been involved in such large-scale undertakings as the construction of national stadiums all over Africa. This approach has proven beneficial to both the ruling elites in Africa, who view the results as symbols of regime legitimacy and power (which suitably impress the local populations), and to Beijing, as it demonstrates China's rising prominence.[83] By engaging in these kinds of projects, along with presenting aid packages and disseminating the notion that China may be a model for Africa, Beijing is very much asserting itself as an equal of Western powers as well as appealing to the African elite classes.[84] Indeed, Arif Dirlik (2006) surmises that the Beijing Consensus draws its meaning and appeal not from some coherent set of economic or political ideas it conveys à la Ramo, but from the alternative it offers to the version of statehood espoused by the US government, which those opposed to Washington and, by extension, the West can draw inspiration from. Shaun Breslin (2007: 2) concurs: "China's alternative path is partly attractive because of the apparent success of the experience of economic reform. Other developing states might also lean toward the Chinese way not just because China's leaders don't attach democratizing and liberalizing conditions to bilateral relations, but also because China is coming to provide alternative sources of economic opportunities (with no democratizing strings attached)."

However, Africa's intellectuals must consider with caution the notion that China offers a viable alternative model of development.[85] For one thing, "the appeal of China as an economic model" wielding soft power (Kurlantzick 2006: 5) overstates the ability of the leadership in Beijing to project and promote an alternative economic type (Yan Xuetong, 2006). Although the thought that economic liberalization can occur within an authoritarian political system might be appealing to some African autocrats, it has its limits, not least for the Chinese themselves in promoting such a message; indeed, China's support of authoritarian elites in Harare and Khartoum has already stimulated anti-Chinese feelings among African civil-society leaders. Furthermore, China's own sustained growth has taken place in a system without democracy or transparency and under a government that has generally shunned policy reforms promoted from outside. This scenario must seem attractive to those African leaders whose rule has no real legitimacy and who are tired of fending off criticisms from the IFIs and the wider donor community.[86]

Yet China's extraordinary economic growth has come about, at least initially, within the context of capable governance, in a region that is itself economically dynamic. Rapid economic growth without democratization, per the East Asian model, was most likely to occur only in a strong developmental state (Öniş, 1991; Evans, 1995; Clapham, 1996; Woo-Cumings, 1999; Leftwich, 2000); the case of China generally confirms this proposition (Ming Xia, 2000), though analysts offer certain caveats (Breslin, 1996b). But contrast East Asia with Africa. Though the strength of the Chinese state has declined somewhat as liberalization progresses (Wang Hongying, 2003), Beijing remains powerful and stable in ways that are beyond the ambition of most—if not all—current African leaders.[87]

Furthermore, the irony is that those who applaud alternatives to Western-dominated IFIs often—sometimes perhaps without realizing it—end up in a position that supports not only the authoritarian status quo in some African states but also the emerging leadership of China. Opposition to neoliberalism—which has considerable appeal—can result in the promotion not of social democracy or even Keynesian liberalism but illiberal authoritarianism. Even within China itself, as Zha Daojiong observes (2005a), there is debate as to whether the Latin American condition of social polarization, international dependency, and economic stagnation will be China's fate if appropriate policies are not implemented (see also Nolan, 2004). These debates often question the capitalist direction of Beijing's current course, again destabilizing the notion of a Chinese model (see Wang Chaohua, 2003; Wang Hongying, 2003; see also Fewsmith, 2001). Even if we disagree with Gordon Chang's forecast that collapse is inevitable (2002), we may grant that critiques of the "China miracle" (Wu Yanrui, 2003) seem to go overlooked by its advocates (Hutton, 2007; Shirk, 2007).

Besides, Martin Hart-Landsberg and Paul Burkett (2005) have demonstrated how market reforms in China have led inevitably toward a capitalist and foreign-dominated developmental path, with massive social and political implications that have yet to be fully determined (see also Hinton, 1991; Sharma, 2007). Even though a key criterion of capitalism—that is, private ownership of the means of production—is not wholly present in China, "profit motivation, capital accumulation, free wage labor, commercialization/marketization[—]in other words, economism (profitmaking, competition, and the rule of capital)[—]is gaining priority as the determinant driving force of societal development" (Li Xing, 2001: 161). This trend has generated social dislocations across the country and caused acutely uneven development between and among regions (Wang Shaoguang and Hu Angang, 2000), such that China's model begins to resemble either crony capitalism or gangster capitalism in the eyes of its critics (Holstrom and Smith, 2000). The rapid growth figures that have defined post-Mao China are arguably a function not of improved efficiency but of a systematic dismantling of the social benefits that facilitated significant levels of economic equality during the socialist-construction period (Hart-Landsberg and Burkett, 2005). China's transition to a liberal market system has been predicated on intensified exploitation of its own labor force (Harney, 2008), which has attracted a mass incursion of foreign corporations (Chossudovsky, 1986) aided by a cadre of compradors (Hinton, 1993). Ironically enough, given the Chinese economy's arguably excessive dependence on exports and FDI (around three-fifths of its exports and nearly all of its high-technology exports are manufactured by non-Chinese firms), foreign companies are routinely denounced within Africa as neocolonialists. In other words, the Chinese model for Africa, one which at least was initially predicated upon extraordinary dependency upon foreign capital, is now being touted by African intellectuals whereas a previous consensus seemingly cast dependency as the key variable for Africa's economic predicament. How such realities fit coherently is unclear.[88]

In "burying Mao" (Baum, 1994)—inherently a process of "smashing the iron rice bowl" (Hughes, 2002)—and "retreat[ing] from equality" (Riskin, Renwei Zhao, and Shi Li, 2001), the deterioration of the Chinese health system, high levels of unemployment, rocketing state debt, regional inequalities, and serious social dislocations across the country have all occurred (Weil, 1996; Chan, 2001; Besha, 2008; Hart-Landsberg and Burkett, 2007; Gao Mobo, 2008). Furthermore, when people speak of China as a model, it is actually only part of the nation they are interested in—namely the coastal and southern regions. The other part—"the central rural belt of poor peasant farmers, the underinvested western regions of Xinjiang, Ningxia, and Tibet, and the ailing industrial areas of northeastern China around Jilin and Heilongjiang provinces"—is overlooked (French, 2007: 105).

At the same time, China's economic revolution has deepened the contradictions of capitalist development in other countries, particularly in China's neighborhood but also elsewhere, and the pathologies associated with the post-Mao reforms are regularly played out wherever Chinese actors operate (which, again, has ironically enough started to produce anti-Chinese sentiment within Africa). Furthermore, in 2004 alone, disparate rural, ethnic, and economic tensions, often stimulated by stresses caused by liberalization, in China provoked 74,000 protests and riots involving more than 3.7 million people, according to China's own security minister, Zhou Yongkang (Keidel, 2006). Meanwhile, 0.1 percent of the households in China possess 41.4 percent of the country's total wealth (*People's Daily*, October 31, 2007; see also Goodman, 2008). Is this a model that any African society wishes to follow?

Arguably, the most we can say about China as a model is that a strong state with an overarching ideology, backed by elites dedicated to development but prepared to indulge in policy experimentation concerning subnational officials and social institutions, can stimulate growth. But that axiom is not specific to China—it applies to developmental state models in general, which Africa has long needed (Taylor, 2005a). As Randall Peerenboom (2007) points out, China is plainly following the patterns of its East Asian neighbors. Perhaps the idea that, in a strong state, authoritarian leaders may maintain control over policy and continue their patronage networks accounts for some of the receptivity of various African countries to the so-called Chinese model. But the key difference between China and Africa is that the former has promoted rapid (albeit uneven) development; with a few exceptions, the latter has not.[89]

▓ The Taiwan Factor

One aspect of Sino-African relations that has lost much of its purchase is the competition between Beijing and Taipei for diplomatic recognition. The search for status, or, more correctly, the desire to maintain status lies at the heart of the Republic of China on Taiwan's (ROC) foreign policy, particularly vis-à-vis its official state-to-state relations; its competition with Beijing for international legitimacy has been a feature of their relations since 1949 (Chen Jie, 2002). However, Taiwan has perpetually been constrained by China's success in marginalizing it on the world stage; as a result, Taiwan has had to satisfy itself with maintaining official state relations with small states.[90] All, with the exception of the Vatican, are in the developing world, including four in Africa (see Taylor, 2002a).

Since the early 1970s, Taiwan's position as a diplomatically recognized entity on the international stage has been weakening.[91] The process of de-recognition started approximately in 1970, when Canada and Italy established diplomatic relations with China; three subsequent watersheds clinched it. First was the admission of China to the UN General Assembly in October 1971; second was the termination of official ties with Taipei by Tokyo in late 1972; and third was the decision in 1979 by Washington, DC, to switch official bilateral ties to Beijing. Between 1971 and 1979, forty-six states came to recognize China instead of the ROC (Larus, 2006). The consistent policy of China is to obstruct Taiwan's relations with the world community and maintain that "China," including Taiwan, is governed by the CPC in Beijing, not the "renegade province" that is, in official parlance, the ROC government (see Taylor, 1998b).

Increasingly, Beijing has used its political and economic muscle to threaten that it will sever relations with any state that establishes or upgrades its relations with the ROC.[92] As a result, Taiwan has full diplomatic relations with only twenty-three countries as of June 2008, as Costa Rica shifted its allegiance to Beijing in June 2007 and Malawi followed suit on December 28, 2007. In Africa, Taipei's current allies are Burkina Faso, The Gambia, São Tomé and Principe, and Swaziland. No other country has been as isolated diplomatically as Taiwan, not even such "pariah states" as Israel or apartheid-era South Africa (Geldenhuys, 1990). Paradoxically, however, even as Taiwan has seen its official status drastically deteriorate over the last thirty years, it has continued to emerge as a major economic player on the global stage and as a democracy—the first ever in Chinese history.

Still, Beijing is able to pursue its aggressive policy against Taipei primarily because of its own ever-expanding economic and political clout. In particular, a seat on the Security Council of the United Nations (and the veto power that goes with it) is China's ultimate trump card, which it plays to dissuade other economically strong or ambitious nations from holding official relations with Taipei (Payne and Veney, 2001).

It is probably true that most Africans do not care much who the "real" China is or with whom official diplomatic ties should be established. In fact, most countries would probably opt for relations with both if it were possible.[93] However, the diplomatic competition is to Africa's advantage (see Taylor, 1998b), particularly insofar as African leaders can play the two Chinas against each other. Indeed, such manipulation has resulted in economic assistance for some countries at a time when the interest of other foreign powers in the continent has continued to decline. Since the 1960s, Taiwan has deployed aid as an inducement for maintaining or establishing official ties with Taipei. This has had the unfortunate effect of causing African countries to sell their recognition to the highest bidder. For instance, in 1996, Senegal switched—for the third time—from Beijing to Taipei to become the recipient of a generous aid package, as had been the case with the previous switches. Similarly, when The Gambia abandoned Beijing in July 1995, a US$35 million aid package awaited Banjul in reward. It was also reported that São Tomé stood to gain US$30 million over three years for recognizing Taipei in 1997—no small amount for a country with an annual GDP of around only US$45 million (see Taylor, 2002a). However, the discovery of oil around São Tomé's waters probably means that its ties with Taipei are approaching their end.

Taiwan is a generous aid partner of those countries who officially recognize Taipei. Yet its generosity has on occasion been exploited by certain African nations that have effectively held Taipei to ransom. A case in point is Niger, which dallied between the two Chinas in an obvious attempt at draw out extra money. In June 1992, Niger agreed to establish diplomatic relations with Taiwan. However, just before the Taiwanese ambassador designate was due to leave for Niamey, Niger suddenly went back on its word and announced it was sticking with Beijing. But the next day, Niger's prime minister contacted Taipei to contradict the announcement. A Taiwanese embassy was established in Niamey, and China departed, denouncing Niger's position. Taiwan immediately began funding medical and agricultural programs and assisted in extracting Niger's uranium deposits. However, this was not the end of the debacle; in 1996, Niger switched back to Beijing, complaining that aid promised by Taipei had not materialized (see Taylor, 1998b).

That one of the most advanced economies in the world was reduced to such an exercise as scrabbling for the favors of Niger (which has a per capita gross national product, or GNP, of less than US$300) illustrates Taiwan's lack of political power in the international arena. Taiwan has since become more circumspect in its dealings with prospective diplomatic partners; those countries seeking a payout from Taipei in return for recognition are likely to be disappointed.[94]

Pragmatically, Taiwan encourages the international community to stop looking at relations with Taipei and Beijing as an either/or matter. Instead, Taiwanese policymakers have adopted what they see as a nonideological and flexible approach to foreign policy. Their policies remain ambiguous vis-à-vis China (Hickey, 2007). On the one hand, Taipei insists that there is only one China, of which Taiwan is a part, and disavows any ambitions for the island's independence *(tai du)*. On the other hand, Taipei emphasizes that it is a sovereign state that should join the international community as an equal. Intricately linked to this contradiction is the ongoing democratization process whereby Taiwan moves toward a more pluralistic society (see Taylor, 2002a). This development has stimulated a whole gamut of new debates within Taiwanese society, including the fundamental question of how to define Taiwan, which have played themselves out in Taipei's foreign policy (Rigger, 2005). Yet as China's economic growth continues at an extraordinary pace, the overwhelming majority of African states are not prepared to risk Beijing's wrath by recognizing

Taipei. The biggest prize, South Africa, fell to China at the end of 1997, and the subsequent defections of Costa Rica and Malawi are indicative of the continuing trend.

▓ The Structure of This Book

The book opens with a discussion of Chinese activities in Africa's oil industries. As of 2008, Africa provides around a quarter of China's fast-growing oil needs, and oil and strategic minerals dominate the profile of Africa's exports to China. The most significant provider to Beijing is Sudan, which began its trade with China in 1996, but the PRC's state-owned oil companies are actively establishing a stake elsewhere as well. Other investments include chromium extraction and processing in Zimbabwe. The major oil companies—CNPC, Sinopec, and CNOOC—were rationalized in 1998 so that they could function more effectively in the global arena. Though they ostensibly operate according to a strategy set by Beijing, coordination seems to be a growing issue. Chinese oil diplomacy in Africa likely has two key aims: to lock in oil supplies to help provide for the Chinese economy's burgeoning energy needs in the short term, and to place Chinese corporations as players in the global oil market in the long term.

Although China's energy requirements have elevated prices and thus income for oil-rich African governments, its attitude of noninterference and its seeming indifference to what happens to the money—where it goes and how it does or does not facilitate development—is probably not helping Africa escape from its infamous "resource curse" (Meidan, 2006). Indeed, Beijing's noninterference policy, based on the stance that "foreign countries should only get involved in a country if invited to by the host state," means that the choices of the host state's elites are paramount.[95] Until and unless the elites themselves promote transparency and prodevelopment policies, no such governance standards will be adopted. In such a depredated milieu, the perpetual question will be: How might Africa engage with and exploit the increased engagement by Chinese companies in order to benefit ordinary people and promote development?[96] Given the average standards of governance in most resource-rich African states, the likely nature of such engagement is evident—and troubling. But it is ultimately a matter for Africans to decide themselves.

A key aim of Chinese involvement in Africa is resource security, but Beijing's entrepreneurs also seek commercial advantages. As China's economy has taken off, the search for more and more markets for Chinese exports has intensified. Africa is seen as a useful and profitable destination, and Chinese imports into Africa—mostly low-cost and low-quality goods—have taken over the marketplaces in most African countries, as any visitor will attest. Chapter 3 looks at how competition from Chinese manufacturers is impacting African industries, focusing especially on the effect Chinese textile exports have had on Africa's apparel industry and its own export competitiveness. Indeed, the impact on local economies of Chinese imports is becoming more and more apparent, leading to growing local resentment.[97] Concerns over unfair Chinese competition and the colonization of Africa by China are invariably linked to such imports. Critics might argue that effective dumping practices across the continent—of which many Chinese businesses stand accused—constitute an infringement of World Trade Organization (WTO) rules; China, they might add, should recognize that—with the exceptions of South Africa and possibly Mauritius—African countries generally lack the necessary technical and monetary resources to bring such issues before the WTO's dispute-resolution panel. As a Nigerian journalist observed, Africa is an easy target for Chinese exporters due to the meager controls on customs; African officials can very often be bribed to look the other way.[98] Beijing appears to recognize that the trade imbalance threatens to sour Sino-African relations—hence the decision, made at the 2006 FOCAC, to more than double the number of African products allowed into China duty free.

It is vital that any analysis of the effect cheap Chinese imports are having on Africa's manufacturing base—particularly the clothing and textile sectors—acknowledges that industries on the continent have been in decline for a long time. A key aim of Chapter 3 is to put Chinese exports to Africa into context and challenge the commonly held view that "China" is to blame for the difficulties of Africa's manufacturing industries. Instead, it cautions against making China a scapegoat for failings that are not Chinese in origin—while conceding that there are issues that need addressing.

Chapter 4 looks at the controversial issue of how the concepts of human rights and good governance fit into Sino-African relations. As we have mentioned, Beijing's relations with all foreign nations are grounded in the Five Principles of Peaceful Coexistence, which rule out interference in domestic affairs and elevates state sovereignty. Critics of Sino-African ties have often emphasized Beijing's no-strings-attached stance on human rights and governance. Clearly, many African states that benefit from Chinese support not only abuse their citizens' civil and political rights—the definition of which may, granted, depend on a Western orientation—but also undermine their economic and social rights, which is the aspect of human rights that Beijing emphasizes. Robert Mugabe's Zimbabwe is a case in point. The chapter suggests that if, while holding fast to the principle of engagement without interference, China actually makes things worse for some in Africa, then its argument that socioeconomic rights are more important for the poor in underdeveloped countries than are "abstract" political rights is potentially awkward, raising the possibility of exploitation by the continent's autocrats. Doing no harm, which is not the same as doing nothing, needs to be part of Beijing's broader African policy. Engaging without damaging is one of the greatest challenges China faces in its African diplomacy, although there are indications that it is beginning to do so, as the chapter details.

Chapter 5 examines another contentious issue in Sino-African relations—arms sales. Chinese arms exporters sell almost exclusively to the developing world, furnishing Africa with cheap defense equipment, much of it small arms. Like many other arms exporters, Chinese companies are cynical; for instance, they supplied both sides in the 1998–2000 border war between Ethiopia and Eritrea. High-level military exchanges between China and Africa are an ever-present feature of Sino-African ties, and Beijing has demonstrated that it is more than happy to supply weaponry to nations regarded by the West as rogue states, invariably invoking the principle of noninterference as its justification. As the chapter demonstrates, Chinese arms have found their way to military forces and police agencies in states that use them in flagrant violation of human rights, Sudan being the example *par excellence,* though not the only one. Furthermore, because the sales are mostly of small arms, control over their distribution or over the wider effect they have on a continent beset by conflict and instability is particularly problematic.

Although all arms exporters face justifiable criticism for their actions, what is especially troubling with regard to Beijing is its no-strings-attached attitude, such that Chinese exporters strike deals regardless of their clients' records on governance and human rights. In fact, cynics might aver that it is precisely the rogue regimes of Africa that provide China with a niche market. The palpable danger is that Beijing's supposed nonpolitical diplomacy simply camouflages its bottom line of profit and resource procurement, which arms sales to Africa possibly facilitate. Although an energy-for-arms link cannot be easily confirmed, the companies involved in arms shipments to Africa are state owned and ostensibly under the direct control of the State Council. Thus China's leadership cannot simply wave away questionable arms deals as the work of irresponsible factories beyond the control of Beijing. However, as the chapter also attests, China's leaders are aware that questions regarding the control of arms sales, particularly small arms, complicates their wish to be seen as responsible players in the global arena. This aspiration gives the international community opportunities to pressure Beijing concerning arms sales, particularly—though not exclusively—to Africa.

Chapter 6 is a study in contrast to the arguably irresponsible arms-sales policies of Chinese companies; it details China's growing role in peacekeeping on the continent. Beijing supports conflict resolution and peace operations in Africa in various practical ways, thus effecting a complete reversal of its previous, long-held policy against so doing. Since 1990, China has contributed over 7,000 peacekeepers to UN operations, and in mid-2007 more than 1,500 Chinese peacekeepers were serving on missions in places such as Democratic Republic of Congo (DRC), Liberia, and Sudan. As of 2008, in fact, China sends more peacekeeping troops abroad than any other permanent member of the UN Security Council (UNSC). China has also contributed financially to peace processes in Somalia and other places. As Chapter 6 further details, the number of Chinese military personnel sent on peace missions has been growing in recent years and is a major positive step in Sino-African relations. However, China's stance on peace operations is closely tied to its attitude on state sovereignty, which limits interventions. Studying how China's position on peace operations has changed, such that Beijing is taking on a greater and greater share of such operations in Africa, is thus a vital part of any wider analysis of Sino-African ties.

Chapter 7 wraps the book up by making the case for a balanced approach to China's intensifying relationship with Africa, avoiding the hysteria that has marked previous accounts and captured the imagination of the popular media, both in Africa and particularly the West. There are both positive and negative aspects to Sino-African ties as they appear in the 2000s, but Chinese policy toward Africa is constantly evolving, and since about 2005, Beijing has clearly been rethinking its policies toward so-called pariah regimes. Indeed, the book concludes that many of Beijing's interests in Africa ultimately coincide with those of longer-established partners; thus engagement with rather than opprobrium toward Beijing is a more realistic and advisable policy for the latter to adopt as they seek to come to terms with the growing Chinese presence on the African continent.

▓ Notes

1. Interview with Western diplomat, Abuja, Nigeria, September 3, 2007.

2. Interview with David Jabati, news editor, *Awareness Times,* Freetown, Sierra Leone, June 7, 2006.

3. Interview with Western diplomat, Abuja, Nigeria, September 3, 2007.

4. Interview with Chinese diplomat, Addis Ababa, Ethiopia, May 15, 2007.

5. Interview with Western diplomat, Abuja, Nigeria, September 3, 2007.

6. Interview with Sanusi Deen, national chairman of the Sierra Leone Indigenous Business Association, Freetown, Sierra Leone, June 7, 2006.

7. Interview with Western diplomat, Asmara, Eritrea, June 29, 2006.

8. Interview with Chinese academic, School of International Studies, Peking University, Beijing, China, September 20, 2007.

9. Interview with Chinese diplomat, Addis Ababa, Ethiopia, May 15, 2007.

10. Interestingly, the Foreign Languages Press in Beijing has started publishing a series of books titled *China in Peaceful Development,* seeking to prove that China has always been a peace-loving nation, even with regard to military strategy (see Huang Zu'an, 2007). However, this argument is undermined by the findings of Andrew Scobell (2003), who argues that a cult of defense within Beijing disposes Chinese elites to rationalize all military operations as defensive.

11. Interview with African Union official, Addis Ababa, Ethiopia, May 16, 2007.

12. Interview with Chinese academic, School of International Studies, Peking University, Beijing, China, September 20, 2007.

13. Interview with Chinese academic, School of International Studies, Peking University, Beijing, China, September 20, 2007.

14. Interview with Western diplomat, Abuja, Nigeria, September 3, 2007.

15. Interview with Chinese academic, School of International Studies, Peking University, Beijing, China, September 20, 2007.

16. Interview with He Wenping, Chinese Academy of Social Sciences, Beijing, China, September 18, 2007.

17. Interviews with Chinese academics, Center for African Studies, Peking University, Beijing, China, September 20, 2007; and School of International Studies, Renmin University, Beijing, China, February 21, 2008.

18. Interview with Western diplomat, Asmara, Eritrea, June 29, 2006.

19. Interview with an official in the Ministry of Agriculture and Food Security, Freetown, Sierra Leone, June 9, 2006.

20. Interview with Western diplomat, Asmara, Eritrea, June 29, 2006.

21. Interview with the acting head of the political-affairs section of the Chinese embassy in Windhoek, Namibia, August 13, 2006.

22. Interview with Chinese academic, School of International Studies, Peking University, Beijing, China, September 20, 2007.

23. Interview with British diplomat from embassy in Beijing, Hong Kong, November 12, 2006.

24. Interview with Pentagon official, Washington, DC, United States, April 5, 2007.

25. Interview with British diplomat, Addis Ababa, Ethiopia, May 15, 2007.

26. Interview with Western diplomat, Asmara, Eritrea, June 29, 2006.

27. Interview with Chinese academic, School of International Studies, Peking University, Beijing, China, September 20, 2007.

28. Interview with British diplomat, Addis Ababa, Ethiopia, May 15, 2007.

29. Interview with Henning Melber, Namibian political economist, Windhoek, Namibia, August 14, 2006.

30. Interview with Robin Sherborne, editor of Namibian political magazine *Insight,* Windhoek, Namibia, August 14, 2006.

31. Interview with David Jabati, news editor, *Awareness Times,* Freetown, Sierra Leone, June 7, 2006.

32. Interview with African Union official, Addis Ababa, Ethiopia, May 16, 2007.

33. Interview with an official in the Ministry of Agriculture and Food Security, Freetown, Sierra Leone, June 9, 2006.

34. Interview with Henning Melber, Namibian political economist, Windhoek, Namibia, August 14, 2006

35. Interview with Henning Melber, Namibian political economist, Windhoek, Namibia, August 14, 2006.

36. Interview with African Union official, Addis Ababa, Ethiopia, May 15, 2007.

37. Interview with Chinese diplomat, Addis Ababa, Ethiopia, May 15, 2007.

38. Interview with the acting head of the political-affairs section of the Chinese embassy in Windhoek, Namibia, August 13, 2006.

39. Interview with Wang Xue Xian, China's ambassador to South Africa, Stellenbosch, South Africa, February 13, 1998.

40. Interview with the acting head of the Political Affairs Section of the Chinese embassy in Windhoek, Namibia, August 13, 2006.

41. Interview with Chinese diplomat, Abuja, Nigeria, September 5, 2007.

42. Interview with Wang Xue Xian, China's ambassador to South Africa, Stellenbosch, South Africa, February 13, 1998.

43. Interview with Chinese diplomat, Addis Ababa, Ethiopia, May 15, 2007.

44. Interview with Xu Mingzheng, general manager of Sierra Leone Guoji Investment and Development Company, Freetown, Sierra Leone, June 8, 2006.

45. Interview with Chinese trader, Gaborone, Botswana, September 25, 2004.

46. Interview with the manager of a Chinese trading company, Massawa, Eritrea, July 1, 2006.

47. Interview with Department for International Development (DFID) official, Freetown, Sierra Leone, June 7, 2006.

48. Interview with African Union official, Addis Ababa, Ethiopia, May 15, 2007.

49. Interview with Ethiopian academic, Addis Ababa, Ethiopia, November 22, 2005.

50. Interview with Chinese academic, Center for African Studies, Peking University, Beijing, China, September 20, 2007.

51. Interview with Shu Zhan, Chinese ambassador to Eritrea, Asmara, Eritrea, June 29, 2006.

52. In 2003, the Ministry of Foreign Trade and Economic Cooperation (MOFTEC) was renamed the Ministry of Commerce after incorporating the former State Economic and Trade Commission and the State Development Planning Commission.

53. Interview with the acting head of the Political Affairs Section of the Chinese embassy in Windhoek, Namibia, August 13, 2006.

54. Interview with Western diplomat, Asmara, Eritrea, June 29, 2006.

55. Interview with an official in the State Department, Washington, DC, United States, April 5, 2007.

56. Interview with a government official, Gaborone, Botswana, September 25, 2004.

57. Interview with African Union official, Addis Ababa, Ethiopia, May 16, 2007.

58. Interview with David Jabati, news editor, *Awareness Times*, Freetown, Sierra Leone, June 7, 2006.

59. Interview with a journalist from the *Abuja Inquirer*, Abuja, Nigeria, September 3, 2007.

60. Interview with an official from the Business Round Table, Abuja, Nigeria, September 6, 2007.

61. Interview with British diplomat from embassy in Beijing, Hong Kong, November 12, 2006.

62. Interview with an official in the Ministry of Agriculture and Food Security, Freetown, Sierra Leone, June 9, 2006.

63. Interview with African Union official, Addis Ababa, Ethiopia, May 15, 2007.

64. Interview with Pentagon official, Washington, DC, United States, April 5, 2007.

65. Interview with British diplomat, Addis Ababa, Ethiopia, May 15, 2007.

66. Interview with Western diplomat, Abuja, Nigeria, September 3, 2007.

67. Interview with Saffie Koroma, National Accountability Group, Freetown, Sierra Leone, June 7, 2006.

68. Interview with British diplomat, Addis Ababa, Ethiopia, May 15, 2007.

69. Interview with Ethiopian academic, Addis Ababa, Ethiopia, November 22, 2005.

70. Interview with Western diplomat, Abuja, Nigeria, September 3, 2007.

71. Interview with Robin Sherborne, editor of *Insight*, Windhoek, Namibia, August 14, 2006.

72. Interview with Lucy Corkin, research manager, Centre for Chinese Studies, Stellenbosch, South Africa, July 31, 2006.

73. Interview with African Union official, Addis Ababa, Ethiopia, May 16, 2007.

74. Interview with Moses Pakote, deputy director of Investor Services, Namibia Investment Centre, Ministry of Trade and Industry, Windhoek, Namibia, August 11, 2006.

75. Interview with British diplomat, Addis Ababa, Ethiopia, May 15, 2007.

76. Interview with Moses Pakote, deputy director of Investor Services, Namibia Investment Centre, Ministry of Trade and Industry, Windhoek, Namibia, August 11, 2006.

77. Interview with Chinese diplomat, Addis Ababa, Ethiopia, May 15, 2007.

78. Interview with Ethiopian academic, Addis Ababa, Ethiopia, November 22, 2005.

79. Interview with Chinese diplomat, Abuja, Nigeria, September 5, 2007.

80. Interview with the acting head of the political-affairs section of the Chinese embassy in Windhoek, Namibia, August 13, 2006.

81. Interview with British diplomat, London, October 17, 2007.

82. Interview with Ibrahim Yilla, director of Asia and Middle East Countries in the Ministry of Foreign Affairs, Freetown, Sierra Leone, June 8, 2006.

83. Interview with an official in the Ministry of Agriculture and Food Security, Freetown, Sierra Leone, June 9, 2006.

84. Interview with Ugandan academic, Mbarara, Uganda, November 2, 2006.

85. Interview with Ethiopian academic, Addis Ababa, Ethiopia, November 22, 2005.

86. Interview with Saffie Koroma, National Accountability Group, Freetown, Sierra Leone, June 7, 2006.

87. Interview with a journalist from the *Abuja Inquirer,* Abuja, Nigeria, September 3, 2007.

88. Interview with Ethiopian academic, Addis Ababa, Ethiopia, November 22, 2005.

89. Interview with government official, Gaborone, Botswana, September 25, 2004.

90. Interview with Taiwanese diplomat, Banjul, The Gambia, March 31, 2008.

91. Interview with an official in the State Department, Washington, DC, United States, April 5, 2007.

92. Interview with Taiwanese diplomat, Banjul, The Gambia, March 31, 2008.

93. Interview with David Jabati, news editor, *Awareness Times,* Freetown, Sierra Leone, June 7, 2006.

94. Interview with Taiwanese diplomat, Banjul, The Gambia, March 31, 2008.

95. Interview with Shu Zhan, Chinese ambassador to Eritrea, Asmara, Eritrea, June 29, 2006.

96. Interview with Christopher Parsons, Ministry of Trade and Industry, Freetown, Sierra Leone, June 8, 2006.

97. Interviews with local market traders, Casamance, Senegal, April 3, 2008.

98. Interview with journalist, *Guardian,* Abuja, Nigeria, September 5, 2007.

Oil
Diplomacy | 2

The growing expansion of Chinese national oil companies into Africa's oil markets is perhaps the aspect of Sino-African relations that most concerns the international community.[1] It should be pointed out that although oil is a major and obvious source of China's economic interest in Africa, Chinese firms are actively seeking resources of every kind: copper, bauxite, uranium, aluminum, manganese, iron ore, and more. However, the issues surrounding oil are of particular interest to Western policymakers studying China's rise (Lyman, 2005; Roughneen, 2006). Indeed, although China and the United States do not rely on one another for energy supplies, the possibility that oil will be the subject of future disagreements between them is arguably high (Zha Daojiong and Hu, 2007) and thus has a bearing on much of the commentary on Sino-African energy policies. Certainly, there is concern that Beijing's procurement of energy supplies will pose a challenge to the global dominance of Washington (Ebel, 2005) at a time when levels of cooperation between the two governments on matters of energy are at best weak (Dreyer, 2007).

A look at Table 2.1 reveals that—with the exception of South Africa, whose industrial economy is well developed—Beijing's main African imports are from oil-producing states.

By the same token, as Table 2.2 illustrates, oil clearly dominates the profile of Africa's exports to China (around 70 percent). This perhaps explains why China's activities in the continent's oil industries have received so much publicity, much of it negative.

Consequently, this chapter explores a key facet of Chinese interest in Africa's resources—oil—along with some of the primary implications thereof.

Table 2.1   Top Five African Sources of Chinese Imports, 2004–2006 (in US$ millions)

	2004	2005	2006
Africa total	15,640.9	21,114.1	28,767.6
Angola	4,717.7	6,580.7	10,930.9
South Africa	2,955.3	3,443.6	4,095.3
Congo-Brazzaville	1,568.9	2,278.0	2,784.6
Equatorial Guinea	995.3	1,486.1	2,537.6
Sudan	1,705.5	2,614.7	1,941.4

Source: Morrison, 2007: 17.

Table 2.2   Composition of Sub-Saharan Africa's Exports to China, 1996–2005

	1996		2005	
Product	US$	%	US$	%
Food and live animals	30,510	2.7	111,265	0.6
Beverages and tobacco	55,244	4.9	130,675	0.7
Crude materials, except food, fuel	563,237	50.3	2,991,326	15.9
Mineral fuel, lubricants	278,530	24.9	13,302,923	70.9
Animal and vegetable products	94	0.0	2,576	0.0
Chemicals, chemical products	31,115	2.8	203,443	1.1
Manufactured goods	145,007	13.0	1,941,324	10.3
Machinery and transport equipment	6,948	0.6	66,893	0.4
Miscellaneous manufactured articles	8,544	0.8	8,868	0.0
Total	1,119,229	100.0	18,759,293	100.0

Source: Mwega, 2007: 4.

▨ China's Energy Needs

The image of China as a nation of bicycle riders is long gone. There are nearly 21.5 million privately owned cars in China, (*Xinhua,* January 9, 2008). What's more, projections for 2010 put the number of privately owned cars in China at 30 million. This growth in car ownership is directly linked to China's 2001 acceptance into the WTO (actively encouraged by Western politicians), which resulted in a reduction of tariffs on auto imports into China even as car-financing schemes backed by international vehicle manufacturers became available to Chinese consumers (Breslin, 2007: 97).

Such figures reflect the central government's ever-growing need to support its economy and, relatedly, to source greater and greater supplies of oil. In 2006, China's dependence on imported oil rose to 47 percent of annual demand, an increase of 4.1 percent since 2005 (*Xinhua,* February 28, 2007) that is expected to rise to around 60 percent by 2020 (*East-West Wire,* October 25, 2006). This energy-security profile represents a major change for China, where the Daqing oil fields in Heilongjiang province fed the economy's oil needs for decades, ensuring the nation's self-sufficiency until 1993. Since then, however, with exponential economic growth and a continuing decline in Daqing's supplies, Beijing has had to look elsewhere. Indeed, crude-oil output from Daqing is expected to fall by 7 percent per year until 2010, "signaling the fast-approaching demise of the country's largest field if new technology isn't found to revive production" (*Xinhua,* March 24, 2004). Overall, China's crude-oil output increased by 1.6 percent, while consumption of crude oil (i.e., the sum of net imports plus output), rose by 7.3 percent (*China Daily,* January 31, 2008). This is an acute problem that has become more and more pressing for energy policymakers (Zha Daojiong, 1999; Lam, 2006). Indeed, in November 2007, Beijing was forced to raise fuel prices by almost 10 percent in an effort to ease the country's worsening supply crisis. Yet at the same time, PetroChina reportedly discovered oil in the Qaidam basin of northwestern China, suggesting big reserves in the region (*Xinhua,* November 13, 2007). Uncertainties, fluctuations in oil supplies, and the constant search for new sources define Beijing's energy concerns.[2]

The rising need to import oil has massive implications for the global oil industry; the International Energy Agency predicts that by 2030, Chinese oil imports will equal current imports by the United States. China's demand for oil is projected to increase to 14.2 million barrels per day by 2025, according to the US Energy Information Administration, which claims, "As the source of around 40 percent of world oil-demand growth over the past four years, with year-on-year growth of 1.0 million bbl/d [barrels a day] in 2004, Chinese oil demand is a key factor in world oil markets" (Energy Information Administration, 2007). Indeed, if China's imports of oil rise, as projected, from 6.5 million barrels a day in 2008 to 14.2 million barrels a day in 2025, the increase will drastically affect both the availability and the global cost of crude oil.[3]

China's exceptionally robust economic growth in the 1990s and 2000s has stimulated the huge upsurge in its demand for oil: between 1995 and 2005, China's oil consumption doubled. As mentioned, in 1993 China became a net importer of oil, the only fuel that can fulfill China's growing transportation and industrial needs for the foreseeable future (Troush, 1999). To address the country's energy-security problems, the new Energy Leading Group, headed by Premier Wen Jiabao, has been set up within the Zhongnanhai government complex to formulate policies whose implementation is handled by the Energy Bureau, a subministerial body under the State Development and Reform Commission (*Asia Times,* June 3, 2005). However, reflecting on issues pertaining to state capacity introduced in Chapter 1, "energy experts doubt that these bodies have sufficient bureaucratic stature to craft and implement a coherent policy for energy security. They also note that the policymaking offices are understaffed and have routinely approached Chinese national oil companies for policy suggestions (when the offices are supposed to be developing national policy to regulate the activities of Chinese oil companies)" (Saunders, 2006: 26). There are also robust debates within China's energy-policy community, with proponents of a strategic vision competing with advocates of market approaches and/or "scientific development" to catch the ear of policymakers (Constantin, 2007). This conflict has further implications for policy coherence.

Experts identify five key ways Beijing seeks to lessen the pressure. One is increased energy conservation—which, "given the rapid economic growth in China and the associated increase in the demand for energy . . . will only moderate the growth in consumption of oil products" (Tjønneland et al., 2006: 27). The second is fuel switching—that is, reducing the dependence on imported fuels by switching to renewable energy and coal, of which China has large domestic reserves. The third involves an increase in domestic oil production, achieved by seeking out new resources and exploiting existing ones more efficiently. However, as we have already pointed out, this approach also has its limits and, at best, can only moderate the rise in China's dependence on imports. Fourth, the central government encourages national oil companies to increase purchases in international oil markets. And fifth, Beijing facilitates their acquisition of oil reserves abroad, which not only reduces the risk of oil shortages in the event of an extended interruption in supplies but also fits with Beijing's broader going-out policies including its efforts to internationalize the activities of the national oil companies and promote an "outward-looking oil economy." These began around 1995 (Christoffersen, 1999), although the first purchase of concession rights by a Chinese national oil company was actually made in 1993, when a subsidiary of CNPC purchased the Talara Block in Peru for US$25 million (Zha Daojiong, 2006: 180). It is the last two policies (buying on the international oil market and acquiring oil reserves abroad) that account, in the main, for Beijing's increased involvement in Africa's oil industry.

However, the ability of the central government to implement a coherent energy policy appears to be diminishing, which explains why the emphasis on external activism seems more energetic than that on the internal measures Beijing might pursue to lessen its energy crisis (Lam, 2006). Indeed, "it is essential to understand China's domestic energy structure in order to understand China's oil strategy and its hunting behavior in its quest for oil" (Yao Yuangming, 2006: 165). As Phillip Saunders puts it:

> Chinese policy on energy security illustrates the limits that competing bureaucratic interests and domestic political considerations can place on policy coherence. Chinese leaders clearly recognize the importance of energy security and have demanded active efforts by government ministries and Chinese national oil companies to secure energy supplies needed to support future growth. . . . However, energy security is an inherently difficult objective that requires coordinating domestic investments in energy production and transmission; domestic price and tax incentives to ensure adequate distribution and efficient use of scarce energy resources; foreign-policy efforts to provide

diplomatic support for access to overseas energy sources; financial efforts to provide resources to Chinese state-owned energy companies; and technological and infrastructure investments to build the capability to extract and transport energy to China in a usable form. (2006: 25–26)

Erica Downs (2007: 49) asserts further that "over the past two decades, the liberalization and decentralization of China's energy sector, which is part of the broader transition from a centrally planned to a market economy, has resulted in a shift of power and resources away from the central government toward the state-owned energy companies. Multiple bureaucratic restructurings have fragmented Beijing's authority over China's energy sector among many government agencies that are understaffed and underfunded."

The question of where to obtain oil, given the declining domestic supply, has increasingly vexed Chinese policymakers:[4] "Oil insecurity has become a major structural insecurity problem largely because of China's growing dependence on foreign oil" (Tang, 2006: 11; see also Lam, 2006). China's perceived energy insecurity is a matter of the availability, reliability, and affordability of oil from overseas (Zha Daojiong, 2005b). Chinese policy analysts have clearly linked energy security with the international political environment; considering the sense of vulnerability arising from China's dependence on foreign oil, they have identified the need to diversify sources of supply, launch pipeline projects, keep the Malacca Straits safe while planning for maritime oil transportation, build up a larger strategic reserve, and encourage oil companies to adopt the going-out strategy and engage in energy diplomacy.

But despite efforts to diversify, the bulk of China's oil imports come from the Middle East. In 2008, imports from the Middle East accounted for about 40 percent of China's total crude-oil imports (*China Daily*, January 17, 2008). The concentration on one geographic source is highly problematic. If oil supplies from the Middle East were disrupted due to heightened conflict or terrorist activity, for example, the implications would be grave. What's more, "the Middle East is in the United States' sphere of influence, and many Chinese strategists see Uncle Sam's military occupation of Iraq and its threat to attack Iran as part of its ambition to monopolize oil supply in the region" (*Asia Times*, February 28, 2007). Beijing has neither the means nor the intention to engage in open confrontation with Washington. However, it is concerned that oil could be used by the United States as a diplomatic weapon to exact leverage (Zha Daojiong, 2005b). This suspicion was heightened in 2005, when Congress stopped an endeavor by CNOOC (a company belonging to the China National Offshore Oil Corporation) from taking over Unocal Corporation, a US oil business, despite an inflated price offer. "This . . . intensified Chinese strategists' suspicion that Washington wants to use oil supply to contain China's development" (Zha Daojiong, 2005b: 51). Consequently, "the strategic question for Beijing is where Chinese oil companies can go to avoid either political or business obstacles, or both, put in place by the international community" (Zha Daojiong, 2006: 182). Ending its overreliance on Middle Eastern oil is thus a genuine geopolitical concern and a matter of national interest,[5] which Beijing is addressing by seeking out resources in other parts of the world, especially central Asia, the South China Sea, Russia, Canada, and Venezuela as well as Africa.

China's Oil Industry

China's oil industry has experienced significant restructuring as domestic needs have become ever-more pressing (Andrews-Speed, Dow, and Gao Zhiguo, 2000). The Chinese government rationalized most state-owned fuel operations in 1998, placing them under the regulatory oversight of the State Energy Administration. In the oil sector specifically, Beijing restructured two firms, namely the CNPC and Sinopec, both of which emerged as vertically integrated oil and petrochemical corporations with interests that stretched across the whole value chain. CNPC had mostly been involved in the exploration of oil and gas fields; its production (the upstream aspect of the industry) soon accounted for 66 percent of China's oil and gas output and 42 percent of its refining capacity. Sinopec, which had formerly focused on refining and delivery, made up 23 percent of oil output, 11 percent of gas output, and 54 percent of refining capacity (Nolan and Zhang, 2002: 21). Both companies are now major players in the world oil industry, more or less involved in all aspects of exploration and production. CNOOC, incorporated in 1982, conducts offshore exploration and production operations (see Jaffe and Lewis, 2002). All three companies continue to be state owned, although the administrative functions of CNPC and Sinopec have been divided from their business-management tasks.

The State Petroleum and Chemical Industry Bureau was established under the State Economic and Trade Commission to assume the administration functions of CNPC and Sinopec. Reflecting a relative openness to policy advice, the CIIS regularly brings academics together with business, military, and government leaders to devise strategies for the country; as a result, "Beijing has been encouraging representatives of state-controlled companies to secure exploration and supply agreements with states that produce oil, gas, and other resources" (Zweig and Bi Jianhai, 2005: 27).

According to Zha Daojiong (2006: 182), "It is hard to tell whether a particular overseas oil or gas venture is the result of the Chinese government directing its state-owned energy company or the domestic energy industry seeking diplomatic assistance from the government, since for over a decade China has lacked a central ministerial agency overseeing the industry." This dilemma further reflects the heterogeneity of contemporary China and the need for caution in talking of a "Chinese strategy" in Africa, especially with respect to sensitive areas such as energy. At best, we can say that there are certain tactics associated with China's national oil companies and their activities in Africa; obvious examples are the acquisition of foreign-energy resources via long-term contracts and of equity investments overseas in order to circumvent overreliance on the open global oil market through either actually acquiring stakes in Africa's oilfields or safeguarding access.[6] Africa is a prime site because, according to CICIR's Chen Fengying, "China confronts foreign competition. Chinese companies must go places for oil where [US] and European companies are not present" (*Washington Post,* December 22, 2004). Indeed, this is a central aspect of the national oil companies' strategy in Africa. Entering markets from which Western oil corporations are excluded (such as that of Sudan) is another important tactic.[7] Still another is to "link access to acreage [with] state-backed financial deals, where[by] acreage is provided in return for soft credit used to purchase Chinese goods and services" (Tjønneland et al., 2006: 30). This approach has been used in a number of African countries, including Angola and Nigeria, as we will see. Forming strategic alliances with the national oil companies of Angola, Nigeria, and Sudan in order to gain access to oilfields has also worked for Chinese corporations, as has outbidding competitors, though the latter "is a risky strategy, as it requires the oil price to remain high for the investments to be profitable" (Tjønneland et al., 2006: 30).

Arguably, Chinese companies saw the opportunities in Africa before other actors did. The latter's concern over the scale of China's activities on the continent[8] reflects the general ambivalence of many Western commentators about the rise of post-Maoist China as well as of other third-world nations such as India (Smith, 2007): "On the one hand, the desire to exploit the vast market that is developing in China is irresistible to global capitalists. On the other, they fear not only [China's] economic power, but the political and military might that is rapidly growing with it" (Weil, 2006: 23). The literature on modern China aimed at popular audiences echoes such fears; compare, for instance, James McGregor's *One Billion Customers* (2005) to *The Gathering Threat* by Bill Gertz and Constantine Menges (2005) and *The Coming China Wars* by Peter Navarro (2006). As the title suggests, the topic of Western confusion is central to Hugo De Burgh's *China: Friend or Foe?* (2006).

Criticism by Western sources is perhaps compounded by the very nature of the national oil companies. Because they are state owned, they are able to expand their activities in Africa even at the risk of paying over the odds in order to outbid competitors.[9] Consider the description by one analyst of such maneuvers:

> Chinese NOCs [national oil companies] . . . are not primarily answerable to public shareholders with short time horizons. They are not overwhelmed by fear of failure. Indeed, they have not had to face major commercial crises. Thus they can afford, or think they can afford, to take a more optimistic view

of technical, commercial, and political risks. Indeed, close support from the Chinese government may . . . lower the political risk in some countries. This lower level of perceived risk, combined with access to loans from state-owned commercial banks, will result in China's NOCs having a lower cost of capital than international oil companies. . . . At the same time, the company may be prepared to evaluate [its] projects with a higher projected oil price than the more conservative [international oil companies]. What is not clear from the outside is which examples of "overbidding" are the result of deliberate strategy and which are the result of inexperience. . . . [But w]here there is competition, the commercial drive of the NOC combined, in some cases, with active encouragement of the Chinese government will necessarily involve the Chinese NOC paying a relatively high price to acquire the target assets. (Xin Ma and Andrews-Speed, 2006: 9)

It is clear that China's national oil companies take the long-term view rather than the short-term view of private Western companies necessitated by considerations of profits and shareholders.[10] Xu Mingzheng, general manager of Sierra Leone Guoji Investment and Development Company, has suggested that Chinese companies are generally farsighted compared to Western companies constrained by shareholder demands of very high profit returns. In addition, management costs for Western firms are relatively high, while for Chinese companies they are much lower, as Chinese salaries are low. Chinese workers are also, according to Xu, prepared to go to places such as Africa and put up with the difficulties of working and living in tough conditions; Western workers are, by implication, not.[11] Thus China's corporations have a distinct advantage over their Western competitors. It is also probable that Chinese corporations are directly pressured (and backed) by Beijing to secure overseas oil and gas assets.[12] Conversely, "it may also be the case that the NOCs are using the government's strategy as a lever to gain government support when it is required" (Xin Ma and Andrews-Speed, 2006: 6).

▓ Chinese Expansion into African Oil Fields

Both the Chinese government and Chinese companies consider Africa rich in natural resources, particularly crude oil, nonferrous metals, and fisheries.[13] Chinese firms have been involved in various deals with the majority of the nineteen African countries that produce oil or have confirmed oil reserves. In fact, as Table 2.3 shows, these companies either have or are chasing oil contracts with every African country that possesses at least half a billion barrels of proven crude-oil reserves.

In contrast to the days of Maoist solidarity, contemporary China's economic dealings with Africa are, in the main, based on a cool evaluation of commercial potential.[14] Indeed, to reiterate, China's rapidly developing oil requirements have helped propel Sino-African trade at the turn of the millennium.[15]

Table 2.3   Proven Reserves of Oil in Africa, January 2007

Country	Oil (in billions of barrels)	Country	Oil (in billions of barrels)
Algeria	12.270	Gabon	2.000
Angola	8.000	Ghana	0.015
Benin	0.008	Libya	41.464
Cameroon	0.400	Mauritania	0.100
Chad	1.500	Morocco	0.001
Congo-Brazzaville	1.600	Nigeria	36.220
DRC	0.180	South Africa	0.015
Côte d'Ivoire	0.100	Sudan	5.000
Egypt	3.700	Tunisia	0.400
Equatorial Guinea	1.100		
Total	114.073		

Source: Oil and Gas Journal, vol. 104, no. 47, December 18, 2006.

But we must also emphasize that Beijing also sees beyond the energy prism and predicts that Africa will play a greater role in future world politics; for example, a *China Daily* journalist asserted in 1998 that "as more African countries improve political stability and make headway in economic growth, the continent's nations will have more say in international affairs" (January 9). Such progress would be to Beijing's advantage if, as is repeatedly asserted, China and Africa indeed share "identical or similar opinions on many major international affairs as well as common interests" (*People's Daily,* October 11, 2000). Specifically, perceptions that China and Africa share a history of oppression by the West and similar levels of economic development are common.[16]

A select listing of recent contracts signed by China's national oil companies gives a flavor of the geographical extent of Chinese interest in African oil. In 2002, Sinopec signed a contract for US$525 million to develop the Zarzaitine oil field in Algeria. In 2003, CNPC purchased a number of Algerian refineries for US$350 million and signed a deal to explore for oil in two blocks, while PetroChina signed a contract with Algeria's Hydrogen Carbide to jointly develop oil fields and construct a refinery. In 2004, Total Gabon signed a contract with Sinopec for exporting Gabonese crude oil into China (*This Day,* February 3, 2004). Angola received a US$2 billion loan in 2005 in exchange for oil deals with China, which added another US$1 billion to the loan in March 2006. Also in 2005, the Nigerian National Petroleum Corporation signed a US$800 million deal with PetroChina to supply 30,000 barrels of crude oil per day to China (Vanguard, July 12, 2005). It was further announced that the Chinese were interested in exploring the reserves of manganese and gold in Côte d'Ivoire, where Sinopec already had investments in an oil field off the coast, overseeing 27 percent of the block (Reuters, June 20, 2006). In 2006, CNOOC agreed to pay US$2.3 billion for a stake in a Nigerian oil and gas field (*This Day,* April 21, 2006); it also signed an offshore-exploration deal with Kenya that would allow it to explore in six blocks covering 44,500 square miles in both the north and south of the country (*East African Standard*, April 18, 2006). Meanwhile, Beijing struck a US$4 billion deal for drilling licenses in Nigeria (*Daily Champion*, May 5, 2006), and Angola's Sonangol announced that Sinopec had taken up a 40 percent stake in the lucrative Block 18 after proposing a US$1.1 billion "signature bonus" from the government on top of its original investment, which amounted to US$1.4 billion (*The Standard,* June 21, 2006).

Chinese oil companies also reportedly signed contracts to begin offshore oil exploration and production in Congo-Brazzaville (Associated Press, June 19, 2006) and began oil exploration in northern Namibia with the intent to establish an oil refinery (*New Era*, April 12, 2006). In addition, Nigeria announced that it would give the first right of refusal on four oil exploration blocks to CNPC in exchange for a commitment to invest US$4 billion in infrastructure. The deal required China to buy a controlling stake in Nigeria's Kaduna Refining and Petrochemicals Company, which yields 110,000 barrels a day, and to build a railroad and power stations (*Daily Trust*, April 27, 2006). Meanwhile, Zhongyuan Petroleum Company started exploratory drilling in the Gambella basin of western Ethiopia (*The Reporter*, March 4, 2006), Chinese oil companies investigated forming upstream joint ventures to exploit newly discovered reserves on the island of Madagascar (Dow Jones, February 24, 2006), and Sinopec and CNPC teamed up to acquire drilling rights to an oil field in Sudan for about US$600 million (Associated Press, November 15, 2005).

Clearly, China's energy interests in Africa are growing exponentially. Indeed, in 2006 China imported 920,000 barrels a day of crude oil, or 31 percent of its total crude imports, from Africa (*Business Day,* February 18, 2007). However, a note of caution needs flagging; many of the African assets held by China's national oil companies are of a magnitude and quality that do not interest Western corporations.[17] Moreover, Chinese national oil companies are still relatively small players on the continent: "The commercial value of the oil investments in Africa of China's NOCs is just 8 percent of the combined commercial value of the [international oil companies'] investments in African oil and 3 percent of all companies invested in African oil" (Downs, 2007: 44).

A central criticism of these contracts revolves around the tactics and strategies by which Chinese corporations enter into them (Shinn, 2006b); Chinese responses have at times been contradictory. For instance, on February 16, 2006, *Chinafrica,* an official Chinese publication, quoted Wang Yingping of CIIS as asserting that "Chinese businesses pay greater attention to protecting the environment when building factories and exploring for Africa's rich reserves in oil, ore, and nonferrous metals"; two months later, it cited, without comment, the assertion by Sierra Leone's ambassador to China that "the Chinese just come and do it. They don't hold meetings about environmental impact assessments, human rights, bad governance and good governance. I'm not saying it's right, just that Chinese investment is succeeding because they don't set high benchmarks" (April 1, 2006). This view has since become a common stimulus for complaint within Sierra Leone.[18]

■ China's Oil Diplomacy in Africa: Two Case Studies

While Western diplomacy in the postmillennium has focused on so-called rogue states, axes of evil, and arcs of extremism, Beijing has taken a very different tack. According to the Chinese ambassador to Eritrea, "There are no rogue states. China has been labeled this in the past and other governments should not criticize"[19]—a position that has itself garnered criticism. A discussion of two different examples—Nigeria and Sudan—illustrates some of the issues that Chinese corporations face in Africa.

Nigeria

Nigeria is rapidly becoming one of China's largest trading partners in Africa, with bilateral trade amounting to more than US$3 billion in 2006. To gauge the exponential rise in Sino-Nigerian trade relations, consider the fact that, in 1998, trade volume was US$384 million. By 2001, it had reached US$1 billion; by 2004, US$2 billion (*This Day,* February 26, 2006). Nigerian exports to China—excluding oil—have quadrupled. Signifying the importance of these increases, Beijing signed a memorandum of understanding with Abuja on the establishment of a strategic partnership in January 2006. Nigeria was the first African country to sign such an agreement with China.

Previously, Chinese firms had been completely excluded from involvement in the Nigerian oil industry by Western oil companies with an established presence in Nigeria.[20] But by December 2004, Sinopec and the Nigerian National Petroleum Corporation (NNPC) signed an agreement to develop Oil Mining Leases (OMLs) 64 and 66 in the Niger Delta. OML 64 has drilled five exploration wells, one of which came across hydrocarbon resources. OML 66 has been far more successful; of its eighteen exploration wells, twelve have discovered hydrocarbon resources (*China Daily,* December 19, 2004). Sinopec also has a contract with the Nigerian Petroleum Development Company (NPDC) and one with Italian company Eni to develop the Okono and Okpoho fields, which have combined reserves of 500 million barrels. In July 2005, CNOOC and NNPC signed a US$800 million contract that guaranteed 30,000 barrels per day to China over a five-year period, to be reviewed every year (*Nigeria First,* July 11, 2005).

Building on such developments, in April 2006, Abuja offered four oil-exploration licenses to Chinese firms in exchange for investments in Nigeria's infrastructure totaling US$4 billion. It then signed seven development agreements with Beijing granting it export credit worth US$500 million (*Vanguard*, April 27, 2006). China agreed to repair the Kaduna Refining and Petrochemicals Company while undertaking other investment projects, such as the construction of a hydropower plant in Mambila, Taraba State, in return for garnering the right of first refusal on oil blocks. A number of the blocks on offer had been relinquished by operators of production-sharing contracts (PSCs) that had run from 1993 to 1998. NNPC also approved CNOOC's acquisition of a working interest in a deepwater area of the Niger Delta. The deal included the lucrative Akpo oil field, which was discovered in 2000. The Akpo field is said to hold 700 million barrels of crude-oil reserves as well as gas reserves of about 2.5 trillion cubic feet (*This Day*, January 9, 2006). CNOOC also took over the commitments of the original contractor of OPL 246, buying a 45-percent working interest in the deepwater block for US$2.3 billion plus an adjustment of US$424 million for other expenses. The former amount will finance the NNPC's 50-percent equity stake in OPL 246; CNOOC will then garner 70 percent of profit oil from the field, while the NNPC takes the remaining 30 percent, as well as 80 percent of cost oil. In winning the contract, CNOOC beat India's biggest oil company, the state-owned Oil and Natural Gas Corporation, which had put in a US$2 billion bid in January 2006 only to see the Indian government blocking the deal on the grounds that it was not commercially feasible. What is interesting here is that the Indian government also deemed OPL 246, which was mired in controversy surrounding the ownership by well-connected former government officials of assets in the billions, too risky.[21]

As it happens, the security of the oil industry in the Niger Delta is increasingly problematic.[22] Following President Hu Jintao's state visit to Nigeria, in April 2006, which resulted in the signing of a US$4 billion infrastructure-investment deal, Nigerian militants from the Movement for the Emancipation of the Niger Delta (MEND) warned Chinese companies to "stay well clear" of the Niger Delta or risk attack.[23] MEND also claimed responsibility for a car-bomb explosion near the port town of Warri, stating that the blast was "a warning against Chinese expansion in the region" and adding that "the Chinese government, by investing in stolen crude, places its citizens in our line of fire" (*Financial Times*, May 1, 2006). Though the Niger Delta produces 90 percent of Nigeria's oil and over 75 percent of the country's export earnings, very little of the wealth has been seen by area residents. About 80 percent of Nigeria's oil and natural gas revenues accrue to just 1 percent of the country's population, such that Nigeria has the second-lowest per-capita oil-export earnings in the world, estimated at US$212 per person in 2004—a figure that compares unfavorably to the 1980 figure of US$589 per person, representing a decline of more than 50 percent. It is also estimated that over 100,000 barrels of oil per day are stolen by well-connected insiders, amounting to a loss of approximately US$1.5 billion per year.

In early 2006, MEND militants began attacking oil installations and kidnapping foreign oil workers, leading to a 20-percent reduction in Nigeria's oil production. MEND appears to be a more efficient organization than the armed gangs of robbers that have sought to extort money from oil companies in the Delta region while engaging in the theft of oil.[24] In an interview with the BBC, a MEND leader stated that his organization "was fighting for 'total control' of the Niger Delta's oil wealth, saying local people had not gained from the riches under the ground and the region's creeks and swamps. He said the Delta had been exploited for the benefit of other parts of Nigeria and foreign companies and ordered all oil companies [including the Chinese] and Nigerians whose roots lie elsewhere to leave the region" (*BBC News Online,* April 20, 2006).

As a result, Nigeria began to turn to China for military supplies to protect the oil fields in 2006, claiming that Washington was tardy in its response to the destabilization of the security situation in the Delta;[25] in the words of Atiku Abubakar, Nigeria's vice-president, "the [United States] ha[s] been too slow to help protect the oil-rich Niger Delta from a growing insurgency" (*Financial Times*, February 27, 2006). A senior Nigerian naval official concurred that Nigeria "felt let down" by the United States' reluctance to provide more support, including 200 boats to guard the Delta; although offering military technical assistance and training, Washington had provided only four old coastal patrol boats. Its reluctance was explained by anxiety over the levels of corruption within and widespread human-rights violations by Nigeria's security forces.[26]

While the Nigerian government accuses MEND leaders of funding themselves through stolen oil, many oil-industry officials claim that corrupt military personnel belong to cartels that steal the oil for sale to criminal syndicates (*Financial Times,* February 27, 2006). Beijing, however, continues to sell weapons to the Nigerian military, frustrating some observers: "When America balked at supplying Nigeria's trigger-happy military, China offered dozens of patrol boats. 'They are impossible. They just don't care what we or anyone else says,' complained a member of one Dutch human-rights advocacy group" (*Guardian,* March 28, 2006).

China's reason for supplying Nigeria's military, however dysfunctional, with armament is very pragmatic: China needs Nigeria's oil. Attacks by MEND in 2006 caused losses in production of at least 500,000 barrels per day, and imports to China fell: "Customs data shows that Nigeria supplied 75 percent less crude to China in the first nine months of this year compared with the same period of 2005, [although] oil exports to China would return to growth if the militant attacks in the Niger Delta region could be halted" (*China Oil Web,* November 6, 2006).

However, arms sales have not stopped MEND's attacks against Chinese interests—and may even have provoked greater efforts to target Chinese workers in the Delta.[27] Five Chinese workers were kidnapped in January 2007 by

MEND; although they were released after two weeks, the *People's Daily* revealed that nine other Chinese workers had been kidnapped in the first two months of 2007 alone (*People's Daily*, March 7, 2007). Indeed, January and February saw an upsurge in crimes against all foreign oil workers in the Delta, as sixty expatriates were kidnapped, two were killed, and one was shot and injured.

Like all other investors in Nigeria, the Chinese have to negotiate the reality of Nigeria's political economy.[28] The most populous country in Africa is, unfortunately, synonymous with corruption and malgovernance, dubbed the "open sore of the continent" by Nigeria's Nobel Prize–winning author Wole Soyinka (1996). Clientelism, patronage, and corruption are absolutely central to its political economy (Barnes, 1986; Reno, 1993; Aluko, 2002). Members of a tiny elite have grown fabulously wealthy at the expense of the rest of the population, "impelled by short time horizons and chronic insecurity [that give] rise to strategies focused on the expedient redistribution of resources rather than the systematic mobilization of resources for production and growth" (Lewis, 2004: 100). Beijing and its national oil companies must, sooner rather than later, face up to the Nigerian condition.

Sudan

Sudan is the third-largest producer of crude oil in sub-Saharan Africa with 563 million barrels of proven reserves—over two times the 262 million barrels estimated in 2001. Chinese companies are now its largest investors, with investments estimated at US$4 billion; as of 2008, Beijing imports 60 percent of Sudan's oil output. Due to economic boycotts imposed by the Western donor community and IFIs over its alleged support for terrorism, the Sudanese government has sought support and help from others. According to Ali Askouri, "The [Islamic] junta wanted its business partner to have the strength and ability to withstand political pressure from Western 'imperialist' countries; the stamina and determination not to be bothered by the protests of human-rights groups; and, above all, [the clout] to be a heavyweight international player that Western imperialist countries would find hard to force out of the country through political pressure" (2007: 72). They found these qualities in China. Khartoum has been appreciative; in the Sudanese president's words, "Our relation with China is built on mutual benefit. China has always supported the unity of Sudan. When our relations became problematic with the international financial institutions, we turned to China. Relations with China have enabled us to overcome economic difficulties" (quoted in Askouri, 2007: 76).

In the mid-1990s, a Canadian company, Arakis Energy, commenced developing the Heglig and Unity oil fields, estimated to hold between 600 million and 1.2 billion barrels of crude. In 1996, Arakis sold off 75 percent of its rights to Blocks 1, 2, and 4 to form the Greater Nile Petroleum Operating Company (GNPOC), a conglomeration of CNPC, which owned 40 percent;

Malaysia's Petronas, which held 30 percent; and the Sudanese state–owned oil company Sudapet, which had 5 percent. This formation helped raise finances to build the 1,000-mile pipeline to the Suakim oil terminal at Port Sudan on the Red Sea. Earlier, in 1995, CNPC had purchased Chevron's concession of Block 6 in Western Kordofan. In 1997, it took the principal position in GNPOC when Arakis sold most of its remaining interests. CNPC trumped its competitors by proposing to Khartoum that it would construct an oil refinery. Arakis then sold its remaining interests in Sudan to a fellow Canadian company, Talisman Energy, in 1998. However, pressure from the Canadian public, compounded by a 2001 lawsuit filed by the Presbyterian Church of Sudan, forced Talisman in 2003 to sell its 25 percent stake in the Greater Nile Oil Project to ONGC Videsh, an Indian oil company. Here, we should point out that the Sudanese government rejected CNPC's bid to increase its share by purchasing Talisman's share itself:

> The Sudanese settled a similar bid by the Malaysian oil company Petronas by awarding it a concession outside GNPOC's domain. Instead, Sudan awarded Talisman's share to the Indian National Oil Company. This chain of events is viewed by many Chinese observers as a reflection of both the Sudanese government's desire to reduce its dependence on one major foreign (i.e., Chinese) company's interests involved in the country's oil exploration as well as the limits of the Sudanese government's inclination to "reward" Chinese business interests in exchange for the Chinese government's support of Sudan in the United Nations. (Jakobson and Zha Daojiong, 2006: 67)

In other words, Khartoum has considerable agency in its dealings with external actors interested in its oil—including the Chinese—and will not hesitate to act when Sudanese interests are at stake. Such power needs emphasizing as it counters Beijing's leverage over Khartoum in other areas—which observers, not least the lobbyists for the Genocide Olympics campaign, tended to exaggerate in any case.[29]

Indeed, Beijing's relationship with the Sudanese regime has become a major cause célèbre that threatens to tarnish China's reputation, impacting Chinese policymaking in turn. A campaign to link Beijing's support for Khartoum despite the crisis in Darfur with the 2008 Beijing Olympics seemed to have rallied China's policymakers.[30] A full-scale foreign policy that played up China's contribution to conflict resolution and encouraged much more proactive explanations of Sino-Africa diplomacy came into effect.[31] The main reason for this public relations exercise is to quell the controversy about Beijing's role in protecting Khartoum from international censure and action (Reeves, 2007).

Analysis of the conflict in Darfur has been covered in depth elsewhere; in short, the conflict began in late 2002 and accelerated in February 2003, when rebel groups—namely the Sudanese Liberation Army/Movement (SLA/SLM) and the Justice and Equality Movement (JEM)—started attacking government police and military targets. Khartoum retaliated with a brutal military campaign, which included encouraging and arming nomads known as the Janjaweed to attack and kill local farmers. According to one report in late 2006, "It is likely that the number of deaths for this conflict in Greater Darfur is higher than 200,000 individuals, and it is possible that the death toll is much higher" (Hagan and Palloni, 2006: 1578). As a result of the conflict, more than 3,500,000 people have been displaced.

The UNSC has been trying to find a resolution to the crisis since it began (Johnson, 2003). Beijing, by contrast, seemed determined to hamper such efforts by abstaining, weakening resolutions, and announcing informally that it would use its veto right if necessary to protect Chinese interests in Sudan.[32] The discovery that China (along with Russia) had been supplying Sudan with attack helicopters, bombers, and other weapons that were used against civilians in Darfur was equally disturbing to the international community. In 2006, a panel of four UN experts recommended seventeen players in the Darfur conflict be sanctioned for obstructing peace. Panel member Ernst Jan Hogendoorn singled out China with the claim that it "has been and continues to be a major supplier of light weapons to the government of Sudan and many of the neighboring states"; although the panel "found no evidence China was defying the embargo and supplying arms directly to Darfur . . . weapons [it] had sold to Khartoum were likely to end up there" (*Reuters,* June 19, 2006). Later, however, Amnesty International compiled a report stating that "Chinese strike aircraft and Russian helicopter gunships have been photographed at three airports in Darfur. Their presence violates UN Resolution 1591, which ban[s] Sudan from transferring any weaponry to Darfur without the Security Council's official permission" (*Daily Telegraph,* May 10, 2007). The report further argued that "the irresponsible transfer of arms to Sudan and its neighbors are a significant factor in the massive human-rights catastrophe in Darfur and its spread into eastern Chad" (quoted by *Associated Press,* May 8, 2007). Furthermore, it was alleged that "China sold arms and ammunition worth [US$20 million] to Sudan in 2005, along with spare parts worth [US$60 million] which could have been used to keep military aircraft airborne" (*Daily Telegraph,* May 10, 2007).

Such reports provoked a grassroots movement, primarily in the United States, to call negative attention to the Chinese government's alleged complicity in Darfur.[33] Linking Beijing's support for Khartoum to its hosting of the 2008 Olympics, campaigners renamed the latter the Genocide Olympics. US newspaper editorials in late 2006 declared that "the Chinese leadership must be forced to make a choice: work now to halt genocide in Darfur or see the Olympic Games used, at every turn, as a means of highlighting the Chinese role in sustaining the ultimate human crime" (*Boston Globe,* December 17, 2006); the *Washington Post,* for its part, ran an article titled "Responsible China? Darfur exposes Chinese hypocrisy" (September 6, 2006).

Alarmed by the possibility that China's coming-out party would be spoiled, Beijing embarked on a major public-relations exercise to convince the world of its positive role in Sudan. Washington provided a major impetus in April 2007, when the chairman of the Senate Foreign Relations Committee, Joseph Biden, and ninety-six other senators wrote a letter to Hu Jintao calling on him to use his influence to help end the violence in Darfur. Soon thereafter, on May 10, 2007, the Chinese government appointed Liu Guijin the special representative of African affairs, with a particular remit for Darfur. Liu was a veteran diplomat in Africa, having served as the Chinese ambassador to both Zimbabwe and South Africa as well as director general of the Department of African Affairs. China's foreign policy is still essentially predicated on state-to-state relations; although Beijing felt it could ignore the Genocide Olympics campaign of nongovernmental activists, the involvement of Washington legislators compelled it to move on the issue.[34]

At the same time, the Chinese media began to publicize Beijing's constructive role in Sudan; for instance, the *Beijing Review* declared that "since the Darfur issue emerged, China has been in constant communication with the relevant people, playing mediator, promoting dialogue between top leaders, dispatching envoys, [and] discussing the problem in the UN assembly" (*Beijing Review,* June 7, 2007). Western diplomats likewise began to assert that there had been a sea change in China's position.[35] A US special envoy to Sudan, Andrew Natsios, told a Senate panel that the Chinese "have been largely supportive of our efforts to resolve the Darfur situation" (State Department, 2007); the then British foreign secretary, Margaret Beckett, joined in, asserting that, "on Sudan, I know there has been some criticism of China, but actually, China has played really quite a positive role, particularly in the negotiation of the Darfur peace agreement" (*Financial Times,* May 18, 2007).

Beijing has clearly become more sensitive to accusations about its role in Sudan. The February 2008 resignation of Steven Spielberg from his post as an adviser to the Beijing Olympics cast China's role in Sudan in a painfully unfavorable light, leaving leaders to exercise damage control, further compounded by protests as the Olympic torch progressed around the world in early 2008.[36] Yet China is hidebound by its intimate relationship with Khartoum and the billions of dollars it has invested in Sudan as well as by its adherence to the position that "China does not support bad governments. What it does is engage with them, but [it] does not tell them what to do."[37] Beijing's leaders are thus willing to place only limited pressure on the Sudanese government.[38] For instance, even as they talked up China's positive influence on Sudan, they tried to talk down the notion that sanctions or isolation could work. We should, however, point out that China had no reservations regarding sanctions against apartheid-era South Africa (see Taylor, 2000).

In February 2007, President Hu Jintao made a visit to Khartoum, notable for the fact that Hu offered up what he called the Four Principles of dealing with the Darfur issue. Ambassador Wang Guangya was reported as saying that "usually China doesn't send messages, but this time, during . . . Hu Jintao's recent visit to Sudan [it] did . . . It was a clear strong message" (*Xinhua,* February 3, 2007). The Four Principles were:

1. Respect Sudan's sovereignty and territorial integrity.
2. Solve the issue by peaceful means and by sticking to dialogue and coordination based on equality.
3. Take into consideration the overall situation and, from a long-term perspective, respect and address each other's reasonable concerns.
4. It is imperative to improve the situation in Darfur and living conditions of local people (*Xinhua,* February 3, 2007).

The first principle is problematic given that Khartoum has been insistent on invoking its state sovereignty to prevent the deployment of international forces to Darfur: "Notably, China says nothing about the principle of a 'responsibility to protect' framed in the UN World Summit Outcome Document (September 2005) specifically so as to supersede claims of national sovereignty" (*Sudan Tribune,* February 4, 2007). With regard to the second principle, one critic scoffed, "one way of understanding 'peaceful means' is as a code phrase for 'no humanitarian intervention in Darfur,'"; the same could be said for the phrase "sticking to dialogue" (*Sudan Tribune,* February 4, 2007). The other principles are prosaic and arguably do little to address the ongoing conflict.

However, as we have noted, Beijing's policies toward Africa are in a process of evolution. China's position on the Darfur issue has evolved from a rather inactive if not amoral to a very clear and active one. Chinese diplomats now seek to mediate on the Darfur issue by clarifying the options open to Khartoum and building trust as a means of reaching a practicable consensus. According to one commentator, from the Chinese perspective, this policy has been successful, as it has increased Beijing's moral influence, reassured its partners both in Africa and the West, and protected Chinese business interests in Sudan (primarily those involving oil) while holding to its principles vis-à-vis sovereignty and state consent (Holslag, 2008).

▓ Conclusion

Any analysis of Chinese involvement in Africa's oil industries needs to be balanced, avoiding the hyperbole that has characterized some accounts (see, for example, "China Covets African Oil and Trade," *Jane's Intelligence Review,* October 12, 2004; *Newsweek,* December 20, 2004; and Brookes and Shin Ji Hye, 2006). China's demand for energy resources has inflated prices, bringing a windfall to African states. What African leaders do with the influx of receipts is the key[39] to the big question: How do governments engage with the phenomenon of Sino-African relations and encourage China to use its influence to benefit ordinary people and promote development despite the corruption and/or incapacity of many African leaders?[40] Here, Beijing's stance of noninterference seems unhelpful.

African nations wishing to avoid the problems that tend to accompany overdependence on one particular commodity (such as oil) and/or to move beyond their roles as suppliers of primary products will face a challenge if the commodity boom stemming in part from Chinese demand "give[s] rise to a sense of complacency" that prevents them "from undertaking the necessary measures to make growth sustainable in the medium term (i.e., investment in human capital and infrastructure, institutional reform, etc.)" (Deutsche Bank Research, 2006: 12). Certainly, overreliance on commodities such as oil threatens to make African nations especially vulnerable to negative price shocks given that no industrialization is taking place and most of Africa's oil exports are unrefined.[41] But the problem of instability is not specific to Chinese involvement, and Beijing can hardly be blamed if African states do not use their profits wisely or seek to diversify their economies.[42] China's increased interest in Africa's oil threatens to deepen Africa's dependency, but only because many African governments appear fundamentally unable to manage their own resources.[43]

James Tang (2006: 31) remarks that "as China has become more involved in regions where the Chinese presence formerly was limited, Beijing has encountered new challenges, such as the humanitarian problem in Sudan." We might aver that the strategies adopted by an emerging power in search of opportunities and those of an established power looking to protect its investments in an unstable environment are intrinsically different and that this difference accounts for some of China's actions. But the question is, how long is it going to take for Beijing to move from one stance to the other? Another crucial question is, how long can it maintain a position predicated on noninterference, particularly as Beijing becomes more and more integrated into the global order and begins to face the responsibilities thereof?[44] Indeed, although Beijing sometimes comes into conflict with the West as it increases its presence in Africa and the developing world in general, maintaining good relationships with major Western powers remains a key foreign-policy concern. Negative perceptions of China's activities in Sudan arguably jeopardize such harmony, playing into the hands of critics who like to speak of the "China threat." Chinese diplomats seem aware of this, asserting that "China's policy of noninterference is appropriate for Beijing's diplomacy, but China has not been very successful in explaining this to the world. Consequently, we are concerned that people are 'misinterpreting' our diplomacy."[45]

Meanwhile, features of Sino-African oil diplomacy resemble the West's own interactions with Africa. After all, not all Western actors possess exemplary records in Africa. French policy toward oil-rich nations such as Gabon has never been guided by liberty, equality, and fraternity.[46] Washington's relations with oil-rich nations such as Saudi Arabia aren't hampered by concerns over democracy. Business, as far as many actors are concerned, is business; thus their criticism of China's oil diplomacy in Africa is somewhat hypocritical.[47] Moreover, point out Linda Jakobson and Zha Daojiong (2006: 62), the lack of a global policy structure for oil trade means there is "ample space for both exporting and importing countries to maneuver by mixing economics with politics." Those activities by China's national oil companies that are routinely criticized are in fact reflections of the absence of any overarching architecture, which, it must be said, has served Western oil corporations' interests for a very long time.

But this is not the whole story. There is a growing consensus among the more responsible African governments on where the continent should be heading. However, "while in some countries China's involvement appears benign, in others its approach undercuts efforts by the African Union and Western partners to make government and business more transparent and accountable" (*Africa Research Bulletin,* February 16–March 15, 2006: 16855). Indeed, their key concern is that, despite Beijing's pledged support of the New Partnership for Africa's Development (NEPAD), some of the tactics Chinese actors employ in pursuit of resources threaten to reintroduce practices that NEPAD and the African Union (AU) are ostensibly seeking to end (see, for instance, Liu Guijin, 2004). Meanwhile, less engaged African leaders eye the allure of Chinese investment—coming as it does with very few strings attached—and wonder why they should bother any longer with NEPAD.[48]

The key issue in many oil-rich states with which Chinese corporations engage is that they are actually relatively weak on the ground where the oil is being exploited, while the resilience of partnerships between producers and oil companies (most of them Western) is quite remarkable (Soares De Oliveira, 2007). Nigeria's Niger Delta is a classic example, as the supposedly sovereign government of Nigeria has essentially lost control of those oil-producing areas where Western companies have cut deals with local militias to protect their assets. Can China's national oil companies emulate their Western counterparts even as Beijing preaches the importance of state sovereignty and noninterference?[49]

These problems are compounded when one considers the character of many African states in light of what is known as the resource curse. Chinese traders in African oil must hereby face the issues that other actors have to confront. The tendency of the oil industry to undermine democracy and accountability in the developing world and particularly in Africa is long-standing. Thus, in African countries that are prospecting for oil or that are suspected of having oil deposits, such as Sierra Leone, debates about the costs and benefits of exploitation have become politically important.[50] The discovery of oil in Uganda triggered similar debate (see *East African,* July 10, 2006, and *The Monitor,* July 12, 2006).[51] David Leonard and Scott Straus argue that Africa's enclave economies (which export extractive products concentrated in relatively small geographic areas) are particularly problematic. Revenue generation is confined to small locales whose prime markets are international. This situation makes concern for "the general economic health of areas outside the enclave quite secondary, if not irrelevant. In enclave economies, then, elites gain little from any deep, growing, economic prosperity of the masses of the population" (Leonard and Straus, 2003: 13). Although individuals involved in such enclaves may benefit handsomely, the system fundamentally fails to promote broad economic growth and development (Yates, 1996).

Indeed, the idea that resources should be channeled toward the nebulous goal of national development is not on the agenda of many African elites for whom profit and power do not depend on productive development but on control over resource-rich areas or on market manipulation (Gary and Karl, 2003). Control over even relatively limited geographic areas is sufficient for their survival, as Africa's so-called resource wars attest. Ultimately, "enclave economies do not need functioning states or infrastructure to generate revenues for elites" (Leonard and Straus, 2003: 16). In such circumstances, affluence and underdevelopment go hand in hand (Joseph, 1984). This is a problem that all actors in Africa's resource-rich states must consider and manage.[52] As of 2008, Western companies have fared no better than others, in spite of their much longer engagement (see Wright, 1997; Chandler, 1998; Cesarz, Morrison, and Cooke, 2003; and Afeikhena, Adjibolosoo, and Busari, 2005). The dirty politics of African oil have been practiced for a long time (Shaxson, 2007; Soares De Oliveira, 2007).

However, it is the specific nature of Beijing's interactions with resource-rich African countries that appears particularly problematic. Dan Zhou, chief analyst at CEB Monitor Group in Beijing, points out that China has emerged as an attractive partner in Africa and central Asia in four ways: Its "intensifying demand drives up prices for its products, which are largely raw materials such as oil, zinc and copper[; it] sets virtually no standards for political transparency or economic reform to get deals done[; it] ignores internal human-rights abuses as an impediment to dealmaking[; and] it is a one-stop shop, offering not just investment, trade, skilled workers, and military weapons but also diplomatic protection in the form of its United Nations Security Council veto" (quoted in Markman, 2006). The distinct opacity of the national oil companies' dealings in Africa compounds suspicions of Chinese motives. As one Chinese scholar has admitted, "China shoulders much of the blame, as it has been poor at making its energy transactions with countries such as Iran and Sudan transparent. Lack of transparency fuels speculation that China has a well-coordinated project for countering US influence, particularly when it comes to dealing with what the United States labels 'rogue states'" (Zha Daojiong, 2006: 183–184).

Yet it is important to note that the stereotype of Beijing as China Inc., advancing centralized strategies around the world, is passé. Erica Downs notes that "when it comes to choosing where to invest," China's national oil companies are almost always in the driver's seat, and the Chinese government, while occasionally offering general advice about the direction they should travel (for example, "invest in Morocco"), is often just along for the ride with little idea of the final destination. Sudan's recent omission from the Chinese government's catalog of countries that Chinese companies are encouraged to invest in is a case in point: This absence has not prevented CNPC from continuing to invest there. (2007: 48)

Chen Shaofeng concurs:

Most studies . . . take a static view of China's motivations, identifying both the government and the national oil companies . . . as the same interest entity or regarding the latter merely as an extension of state policy. Consequently, they tend to explicitly and implicitly look at every NOCs' behavior in the foreign markets as the strategic actions of Beijing, which . . . is untrue. . . . China's oil diplomacy has been driven not only by the government's learning skill and strategic concerns with respect to national and economic security, social stability and foreign strategy, but also by the NOCs' strong commercial motives to "go abroad" and the personal incentive of their management. (2008: 79–80)

We must not exaggerate the Chinese government's ability to manage Chinese business on the African continent. Although the foreign policy makers at Zhongnanhai may seek to coordinate Chinese activities abroad, they face serious difficulties in convincing commercially motivated actors to comply:

The central leadership has made efforts to align key Chinese business interests with its new diplomacy. Most notably, in August 2006, it convened the Politburo, government ministers, Chinese ambassadors, provincial governors, party secretaries, officials from state-owned enterprises, and senior officials from the People's Liberation Army at the Central Foreign Affairs Work Conference, the largest foreign-policy gathering in China's recent history. Participants discussed how the behavior of Chinese companies abroad risked damaging the country's image, [how] to establish a more coherent grand strategy, and how to strengthen China's soft power. But these efforts have had little discernible effect on China's arms sales or the activities of Chinese energy companies in pariah states. (Kleine-Ahlbrandt and Small, 2008: 51)

In such a milieu, where China's energy needs have raised prices and hence receipts for African governments, the stance of noninterference means that the values of the host country's elites wholly determine the conduct of China's actors. Until and unless the host elites themselves advance transparency, prodevelopment policies, and equitable growth—and prove able to enforce such ideals—no course of intervention will be taken.[53] Given the standards of governance in most oil-rich African nations, this prospect is not on the immediate horizon. While ultimately it is a matter for Africans to decide themselves, the official Chinese position on such issues is not likely to help.[54]

Overall, Chinese national oil companies have two main advantages over private firms operating in Africa. Their operations can be incorporated into larger, state-backed financial-support programs that obscure the costs and benefits of their involvement compared to that of private companies engaged in open competition and international tendering. Moreover, the national oil companies are often prepared to deal with regimes regardless of their international standing or human-rights records.[55] In contrast to many Western oil companies (which may be tempted but unable to follow suit), Chinese corporations can generally obtain their government's support for such dealings (Tjønneland et al., 2006: 34). It is doubtful that either Beijing's policymakers or the managers of the national oil companies will wholly abandon this way of doing business; presumably, they perceive themselves to be bringing development to Africa, and they are intensely suspicious of the West's supposed concern for human-rights violations occurring in the name of oil extraction. Post-Unocal, it's no surprise that some policymakers in Beijing believe that the United States "bends over backwards to deny Chinese access to energy resources," seeking to raise obstacles to national oil companies' engagement in oil deals outside of US spheres of influence (Zha Daojiong, 2006: 184). Arguably, Unocal has in fact "serve[ed] as justification for ignoring [US] attempts at dissuading China from engaging 'rogue states' for energy" (Zha Daojiong, 2006: 184). Besides, a change in policy that lessened the advantages China's national companies enjoy in Africa could destabilize the energy security situation back home in China. Negative Western reactions to China's activities in Africa's oil industries have a historical precedent in the hostility many commentators expressed in the late twentieth century in the face of Japan's seemingly imminent rise; Western bookshelves were stocked with such titles as *The Coming War with Japan* (Friedman and Lebard, 1991) and *Yen! Japan's New Financial Empire and Its Threat to America* (Burstein, 1988). As Zha Daojiong (2006: 182) notes, "International reaction to China's pursuit of supply security through offshore energy sources, particularly oil and gas, has put Beijing on the defensive. In some ways this is a repetition of the Japanese experience in the 1970s and 1980s, when there were serious debates about the impact on the world's economic and political structures of Tokyo's pursuit of high economic growth." Stanley Lubman (2004) adds that much anti-Chinese rhetoric, particularly in Washington, springs from lobbyists with political agendas informed by their paymasters (who are often linked to US oil interests) as well as from uninformed staff, particularly in Congress. Again, contextualization is needed.

For African elites weighing up the costs and benefits of engaging with Chinese versus Western oil companies, the former look increasingly attractive for reasons other than the fact that they do not generally come with political baggage involving transparency and human-rights issues. China's national oil companies—working in tandem with the government—are more prepared than Western firms to aid a host country in constructing entire sectors of the oil industry.[56] These include building "local refining facilities and a petrochemical industry in addition to . . . infrastructure not directly related to oil exploration":

> In contrast, American and European oil companies, with a long history of operating in such oil-rich African countries like Nigeria, often operate by taking out crude oil and reselling oil products to those countries. Also, some Western observers have noted Africa's need for technical assistance. Chinese companies are estimated to be involved in 900 investment projects in Africa. Analysis of the wide range of Chinese economic activities in Africa in recent years has at least in part supported the predominantly Chinese view that it would be a mistake to ascribe one single motive to the relationship between African nations and China. More than energy is at stake. (Jakobson and Zha Daojiong, 2006: 67)

The strategic importance of Africa for the global supply of energy, which is becoming ever more apparent, combined with the robust growth of Chinese involvement in the continent's oil industries, places great responsibility on Africa's leaders, which they have generally failed to assume (Soares De Oliveira, 2007). According to one informant, "China could be a very good partner for Africa, but this is dependent on serious governments and how they engage and fashion the relationship."[57] One way this could be assisted would be for the international community to encourage China's national oil companies to take part in initiatives such as the Extractive Industries Transparency Initiative (EITI). Yet the problem remains that "Africa is like a drowning man and so will accept any help or any investment with no questions asked. No one asks whether the Chinese investment is good for the continent, as there is little planning or vision by our governments."[58] Obviously, the severity of this problem varies across the continent, but a big question remains. As a Western diplomat set it out, there are two possible scenarios for future Chinese relations with oil-rich economies. In one, China is willing to help build and refurbish infrastructure, plays fairly in its trade relations, and seeks to control its corporations' activities if and when they misbehave (whether it would be able to do so was not addressed). In the other scenario, China does whatever it can to access minerals, unconcerned with reform or good governance even to the point of supporting autocratic regimes.[59] This worst-case scenario would actually work against Beijing's interests in the long term, as broader geopolitical developments encourage Chinese policymakers to fashion China into a responsible power, in line with their diplomatic rhetoric.

The international community (i.e., the West) is generally preoccupied with analyzing how Chinese actors in the developing world's energy industries can wield their growing commercial influence responsibly. In turn, Beijing is increasingly zealous in assuring the world of its desire to be a responsible power. "The challenge," observes Zha Daojiong, "is for China and other leading energy-consuming countries to cooperate in defining and addressing the political and social challenges that arise in many of the oil states of the world" (2006: 183). But ultimately, it is for the people of Africa to determine their fate. Outsiders can, at best, provide a supporting role.

▨ Notes

1. Interview with State Department official, Washington, DC, United States, April 5, 2007.
2. Interview with Chinese academic, School of International Studies, Peking University, Beijing, China, September 20, 2007.
3. Interview with State Department official, Washington, DC, United States, April 5, 2007.
4. Interview with Chinese diplomat, Abuja, Nigeria, September 5, 2007.
5. Interview with Western diplomat, Asmara, Eritrea, June 29, 2006.
6. Interview with Chinese academic, School of International Studies, Peking University, Beijing, China, September 20, 2007.
7. Interview with Lucy Corkin, research manager, Centre for Chinese Studies, Stellenbosch, South Africa, July 31, 2006.
8. Interview with Lucy Corkin, research manager, Centre for Chinese Studies, Stellenbosch, South Africa, July 31, 2006.
9. Interview with Western diplomat, Asmara, Eritrea, June 29, 2006.
10. Interview with Western diplomat, Abuja, Nigeria, September 3, 2007.
11. Interview with Xu Mingzheng, Freetown, Sierra Leone, June 8, 2006.
12. Interview with State Department official, Washington, DC, United States, April 5, 2007.
13. Interview with the manager of a Chinese trading company, Massawa, Eritrea, July 1, 2006.
14. Interview with Chinese diplomat, Addis Ababa, Ethiopia, May 15, 2007.
15. Interview with Shu Zhan, Chinese ambassador to Eritrea, Asmara, Eritrea, June 29, 2006.
16. Ibid.
17. Western diplomat, Abuja, Nigeria, September 3, 2007.
18. Interview with David Jabati, news editor, *Awareness Times,* Freetown, Sierra Leone, June 7, 2006.
19. Interview with Shu Zhan, Chinese ambassador to Eritrea, Asmara, Eritrea, June 29, 2006.
20. Interview with Western diplomat, Abuja, Nigeria, September 3, 2007.
21. Interview with Western diplomat, Abuja, Nigeria, September 3, 2007.
22. Interview with Chinese diplomat, Abuja, Nigeria, September 5, 2007.
23. Interview with Chinese diplomat, Abuja, Nigeria, September 5, 2007.
24. Interview with Western diplomat, Abuja, Nigeria, September 3, 2007.
25. Interview with a representative from the House of Representatives, Abuja, Nigeria, September 3, 2007.
26. Interview with Pentagon official, Washington, DC, United States, April 5, 2007.
27. Interview with a journalist from the *Abuja Inquirer,* Abuja, Nigeria, September 3, 2007.
28. Interview with Western diplomat, Asmara, Eritrea, June 29, 2006.
29. Interview with Shu Zhan, Chinese ambassador to Eritrea, Asmara, Eritrea, June 29, 2006.

30. Interview with He Wenping, CASS, Beijing, China, September 18, 2007.

31. Interview with Chinese diplomat, Addis Ababa, Ethiopia, May 15, 2007.

32. Interview with African Union official, Addis Ababa, Ethiopia, May 16, 2007.

33. Interview with State Department official, Washington, DC, United States, April 5, 2007.

34. Interview with He Wenping, CASS, Beijing, China, September 18, 2007.

35. Interview with British diplomat, Addis Ababa, Ethiopia, May 15, 2007.

36. Although most protests centered around the issue of Tibet, it was noticeable that in the UK and United States at least, protestors also raised the issue of alleged Chinese complicity in Darfur.

37. Interview with Chinese diplomat, Addis Ababa, Ethiopia, May 15, 2007.

38. Of course, China is not alone in compromising ostensible principles insofar as they clash with commercial interests. In late 2006, commercial considerations seemingly compelled the Blair government in London to halt a major criminal investigation into alleged corruption by a British arms company. The attorney general, Lord Goldsmith, ended a Serious Fraud Office inquiry into the alleged bribery of Saudi Arabian officials to secure a multi-billion-dollar arms deal, explaining that the invesigation would "endanger Britain's security if [it were] allowed to continue" (*Guardian,* December 15, 2006).

39. Interview with African Union official, Addis Ababa, Ethiopia, May 15, 2007.

40. Interview with Christopher Parsons, Ministry of Trade and Industry, Freetown, Sierra Leone, June 8, 2006.

41. Interview with African Union official, Addis Ababa, Ethiopia, May 16, 2007.

42. Interview with Chinese diplomat, Abuja, Nigeria, September 5, 2007.

43. Interview with African Union official, Addis Ababa, Ethiopia, May 16, 2007.

44. Interview with Henning Melber, Namibian political economist, Windhoek, Namibia, August 14, 2006.

45. Interview with Chinese diplomat, Addis Ababa, Ethiopia, May 15, 2007.

46. Interview with Ethiopian academic, Addis Ababa, Ethiopia, November 22, 2005.

47. Interview with Robin Sherborne, editor of *Insight,* Windhoek, Namibia, August 14, 2006.

48. Interview with Henning Melber, Namibian political economist, Windhoek, Namibia, August 14, 2006.

49. Interview with Western diplomat, Abuja, Nigeria, September 3, 2007.

50. Interview with Sanusi Deen, national chairman of the Sierra Leone Indigenous Business Association, Freetown, Sierra Leone, June 7, 2006.

51. Interview with Ugandan academic, Mbarara, Uganda, November 2, 2006.

52. Interview with Western diplomat, Abuja, Nigeria, September 3, 2007.

53. Interview with DFID official, Freetown, Sierra Leone, June 7, 2006.

54. Interview with a representative from the House of Representatives, Abuja, Nigeria, September 3, 2007.

55. Interview with Western diplomat, Abuja, Nigeria, September 3, 2007.

56. Interview with a representative from the House of Representatives, Abuja, Nigeria, September 3, 2007.

57. Interview with African Union official, Addis Ababa, Ethiopia, May 16, 2007.

58. Interview with Saffie Koroma, National Accountability Group, Freetown, Sierra Leone, June 7, 2006.

59. Interview with Western diplomat, Abuja, Nigeria, September 3, 2007.

The Impact of Cheap Chinese Goods | 3

One of the more contentious issues surrounding Sino-African relations involves the export of cheap manufactured goods from China to Africa, which is blamed for a decline in African exports—particularly of clothing and textiles. Official statistics indicate that there has indeed been a great increase in African imports from China, making a massive 712-percent jump from US$895 million in 1996 to US$7.3 billion in 2005. China's share of Africa's imports went from 2.5 percent in 1996 to 7.4 percent in 2005, and this trend is likely to continue (Mwega, 2007: 5). In the minds of many African observers, it is the cause of a concomitant trend, namely the decline of Africa's manufacturing sector. Chinese producers, they and other critics claim, are both cornering the global market in sectors where African exporters compete for share and flooding the continent's own market, crowding out locally produced goods.[1] Strong condemnation is thus coming from many African trade unions and civil-society organizations as well as from African producers.[2] For instance, the International Textile, Garment, and Leather Workers Federation's Africa chapter, representing trade unions from South Africa, Zimbabwe, Mozambique, Lesotho, Swaziland, and Zambia, issued a joint statement in 2005 asserting that they had "identified the challenge of Chinese imports flooding into global and local markets as a fundamental challenge for the industry, its workers and their jobs. . . . Increasingly, the trade pattern between the African continent and China is becoming colonial in character, with African countries exporting raw materials to China and importing finished products" (*Business Day,* September 27, 2005).

Similarly, in Ethiopia, the Chamber of Commerce and Sectoral Association have voiced concern about the growing "takeover" of the domestic market by Chinese-owned firms with cheap products. According to one report, "Products produced from fake and cheap materials in China and imported to Ethiopia are saturating the market at the moment and as a direct result of this, homemade products have been thrown out of competition" (*The Reporter*, June 30, 2007). Ethiopian entrepreneurs have linked the closure of a growing number of private businesses to "unfair" Chinese competition, while the Chamber, intriguingly enough, has demanded that "Western powers should intervene to save private business activity, which [is] under threat in Ethiopia" (*The Reporter*, June 30, 2007). In Nigeria, "one complaint by Nigerian investors is that Nigeria is fast becoming a dumping ground while indigenous companies are dying" (*Daily Trust*, February 23, 2007); likewise, in Kenya, "unease seems to be rising as Chinese businesspeople become significant players and, in some cases, overtake Kenyan locals" (*Inter Press Service*, July 18, 2007).

China is extremely conscious of its international reputation and is particularly concerned about how it is perceived in Africa, where its leaders are keen to stress that they will never make the mistakes the colonialists made.[3] Indeed, Wen Jiabao insists that they "are truly sincere in helping Africa speed up economic and social development for the benefit of the African people and its nations" (*China Daily*, April 16, 2007). Unlike Chinese imports from Africa, which are geographically concentrated and overwhelmingly centered on oil and other primary commodities, Chinese exports to Africa—mostly manufactured products—stretch across the continent. In fact, in 2004, 87 percent of Africa's imports from China were manufactured or processed goods, with textiles making up 36 percent. Meanwhile, "African manufactured goods struggle to maintain a foothold in the Chinese marketplace, accounting for only 13 percent of exports. Regardless of the supposed economic generosity that China exhibits, a picture can be construed of China giving with one hand while taking away with the other" (Thompson, 2007: 1).

The growing perception that Chinese commerce is damaging African interests must worry Beijing, especially when respected African commentators such as Fantu Cheru (2007) characterize Sino-African relations as "recolonization by invitation." Policymakers in Beijing must also be troubled when a newspaper as prestigious as *The East African* accuses China of "dumping" cheap products in Africa or reports that "Chinese products are killing [or] undermining local industries and potential benefits such as value addition, industrialization, and job creation" (*East African*, July 3, 2007).

This chapter aims to examine this conflict and demonstrate the paradoxes and contradictions at its heart. It argues that China is being unfairly castigated for many problems, such that Chinese imports into Africa—and the Chinese themselves—are in danger of being made scapegoats for the failure of many African economies postindependence to industrialize and build their own manufacturing bases.

Because the clothing and textile industry is considered vital to both high employment levels and Africa's future development,[4] any perceived threat to its well being and security is magnified and arguably exaggerated. As a labor-intensive manufacturing sector, the industry constitutes a first step in the industrialization process. Historically, most successful economies started off with an expansion of light industry; those that focused on heavy industry prior to laying such groundwork invariably failed.[5] That is why discussing the purported effect of China's exports on Africa's manufacturing sector, particularly the textiles and clothing sector, in depth is so important; merely laying blame on China for Africa's woes may be somewhat fashionable, but it is not constructive. Perspective needs to be maintained.

For the purposes of this chapter, it is important to point out that the overwhelming bulk of imports into Africa from China are final manufactured products. As a result of low labor costs and generally efficient production and transport infrastructures, exports from China—particularly clothing and textiles, as well as low-level electronics—are low priced.[6] They are indeed taking over Africa's markets, as visitors to any African marketplace will attest, and the perception that this phenomenon is having major implications for indigenous manufacturers in Africa threatens to complicate China's relations with a number of African nations. That said, some African countries appear to have made a conscious decision to encourage Chinese business as a means to lessen dependency on other trade partners. In Namibia, for instance, one informant asserted that the country had been very dependent on South Africa and Europe for its imports until diversification became a key objective of the Namibian government; China has helped not only by diversifying the productive base but also by providing cheaper inputs and supplying affordable goods for low-income people.[7]

We can also link the supply equation for Chinese-made exports to Africa to the state of the global market and to changes within China's political economy. Much of China's export growth is driven by the dynamics of its productive base and the impulses associated with liberalization and globalization (Zheng Yongnian, 2004). As a report in the *People's Daily* from August 31, 2005 puts it, "Chinese textile manufacturers . . . get no more than 10 percent of total profits in trade. The remaining 90 percent is shared by foreign-brand owners, wholesalers, and retailers, mostly Americans." Domestic oversupply and the bargaining muscle of conglomerates such as Wal-Mart have served to drive down costs and erode profitability—even as the developed world erects trade barriers and quotas to Chinese imports: "It is in the corporate strategy of major US companies that we find at least part of the reason for the growth of Chinese exports" (Breslin, 2007: 147). In short, the impetus to find new export markets is intense, especially as the Western notion that "profit is the ultimate goal for all enterprises" gains credence (*People's Daily,* August 31, 2005; see also Cheung, 1998). Dynamics that are beyond the control of either the African importers or even the Chinese exporters but that are central to the globalized, capitalist world order bear some responsibility.

Still, the pressure to export is propelling the spread of small-scale, Chinese-run retail emporiums across Africa, down to the smallest village.

Heidi Haugen and Jørgen Carling (2005) show that such omnipresence is a function of market saturation, as do interviews with Chinese traders in various African countries. Essentially, a pattern emerges whereby one or two Chinese entrepreneurs set up shop selling cheap products, followed by other Chinese who have heard of their success or by the Chinese nationals they employed. However, since they all sell the same sorts of products, competition between them increases, leading to a fall in prices and a concomitant decline in profits. This in turn propels some traders to seek out new markets in other towns,[8] where the process is repeated, until one finds Chinese shopkeepers in the smallest villages, eking out livings. In other words, dynamics intrinsic to market competition explain why African markets are saturated with Chinese-made products (and Chinese-owned stores). Meanwhile, Africans simply see a Chinese incursion everywhere.

The effects for Africa of China's rise in global commerce are both direct and indirect. The key direct impact is that Chinese imports compete with and displace African-made products. Indirectly, Chinese exports to the world market affect supply and demand as well as prices and may prove to be just as—if not more—damaging to Africa's manufacturing base as the more observable influx of cheap Chinese imports.[9] The indirect consequences for the export potential of Africa's manufacturing industries are thus what we turn to first.

■ The Indirect Effects of China's Rise on Africa's Manufacturing Sector

Between 1987 and 2005, China's export stake in the world market went from 1.6 percent to 7.2 percent. Although it is true that a considerable share of these products do not impact African exports, Chinese exports do vie with—and usually crowd out—African exports in third-country markets, particularly clothing and textiles, as we will see below. This is an important issue for Africa as the sector is labor intensive and thus impacts income, livelihoods, and poverty levels.[10] In 2004, clothing and textiles exports made up 4.7 percent of sub-Saharan African merchandise sold abroad and 18.7 percent of all manufactured goods exported from the continent (WTO, 2005). Africa's major clothing and textile exporters are Kenya, Lesotho, Madagascar, Mauritius, South Africa, and Swaziland, all of which have been strongly affected by the rise of China's economy.

Indeed, a significant portion of these countries' economies depends on these exports. For instance, in Lesotho, light manufacturing has accounted for an average 17 percent of GDP in the past ten years and for 99 percent of exports to the United States, predominantly clothing and apparel. In 2004, the manufacturing sector in Kenya accounted for over 20 percent of the country's GDP and "provided employment opportunities to about 300,000 people in the formal and

3.7 million persons in the informal sectors of the economy" (Hayes, 2003: 4). Kenya's textile subsector is significant, forming "one of the key[s to] the country's strategy for economic recovery" (Omolo, 2006: 148). The number of people employed by Africa's textile and clothing industry has long been relatively significant. In 2004, the sector in Kenya employed 32,095 people; in Madagascar, 75,600; in Mauritius, 67,249; in Lesotho, 53,087; and in Swaziland, 30,000 (Traub-Merz, 2006: 19). In South Africa in March 2005, the traditionally robust textile and garment industry employed almost 143,000 people and contributed 12 percent to total manufacturing employment (Vlok, 2006: 229).

Unfortunately for these sectors, manufacturing export prices fell globally in the 1990s and continue to fall in the 2000s, mainly due to the cheapness of exports from China and, to a lesser extent, India (Kaplinsky, McCormick, and Morris, 2006). This drop has had an important impact on Africa's export competitiveness. Equally problematic, however, is what has occurred since the rescinding of privileges afforded African exporters. A primary case in point involves the events that occurred after the demise of the Agreement on Textiles and Clothing and the earlier Multi-Fiber Agreement (MFA) of the WTO. In many respects they are intimately tied to the impact of the African Growth and Opportunity Act (AGOA) on Africa, which was greatly beneficial to a number of African economies, as will be explained.

AGOA, which became law in the United States in May 2000, offered "tangible incentives for African countries to continue their efforts to open their economies and build free markets," providing "reforming African countries with the most liberal access to the US market available to any country or region with which the United States does not have a Free Trade Agreement" (US Department of Commerce, 2007: 1). Due to the fact that, with the limited exception of Mauritius and South Africa, no African exporters of clothing were able to satisfy the act's rules-of-origin, modifications were made (extending at first to September 2005 and then to September 2007) to permit least developed African countries to employ materials from the cheapest contractors worldwide. This provision had an important impact on textile manufacturing in Africa, because as soon as it came into effect, various foreign companies, mostly Asian, set themselves up in Africa as a means to evade the obstacles placed on them by the MFA.

The MFA (officially replaced by the Agreement on Textiles and Clothing in 1994, but still largely known as the MFA) was a derogation from the rules of the world-trading system, allocating export quotas to low-cost developing countries while limiting the amount of imports to states whose domestic textile industries were negatively affected by them—in de facto terms, imports from Asia and particularly China. The rationale behind the MFA was to allow developed countries to set quotas on textiles and clothing imports, giving them space to reorganize their domestic industries prior to granting poorer economies the opportunity to compete for market share. The effect, however, when combined with that of trade preferences such as were granted by the AGOA, was that the global apparel industry took advantage of Africa's unexploited quota access to the European and American markets in a process that became known as "quota hopping" (Curran, 2007). Triangular production networks developed whereby Asian firms made products in least developed economies—chiefly, though not exclusively, in Africa—for export to Western markets (Gereffi, 1999).

Under the AGOA, African exports of textiles and clothing to the United States boomed. In 2000, the value of sub-Saharan Africa's apparel exports to the US was $776 million; by 2004, it had reached $1,782 million, an increase of 130 percent. Table 3.1 breaks down the figures by country.

However, we must point out that the growth period for African clothing exporters is viewed by many commentators as artificial, created by the exploitation of the MFA via the AGOA. Given the very low level of textile-production capacities in most African countries, it was the foreign sourcing of yarns and fabrics that enabled African economies to enjoy the boom in clothing exports in the first place. A look at Table 3.2 reveals that the vast majority of "African" clothing being exported to the United States in 2004 (taken as a snapshot year for illustrative purposes) was made using foreign fabrics.

Since China is being held responsible for the post-MFA collapse of the industry, we should also note that, according to Munir Ahmad (2005: 11), a sizeable proportion of the fabric in question was Chinese.

▓ The Collapse of Africa's Clothing Exports

The MFA expired on January 1, 2005, affecting 86.5 percent of American quotas and 73.3 percent of European Union (EU) quotas (Williams, Kong Yuk-Choi,

Table 3.1   US Textile and Clothing Imports from AGOA Countries, 2000–2004 (import values in US$ millions)

Exporter	2000	2003	2004	2004/2000 (percentage)
Lesotho	140	393	456	225
Madagascar	110	196	323	195
Kenya	44	188	277	529
Mauritius	245	269	226	−8
Swaziland	32	141	177	455
South Africa	163	253	164	0
Namibia	0	42	79	n/a
Malawi	7	23	27	276
Botswana	8	7	20	140
Zimbabwe	20	5	n/a	n/a

Source: Ahmad, 2005: 8.
Note: "n/a" stands for "not available."

Table 3.2   AGOA Exports to the United States, 2004 (in US$ millions)

Exporting Nation	Total Value of Exports (in US$ millions)	Amount Made with Foreign Fabrics	Percentage Made with Foreign Fabrics
Lesotho	455.6	446.4	98
Madagascar	323.1	297.8	92
Kenya	277.3	271.4	98
Mauritius	226.5	145.2	64
Swaziland	178.7	175.6	98
South Africa	163.9	111.0	68
Namibia	78.9	75.9	96
Malawi	26.8	25.5	95
Botswana	20.3	20.1	99

Source: Ahmad, 2005: 10.

and Yan Shen, 2002) in what was known as "clothing's big bang" (Curran, 2007). With this, Africa's temporary textile boom was over; as Ugandan newspaper *New Vision* put it, "Then came the end of the World Trade Organization's Multi-Fiber Agreement . . . and the resulting flood of Chinese apparel onto the world market" (December 3, 2006). Consequently, market share that had been enjoyed by African exporters was taken over by Chinese manufacturers. At the same time, many of the Chinese companies that had relocated to Africa during the MFA era moved back to China.[11] Granted, the expiry of the MFA is a global, not merely an African, concern; Christian Aid suggests that 27 million workers around the world may ultimately lose their jobs in its aftermath (Christian Aid, 2004).

In addition, uncomfortable as it may be to mention, the African clothing and textile manufacturers generally failed to prepare themselves for the post-MFA period.[12] Their governments certainly did very little, if anything, to guard against the long-predicted ramifications of the agreement's expiry. In contrast, Chinese manufacturers, in tandem with Beijing, were prepared. In fact, as 2005 neared, the Chinese government supplied the industry with billions of dollars "in the form of free capital, direct and indirect subsidies, and a host of other 'incentives' to drive competitors out of the markets and create an environment where no one, including the lowest-cost producing countries in the world, [could] compete with China," as the president of the National Council of Textile Organizations, Cass Johnson, has observed (quoted by Mutume, 2006: 18). In fairness to the African companies, however, we should add that the yuan has been undervalued by 20 to 40 percent for a long time, making Chinese imports into Africa even more attractive to retailers and consumers.[13]

To return to the post-MFA milieu, African textile and apparel manufacturers saw a particular decline in exports to the United States, a key market, in 2005. Indeed, they fell by 15.6 percent from 2004. In contrast, US imports from China went up by a massive 43.76 percent from 2004 to 2005, despite safeguard quotas on some of the key product categories. In essence, China doubled its market share in 2005, accounting for 33 percent of US textile and clothing imports, compared to 16.8 percent in 2004. The flood of Chinese imports into the West was dramatic enough to cause serious concern in Washington and the capitals of Europe, where the phenomenon crystallized under the rubric of the "bra wars" of 2005 (*Daily Telegraph,* August 25, 2005). As we have seen, as soon as quantity restrictions were removed, Chinese textile and clothing exports to the United States and the EU increased so rapidly that, within a few weeks, both the United States and the EU reimposed quotas on a number of items. In mid-2005, the EU made an agreement with Beijing that limited ten Chinese clothing products to an annual growth of between 8 and 12 percent until 2008; in November, the Americans made a similar agreement, effective January 2006 through 2008, that covered thirty-four products. These deals were expected to afford African producers "temporary relief. They are now left with [two or three] years during which quota[s] and preferential access will be maintained before they may be thrown into a full-blown competition with other [textile and clothing] suppliers" (Traub-Merz, 2006: 27). This was an important turn of events given the dramatic post-MFA decline in Africa's share of the American market. Table 3.3 attests to this fact via figures provided by the Corporate Council on Africa in its periodical, *The Africa Journal.*

As we can see, the country hardest hit by the removal of the MFA quotas was South Africa, whose AGOA exports shrank by nearly 50 percent. This was partly because it does not benefit from the provisions granted to least-developed countries, including access to imported materials via the derogation on market entry.[14]

**Table 3.3   US Textile and Apparel Imports from Africa
(in million square-meter equivalents)**

Country	2004	2005	Change (percentage)
Botswana	5.835	7.688	31.77
Cape Verde	1.146	0.914	−20.28
Ethiopia	2.606	2.141	−17.86
Ghana	9.331	6.438	−31.01
Kenya	73.396	74.079	0.93
Lesotho	111.163	95.251	−14.31
Madagascar	69.414	62.572	−9.86
Malawi	7.795	6.965	−10.65
Mauritius	37.546	29.325	−21.89
Namibia	18.938	16.092	−15.03
South Africa	57.356	28.928	−49.56
Swaziland	61.469	55.015	−10.50
Tanzania	1.541	1.664	7.94
Uganda	1.477	1.762	19.27
Sub-Sahara	462.268	390.375	−15.55

Source: Corporate Council on Africa 2006: 19.

To reiterate, in the period between 2001 and 2004 when both the AGOA and the MFA were in effect, some African economies enjoyed an expansion in clothing and textile exports, especially to the United States, that halted dramatically in 2005: "Indeed, Africa enjoys the dubious distinction of having suffered the largest decline in textile and apparel trade despite having the most generous trade preference program under AGOA" (Corporate Council on Africa, 2006: 20). This situation is unlikely to get better given the agreement made at the WTO meeting in Hong Kong in December 2005 that quota-free/duty-free status would be granted to imports from all LDCs (Wilkinson, 2007: 253). If the trends of the past few years continue, the beneficiaries of this agreement will likely be countries such as Bangladesh, Cambodia, India, and Pakistan, not African states: "If already competitive LDCs such as Bangladesh and Cambodia obtain duty-free access to the US market for their apparel exports, there is a serious risk that the decline in apparel imports from Africa will only accelerate" (Corporate Council on Africa, 2006: 20).

As Raphael Kaplinsky and Mike Morris show (2006: vi), the post-MFA closure of apparel factories in a number of African countries was considerable; in Lesotho and Swaziland, for instance, there was a 28.9-percent and a 56.2-percent decline in employment in the clothing sector, respectively. Such declines are deeply challenging for the societies and economies concerned: "It is not just the degree of job loss (particularly in Lesotho and Swaziland) which is of concern but the nature of the jobs [that] have gone. It mostly involves women, and the impact on their families is severe (in South Africa, for example, it is estimated that approximately four people are supported for every job in the formal sector). For countries without alternative sources of employment, this employment-decline has major poverty implications" (Kaplinsky and Morris, 2006: vii). Indeed, in many of the countries affected, economic diversification is highly limited, so it is unlikely that those who have lost their jobs will find work at a comparable level of pay (Nordas, 2004: 30–31).

This is where China comes in. On the one hand, Beijing's insatiable demand for minerals encourages a trend that reifies Africa as a supplier of primary products and a player in the mineral and energy sectors, which are highly capital intensive and boast relatively low levels of employment; the owners are mostly multinational corporations and/or comprador elites (see Chapter 2).[15] On the other hand, China's manufacturing exports have the unintended consequence of eroding what little is left of Africa's manufacturing base, which is relatively labor intensive.[16] In other words, "because of its impact [both] on poverty levels (through employment) and on income distribution (through changing forms of economic specialization), China's poverty-related impact on [sub-Saharan Africa] is likely to be significant" (Nordas, 2004: 30–31).

We can gauge the potential impact of Chinese exports by looking at Export Similarity Indexes (ESIs; see Table 3.4), which are measures of overlap

Table 3.4   Export Similarity Index, Eighteen African Countries and China

	Year	China (percentage)		Year	China (percentage)
Botswana	2001	5.8	Nigeria	2003	1.7
Cameroon	2003	6.6	Rwanda	2003	8.8
Ethiopia	2003	4.3	Senegal	2003	14.5
Ghana	2000	10.6	Sierra Leone	2002	4.5
Kenya	2003	19.3	South Africa	2003	27.7
Lesotho	2002	17.8	Sudan	2003	2.6
Malawi	2003	10.6	Tanzania	2003	11.0
Mozambique	2002	6.4	Uganda	2003	8.0
Namibia	2003	18.7	Zambia	2002	11.0

Source: Jenkins and Edwards, 2006: 219.

between the value of products different countries export. The ESI that compares China to selected African economies is relatively high.

The share of exports from sub-Saharan Africa that confronts serious competition from China varies from country to country but is extremely high in many. For instance, in Lesotho, it is 89.1 percent; in Mozambique, 73.4 percent; in Malawi, 64 percent; in Namibia, 55.4 percent; in Senegal, 44.1 percent, in South Africa, 54.4 percent; and in Zambia, 82.4 percent (Jenkins and Edwards, 2006: 220). In addition, around a third of the exports from Ghana, Kenya, Tanzania, and Uganda face stiff competition from Chinese exports. Although this is not China's fault, it is a serious problem (Kaplinsky and Morris, 2007). The cases of Nigeria and South Africa are useful in this regard, demonstrating the multiplicity of factors that play out vis-à-vis China's role in Africa's manufacturing environment. They also show that endogenous issues, often overlooked in the debate, are just as important.

▓ Nigeria and the "Chinese Invasion"

Nigerian accusations against Chinese importers often overlook the internal problems that Africa's manufacturing sector confronts. It is commonly held that the flooding of Nigeria's markets with cheap Chinese products has had the effect of undermining Nigerian commercial operations and putting Nigerians out of work.[17] Textiles and garments constitute the majority of China's exports to Nigeria, accounting for 15 percent of its total exports, a fact that fuels grave accusations:

> The Nigerian textile industries are in the process of shrinking as a whole or shutting down entire plants for good. The main culprit behind the Nigerian debacle is the Chinese invasion of Nigerian markets. Chinese fabrics in the

Nigerian markets are readily and cheaply available for the Nigerian consumer, and the latter is compelled to buy Chinese rather than Nigerian textile products. Because China is endowed with massive intensive labour potential and relatively skilled manpower in its respective industries, Chinese products, including textile fabrics, are now ubiquitous in African markets. Nigerian fabrics are more costly to the Nigerian than the Chinese fabrics, and no amount of national fervor can salvage the Nigerian textile factories from their present crisis. (Institute of Development and Education for Africa, 2005)

According to Issa Aremu, general secretary of the Textile, Tailoring, and Garment Union, the mass importation of textiles—both secondhand from Europe and new garments, mostly from China—has led to the closing down of sixty-five Nigerian textile mills and the laying off of a total of 150,000 textile workers over the course of ten years; furthermore, "more than 1 million other persons whose jobs are linked to the textile industry, such as traders and cotton farmers, have lost their means of livelihood as a result of the closures" (*Koinonia International,* February 15, 2005). Consequently, on April 6, 2005, Nigeria's Ministry of Finance issued a revised list of prohibited imports. Among the many items listed were about twenty types of Chinese manufactured products, including textiles, footwear, cases and bags, cement, and ballpoint pens.[18]

However, as we have argued, blame for the collapse of Nigeria's local textile industry cannot be laid solely at the door of Chinese manufacturers. It is in fact very difficult to assess whether Nigerian textiles could compete with Chinese imports because the playing field is not level due to the domestic fees that Nigerian manufacturers have to disburse, notably on energy and transport.[19] This situation is directly linked to the chronic inefficiency, misadministration, and corruption within Nigeria's service industries.[20] For instance, Nigeria has the world's tenth-largest reserve of gas, as well as plentiful supplies of coal and the potential to develop a vigorous hydroelectric resource. Yet Nigeria generates only 3,000 megawatts of electricity, even though the domestic demand is around 6,000 megawatts (*People's Daily,* November 17, 2005). In fact, in February 2007, the state-owned Power Holding Company of Nigeria announced that power generation had dropped by almost 60 percent to under 1,500 megawatts—this for a population of over 140 million, despite the government's claim to have spent over US$2 billion on the power sector over the previous six years (*This Day,* February 4, 2007). The result is that "companies are run on generating sets powered by expensive fuels that are sometimes a scarce commodity in spite of the country being the seventh largest producer of crude oil in the world. As a result, the cost of doing business is dear, and products are expensive" (*This Day,* February 4, 2007). In such a setting, it is virtually impossible for even the most efficient Nigerian textile manufacturer to compete with Chinese producers. Indeed, it is very difficult for Nigerian manufacturers to compete at all.[21] And it is not only textile businesses that are feeling the pressures caused by Nigeria's crumbling power infrastructure. In early 2007, Michelin, the transnational tire manufacturer, announced the closure of its factory in Port Harcourt because of high production costs stemming from the lack of a dependable power supply. The closure of the plant "clearly signal[ed] the process of deindustrialization in Nigeria with its deleterious effect on the nation's economy" (*Times of Nigeria,* February 17, 2007).

Thus finished goods from China are arriving into a market without domestic competitors, whose potential has been undermined not only by the low prices of the Chinese imports but by the Nigerian government's own incompetence.[22] As one informant put it, "Textiles are a good example of Nigeria's domestic problems—the cost and productivity of Nigerian products [are] just completely outcompeted by Chinese goods, but that is not China's fault."[23] Nigeria is not the only example, however. The World Bank reports that "if the Zambian and Kenyan power systems were of the same quality as their Chinese counterparts . . . the cost savings for Zambian and Kenyan firms would be equivalent to nearly their entire wage bills" (Mutume, 2006: 19). Problems of competitiveness and efficiency also plague South Africa's clothing sector, complicating the impact of Chinese imports, as we will now see.

■ South Africa and Chinese Imports

As has already been pointed out, South Africa suffered exceptionally badly after the elimination of the MFA quotas, undergoing a decline of 34 percent in clothing and textile exports in 2005—while China's exports increased by 65 percent. This decrease has proven a challenge for Pretoria, not least because the industry garners annual sales of over 20 billion rands (approximately US$2.75 billion) and employs some 200,000 people, accounting for about 15 percent of total formal employment in South Africa (Textiles and Clothing Core Team, 2006: 3). Having a manufacturing base of its own (a rarity for much of Africa), Sanusha Naidu (2006: 474) estimates that, in 2006, 74 percent of all garments imported into South Africa were Chinese; by contrast, Walter Simeoni, president of the South African Textile Federation, claimed in 2005 that Chinese clothing represented 86 percent of the total garments imported into South Africa, adding that "all this was achieved within the past three years" (*Inter Press Service,* January 24, 2005). Pressure on South African manufacturers has been compounded by the elimination of the MFA and the subsequent substantial loss of jobs; between July 2004 and July 2005 alone, 40,000 jobs were lost in the South African clothing sector (Kaplinsky and Morris, 2006: 21). It should be reiterated here that, unlike most other African economies, South Africa cannot access low-priced fabric from Asia for products destined for the US market without forfeiting the AGOA's preferential tariffs, as it is not recognized under the AGOA as an LDC.

Thus it appears that South Africa is being drawn into a trading relationship with China characterized by its need to export raw materials and capital-intensive commodities even as its labor-intensive industries undergo heavy pressure from Chinese imports. The burden on developing nations to export primary products while importing manufactured goods has long been an attribute of colonial and neocolonial economic relationships. In 2006, a Nigerian observer of the trend in Sino-African economic relations described it thus:

> Africa has become China's main source of energy and raw materials, but industrial products originating from Africa is yet to make an appreciable entry into the Chinese market. This is indeed a huge lacuna in the China Africa co-operation, and except it is quickly addressed by both sides, the relationship will in future come to resemble the Europe/America and Africa relations, that is lopsided, dependent and even detrimental to Africa. The Chinese may not will it, but if the trend of economic co-operation between the two sides continue to feature its current disequilibrium, imbalance and a pattern of disarticulation where Africa exports only primary products and received in return, finished Chinese goods then the future of China-Africa co-operation will be fraught with unforeseen difficulties. (*Daily Trust*, November 8, 2006)

And in fact, as we noted in Chapter 1, President Thabo Mbeki, addressing students at a congress in Cape Town in late 2006, warned that Africa must not allow itself to be a mere supplier of raw materials in exchange for China's manufactured goods, as there was an intrinsic danger in establishing a highly asymmetrical relationship. Wilfred Collins Wonani of the Chamber of Commerce in Mulungushi, Zambia, has argued likewise: "Sending raw materials out, bringing cheap manufactured goods in. This isn't progress. It is colonialism" (*New York Times,* August 21, 2007). Other commentators have been just as critical; the influential South African publication *Business Day,* for instance, editorialized in 2007 that "our own textile industry has been crippled by cheap Chinese imports made possible only because of China's appallingly poor labor policies" (July 11). The influx of Chinese imports into South Africa has also eroded belief in the idea that Sino–South African trade relations can be win-win, despite Chinese assertions to the contrary. The notion that China poses a serious threat to South African interests seems to be developing quickly. A 2005 editorial from one South African newspaper is worth quoting at length:

> South African politicians and officials would do well to consider the advice of China's reformist leader, Deng Xiaoping: "Seek truth from facts." China's attraction as an ideological and strategic counterweight to the dominance of the West has led to a desire to cozy up to the Asian dragon. But the reality of Chinese engagement in Africa—and in South Africa itself—should give us pause, especially in the rush to conclude a free-trade agreement with the economic giant. China's foreign policy has generally been characterized by an approach of unsentimental and aggressive self-interest, and we would be fooling our-

selves if we did not adopt the same approach. . . . The flood of cheap Chinese imports has been a significant threat to local manufacturers, particularly in the clothing and textile industry, which has seen a jobs bloodbath. . . . In the light of the demonstrable impact on the South African market, it is sobering, at best, that the official Chinese position is that South Africa needs no protection from Chinese imports and that an "asymmetrical" trade deal is unacceptable. It may be a generalization, but the record of Chinese adherence to minimum labor standards in local South African businesses has also left much to be desired. This is not to say that we should not engage China, but to argue that the sense of starry-eyed ideological solidarity that surrounds some of our attitudes to Beijing represents a serious trap. (*Mail and Guardian,* May 28, 2005)

Responding to such concerns, the South African government implemented quotas on Chinese imports in an assortment of clothing and textile categories as of January 2007. Its main rationale involved job losses allegedly caused by cheap Chinese imports; the goal was to provide clothing and textile businesses a respite from such pressures, allowing them to eventually improve competitiveness and thus regain domestic- and export-market shares. However, the South African government has continued to take a reactive, not a proactive, stance toward the textile industry's problems.[24]

What is more, trade data from the first three months of 2007 suggests that the tactic of introducing quotas was not succeeding: "While imports from China in the HS[25] lines targeted by the quotas have been reduced by around 35 percent, aggregate imports in these categories have only marginally decreased—clearly other countries have replaced China as the importer of choice. Figures show that, among others, Pakistan, Zimbabwe, and Vietnam have shown significant gains in the first quarter of 2007. In other words, the quotas have led to a diversification of import sources. Local producers do not seem to be in any better position than before the quotas" (Van Eeden, 2007). Put another way, it is not (or not only) the Chinese who are damaging South Africa's clothing and textile industry, which appears incapable of competing with cheaper producers irrespective of their origins. In fact, "South Africa has been hemorrhaging clothing jobs since acceding to the WTO ATC in 1995. The industry was highly protected during the apartheid years and [remains] characterized by uncompetitiveness and inflexible production methods" (Van der Westhuizen, 2007: 257).

Importers, including retailers, have been compelled to find alternative sources of supply, but they have "not switched predominantly to sourcing locally. This raises questions about South African clothing and textile firms' supply capacity and their competitiveness" that are unrelated to any immediate "China effect" (Hartzenberg, 2007: 2). The appreciation of the rand by roughly 50 percent between 2002 and 2004 is also an important factor unrelated to Chinese import practices, as it made South African exports (as well as those from Lesotho and Swaziland, whose currencies are pegged to the rand) more expensive and less competitive.

This is not to absolve China totally. According to Etienne Vlok (2006: 233), "The principal reasons for the decline in [South Africa's clothing] industry are structural, but the current crisis was largely caused (and the long-term survival of the industry is seriously threatened) by a sharp surge in imports, especially from China. . . . This is also linked to the development of post-quota international textiles trade . . . characterized by the dominance of China." Still, to quote one South African official interviewed for an article on Sino-South African relations, "Why can't South African producers make the same product for a competitive price? The Chinese have to pay for transport, pay duties, and pay taxes to get the product here, and still it is cheaper. It is bad for the people working in the textile factories, but they have to move on or become more competitive" (*UN Integrated Regional Information Networks,* March 23, 2006). In fact, the Chinese government has indicated that it is "willing to help Africans improve the competitiveness of their textile products," not only agreeing to fund a US$2.5 million training program in South Africa's garment and textile industry but also promising to make "preferential loans available to South Africa in modernizing its textile industry if [they are] needed" (*Xinhua,* October 18, 2006). These offers are potentially helpful, as Africa needs to start processing local raw materials into finished goods for export rather than exporting raw cotton and cloth, which is largely pointless given the huge subsidies enjoyed by those sectors in the developed world that import them.

That said, there are aspects of Chinese business practice that are problematic and that might even defeat the purpose of Beijing's offers of assistance. A quite pernicious example is the fact that some Chinese manufacturers illicitly copy African designs. Piracy and intellectual-property theft is endemic in China (Mertha, 2007); as Chinese traders expand further overseas, these pathologies of the liberalization process are making themselves felt in the most remote corners of Africa. Although they are not linked to any official policy of the Chinese government, they damage China's image in Africa by contributing to the popular impression that China is ripping off Africa at multiple levels.

▓ Designed in Africa and Made in China— but Who's Buying?

Although the problem of the intellectual theft of African clothing designs by Chinese cloth manufacturers is growing across Africa, it is especially prevalent in West Africa.[26] Traditional African patterns, many of which are printed in wax, are—as any visitor to Africa will attest—popular for both men and women throughout West Africa and beyond. However, Chinese copies of traditional and contemporary African designs are appearing more and more often in African markets, undercutting indigenously manufactured items.[27] In

Ghana, approximately 150 million yards of African prints worth up to US$250 million are sold domestically each year (*BBC News,* August 30, 2006). Yet only around one quarter of Ghanaian demand for such prints is met by locally produced textiles; in 2006, sales for one local company involved in designing and manufacturing African clothing "[fell] by between 50 percent and 75 percent, as customers [bought] Chinese copies of locally produced designs" at prices that were cheaper by one-third to one-half (*BBC News,* August 30, 2006). A 2007 report observed that "textiles that come from China do not only carry the designs of Ghanaian cloths but . . . appear [to be] made in Ghana[ian] cloth. Although the Chinese textiles are not durable compared to made-in-Ghana cloth, they sell far below Ghanaian textiles. Consequently, most retailers of textiles from local textile companies such as Akosombo Textile Limited (ATL), Printex, and Ghana Textiles Prints (GTP) are said to have abandoned the local cloth and are now selling wax prints from China, which [are] far cheaper" (*Public Agenda,* August 3, 2007). The situation has apparently gotten so bad that "industry watchers are wondering [about] the fate of tertiary graduates who pursue industrial-art courses with textile options on the labor market as the sector faces total collapse" (*Public Agenda,* August 3, 2007). Since the demise of Ghana's own textile industry, domestic printed cloth has mostly been composed of imported raw materials, mainly from the Netherlands. But whereas the importation of raw materials such as cotton has historically been complementary to local production, the influx of cheap African prints from China has begun to seriously stifle Ghanaian production. Many of the Chinese copies come into West Africa and particularly Ghana via Lomé in Togo. Indeed,

> Togo remains central . . . as a trade hub for illegal Chinese imports of reproduced African prints. Official trade statistics of China-Togo trade indicate a 27-percent growth rate in 2005 with [US]$508 million of trade value. This indication poorly reflects its actual trade volume, and, most importantly, its reexportation [role] (notably [via] smuggling networks) . . . in the vibrant transborder trade with West Africa's largest consumers of African prints, Nigeria and Ghana—namely those countries whose textile industries have been so severely affected by the export of Chinese-produced African prints. (Sylvanus, 2007: 1)

Unfortunately, as elsewhere in Africa, the clothing and textile industry in Ghana formerly contributed much to the local economy and the country's GDP; it had also employed a sizeable number of women and otherwise jobless youths.

Worryingly, the competitive edge that creativity and market knowledge might give a local company is instantly eroded by the arrival of Chinese fabrics that simply replicate indigenous designs and by the development of Lomé "from a trade hub of European-produced fabrics to a trade hub of Chinese imitations" (Sylvanus, 2007: 2). And there does seem to be evidence that the illegal copying is systematic and widespread, restricted neither to the fabric industry nor to Chinese–West African trade. In Kenya, there are accounts of Chinese traders visiting market stalls to see what is on sale and then hurriedly reproducing such items; according to one local vendor, "Sometimes it happens with a camera. They pose as customers and pretend to be taking general pictures. . . . The next thing we know, they have duplicated the goods and are trading in them. They are edging us out of business. Soon we will have no customers" (quoted in *Inter Press Service,* July 18, 2007). In Sierra Leone in mid-2006, one informant claimed that Chinese entrepreneurs were observed interviewing local people in the markets to ask what sorts of things Sierra Leoneans wanted and wore. Soon after, the market was full of Chinese imports that coincided with locals' responses.[28]

But like many issues surrounding Sino-African relations, the topic is not one-dimensional. Yes, it is true that some Chinese entrepreneurs engage in shady business practices, including intellectual property theft. They indeed sell the resulting designs on the African market and crowd out indigenous producers. But they do so only because they can; they are not being stopped.[29] Explains one commentator, "The problem of counterfeit goods is not unique to China; it affects other countries in the world as well. It is up to African governments to put in place rules and standards that goods from other countries must be subjected to" (*East African,* November 14, 2006). That African governments either lack the ability or choose not to do so is a key issue. For instance, to claim, as a Zimbabwean newspaper did in 2004, that "Chinese residents in Zimbabwe are suspected of engaging in informal trading activities and importing clothes and other cheap low-quality goods without paying taxes or duties" (*Zimbabwe Independent,* October 15) is to ignore the fact that someone with influence within the Zimbabwean state is complicit. Likewise, Chinese managers in Zambia have made it apparent that the main explanation for their noncompliance with Zambian laws is the absence of any enforcement by the Zambian state (Fraser and Lungu, 2007: 52).

In fact, it is highly likely that, in breaking the law, some Chinese importers are taking advantage of not merely the negligent tendencies but the corrupt practices of African statesmen—just as they do in China, where there is a "lack of sufficient political will, corruption, local protectionism, misallocated resources, and training, [as well as] a lack of effective public education regarding the economic and social impact of counterfeiting and piracy" (Israel, 2006: 3). In Ghana, for instance, "It is speculated that some people in government are benefiting from the textile imports" (Quartey, 2006: 143). It is these facilitators of crime, as well as the few rogue Chinese who perpetrate it, who should be held accountable, not the whole Chinese nation. In this respect, it is encouraging that the Southern African Trade Union Council (SATUC) has launched a campaign to mobilize the region's governments, businesses, and labor organizations to ensure that potential investors abide by the law (*Zimbabwe Standard*, May 13, 2007).

Meanwhile, we must also note that consumers are buying these Chinese-made copies. Interviews with market traders in Abuja, Banjul, Freetown, and Praia have revealed that the arrival of foreign textiles has not negatively affected indigenous dealers—but it has granted poorer people the opportunity to buy clothing in traditional designs formerly held to be too expensive. Interestingly, the traders (all women) sold both African-manufactured cloth—mostly from Ghana and Nigeria—and Chinese-manufactured items and respected the consumer's right of choice. They reported that the wealthy tended to buy the relatively high-priced African-made textiles while the less affluent bought Chinese goods.[30] This trend is not restricted to textiles. In a market in Nigeria, traders generally hold two types of electronic goods at their stalls: the brand names, which are relatively expensive but of good quality, and cheap Chinese copies such as Sonny, Samsong, and Pansonik.[31]

Such anecdotes highlight the issue of consumer choice. In Ghana, for instance, "Consumers have argued that although the locally produced, finished fabrics are relatively better in terms of quality, the market for imported products has increased because the products have attractive colors, new designs, [and] a softer and glossier finish" (Quartey, 2006: 139). Indeed, the *East African* has editorialized that "compared with Western products, Chinese products enjoy a better price-to-performance ratio and better meet the needs of consumers" (November 7, 2006), and the fact is that Chinese manufactured goods are highly popular among African consumers despite frequent complaints about their quality. According to one informant, "Chinese products are poor in quality—everyone knows this. But people buy them because they cannot afford anything else."[32] Take the case of Sierra Leone, where Chinese-made clothes are referred to by wags as "PRSP cloth," that is, cloth allegedly suitable as part of an emergency Poverty Reduction Strategy Paper initiative but not for the long term.[33] As the *New York Times* reports, however, Chinese importers generally "give Africans access to goods and amenities that developed countries take for granted but that most people here could not have dreamed of affording just a few years ago—cellular telephones, televisions, washing machines, refrigerators, computers. And cheaper prices on more basic items, like clothing, light bulbs and shoes, mean people have more money in their pockets" (August 21, 2007).

Meanwhile, the Zimbabwean deputy minister of industry and international trade, Phineas Chihota, has noted that "individual businesspeople and some private companies have demonstrated their interest in importing cheap Chinese goods," so "it is locals [who are] fueling [the] trade in cheap Chinese imports" (*Zimbabwe Independent*, October 20, 2006). And the competition brought by cheap Chinese products is not necessarily a bad thing.[34] Sam Ncube of the Bulawayo Affirmative Action Group in fact asserts that competition is healthy and that "people should open up and appreciate that these people [the Chinese] are providing the competition we need" (*Zimbabwe Standard,* August 2, 2004). Affordable alternatives for low-income households are commendable in themselves, although there is a potential long-term downside for the overall economy, as we will soon see.

A common complaint against Chinese traders, echoed by local businesspeople interviewed in Botswana, Ethiopia, Namibia, Nigeria, Sierra Leone, and Uganda, is that they are given preferential treatment by African governments and that the economic playing field has shifted in their favor.[35] Indeed, one informant in Nigeria claims the Chinese get explicitly favorable treatment from the government.[36] However, some context is in order. According to the same informant, outside of Abuja and Lagos, the only foreign businesspeople one sees are Chinese, which suggests that no one else is really interested in investing in Nigeria (excluding those in the oil sector). Thus, "we think they [the Chinese] are good overall."[37] And in fact, as one Nigerian businessman put it, "Our leaders want to demonstrate to the world that they are 'open' but few people want to touch us outside of oil due to our bad governments. The Chinese were [among] the few who took up the invitations and so we roll out the red carpet for them—not because they are favored but because they are the only ones coming."[38]

In some quarters, such as South Africa, the consumer boom that cheap Chinese imports have spurred in the clothing market has had a positive impact on the broader economy despite the ramifications for the indigenous textile industry, at least "as far as total employment and output growth . . . are concerned, since the growth rate in South Africa has been based on the retail sector's expenditures" (Bonga-Bonga, 2006). Of course, it could be argued that the increase in retail employment merely compensates for job losses in the textiles and clothing industries; what's more, it leaves South Africa in the unenviable position of being a consumer rather than a producer with development potential—even if the products consumed are cheaper thanks to China. This sort of economic relationship, arguably reminiscent of forms of neocolonialism, is what Mbeki was in part warning of in his comments on Sino-African relations. An additional argument is that Chinese businesspeople who wish to come to Africa "should come as investors, building factories, not as petty traders who compete for already scarce customers [with] bottom-dollar items like flip-flops and T-shirts" (*New York Times,* August 18, 2007); interviews with African traders in Botswana, Nigeria, Sierra Leone, South Africa, and Uganda reflect this line of thought.

Yet, choice remains a crux of the debate as presented by one South African newspaper: "South African consumers . . . have a role to play." Consumers unhappy about China's domination of the market "must simply do without those cheap goods." However, "after the seemingly interminable consumer party that is the result of relatively low interest rates and cheap imported goods, which in no small measure has contributed to the booming South African economy, giving it all up may be hard to do" (*Business Day,* July 11, 2007). An editorial in a Ugandan newspaper summarizes the situation succinctly: "In most African countries, [Chinese commerce has] resulted in a fall in prices and a wider variety of consumer goods on the market, cutting the daily expense[s] of urban families. . . . At the same time, the Chinese traders are taking away business and income from local traders, who lack the foreign contacts and access to credit" (*New Vision,* June 2, 2007). Interviews with market traders in Abuja, Asmara, Freetown, Gaborone, Kampala, and Windhoek indicate that, like their customers, African stallholders welcome Chinese products—they just don't want the Chinese vendors moving in to outcompete them. This conundrum will not be easily resolved.

■ Conclusion

Any commentator on the effect that cheap Chinese imports are having on Africa's manufacturing base, particularly the clothing and textile sectors, must acknowledge that Africa's industries have been in decline—which some say is terminal—for a long time, certainly prior to the arrival of the Chinese on the scene. For instance, between 1975 and 2000, Ghana experienced a reduction of textile output by about 50 percent while employment in the sector shrank by 80 percent, from 25,000 to only 5,000 people (Traub-Merz, 2006: 17). To observe, as did Abraham Koomson of the Textile, Garments, and Leather Employees Union in 2007, that "the problems with Ghana's textile industry exist and [are] getting worse each day" . . . and argue that "there is the need for government to find out why the sector is collapsing and why Ghana cannot compete with China" (*Public Agenda,* August 3, 2007) is to ignore the fact that the sector all but collapsed long ago. We should add as an ironic aside that the cloth for the 2007 celebration of the fiftieth anniversary of Ghana's independence was made in China (*Public Agenda,* August 3, 2007). Similarly, in Zambia, employment in the clothing and textile sector fell from 25,000 in the 1980s to below 10,000 in 2002; in Kenya, the number of large-scale garment manufacturers has dropped from 110 in the 1980s to 55 in the 2000s (Traub-Merz, 2006: 17). Very little of this has to do with the Chinese per se, although their entry into the African market has undoubtedly worsened matters.

Further, any analysis of the effect that China has had on Africa's exporting ability must account for two factors: export-supply capacity—which is shaped by both production costs and the size of the industrial base and has significant implications for the ability to compete globally—and negative import-demand conditions associated with the state of the US and European markets, which is largely outside the control of African governments.[39] With respect to export-supply capacity, Africa's one-time growth in the clothing- and textile-export sector was, as we have demonstrated, predicated on the use of foreign fabrics and on fortuitous but temporary circumstances, namely trade preferences and heavy investments by Chinese companies taking advantage of the AGOA in the late 1990s and early 2000s. In other words, it was an artificial boom for an industry that had otherwise lost its competitive edge long before. Indeed, it seems apparent that the only factor supporting the growth of much of Africa's export-oriented clothing sector was preferential access to overseas markets, particularly in the United States and the EU. When these privileges were abolished, Africa's success in the clothing and textile sectors evaporated.[40] Furthermore, we must emphasize that this supposed advantage was not only temporary but may eventually have had a negative impact on the industry, as there appears to be a link between tariff preferences and market-access privileges and the cost of units produced (Kaplinsky and Morris, 2006). In fact, Africa's best-protected production sectors are the ones coming under the worst pressure vis-à-vis prices and thus are rapidly losing their market share to China.[41]

This irony is directly linked to the competitiveness of African garment and textile exports for reasons that are often obfuscated. Consider the fact that wages in Africa's most active clothing and textile sectors are high compared to those in Asia. According to Kaplinsky and Morris (2006: 35), Asian producers pay wages of between US$0.15 and US$0.33 per hour, while hourly wages in southern and eastern Africa vary from US$0.44 to US$1.87; Bangladesh and the interior of China pay the least, setting wages at between US$0.15 and US$0.17 per hour, respectively, while South African workers are paid the most, making the aforementioned US$1.87 an hour. But wage levels in other African apparel industries are much lower than those in China or India; a detailed 2005 study of the industry in Ethiopia, Kenya, Madagascar, and Uganda estimated that monthly wages averaged US$205 in China and US$146 in India but only US$90 in Kenya, US$65 in Uganda, US$38 in Madagascar, and US$30 in Ethiopia (Lande et al., 2005: 60). It also found that "the major deficiency is the productivity of COMESA [Common Market for Eastern and Southern Africa] workers in each of the four LDC members that were visited. . . . In fact, productivity is so low as measured in machine output per hour, it more than offsets the lower wages paid in sub-Saharan Africa" (Lande et al., 2005: 59–61). In short, wage levels are not the only factor in determining competitiveness; low productivity poses a similar problem. In Lesotho, for example, "it is estimated that most firms . . . register around 50 percent in labor productivity relative to that in East Asia" (Sandrey et al., 2005: 21). There may even be "pervasive evidence that many [sub-Saharan African] clothing plants have low levels of productivity because of poor organizational procedures, low levels of skill, and inadequate management within plants" (Kaplinsky, McCormick, and Morris, 2006: 13).

Although the International Textile, Garment, and Leather Workers Federation's African chapter claims that southern Africa "could not compete with

Chinese exports because of government subsidies, an artificially weak currency, and the absence of independent trade unions in China, which depressed working conditions and kept costs down" (*Business Day,* September 27, 2005), the reality is somewhat different. Consider first that "one of the primary competitive benefits of Chinese industry is the efficiency with which the infrastructure functions. This includes not just physical infrastructure such as roads, water and power, but also bureaucratic infrastructure such as port clearance, enterprise set-up and the delivery of appropriate certification" (Kaplinsky and Morris, 2006: 43). Now contrast this picture to that of Africa. We have already touched on productivity levels, but infrastructural constraints are equally important. Access to power and water, the development of an educated and incentivized workforce, a solid transport infrastructure, the efficiency of customs and clearing, general political stability—all these conditions and more contribute to productivity. In many countries in Africa, none are optimal.[42] For instance, a study on Ghana's clothing and textiles industry finds that

> the decline in textile exports from 1992 to 1998 can be attributed to internal and external bottlenecks. Ghanaian manufacturers of textiles generally agree that the market for exports is huge but have reservations about operating in some of these markets, particularly within the ECOWAS [Economic Community of West African States] subregion, due to trade barriers. Some of the trade barriers include, among others, imposition of [a] 20 percent duty by Côte d'Ivoire (contrary to ECOWAS regulations), transit tax collected at Benin, extortion by Nigerian authorities, and the risk of currency devaluation. Poor packaging of some manufacturers/exporters also serves as a barrier to exports to markets such as the EU and the United States of America. . . . [as do] poor finishing of products (quality/conformity to standards), technical barriers, [the] inability of some manufacturers to meet export orders on schedule, [and] high tariffs charged in some export destinations of Ghanaian textile, to mention but a few. (Quartey, 2006: 140)

By the same token, the World Bank estimates that "the cost of doing business in Africa is 20–40 percent above that for other developing regions due to high regulatory costs, unsecured land property rights, ineffective judiciary systems, policy uncertainty, and unfair competition from politically connected companies, which results in a few large firms holding very dominant market shares" (Mutume, 2006: 19).

Overall, China's rise vis-à-vis Africa's manufacturing sector could be a positive catalyst for change, enlarging the market for exports from Africa to China, stimulating competition and, in turn, innovation within Africa.[43] But it could also be a negative one, with Chinese goods crowding out exports from Africa in third-country markets and taking the place of indigenous goods in local markets[44] (although African consumers seem quite content with this scenario, which benefits them). The impact of Sino-African trade, however, varies hugely from country to country; a brief chapter on the topic can only touch on some of these variations. Still, a key point is that much of the purported impact of China's exports on Africa may reflect less on Chinese practices and conditions than on those of Africa. Indeed, attempts by African governments to guide and manage Chinese investments leave a lot to be desired. This fact is beginning to plague Chinese entrepreneurs who are being blamed by some Africans for their governments' failings,[45] partly out of a misunderstanding of the nature of Chinese investment. As one South African report put it, "There is nothing essentially wrong with China making inroads into global markets. Everybody tries to do it. What is different here is that some African governments seem to believe it's not strictly a hard-nosed relationship but one that is altruistically motivated" (*Business Day,* February 21, 2005). Tellingly, "the Chinese practice of offering 'gifts' to smooth the way for later ventures often serves to bolster this perception of magnanimous comradeship" (*Business Day,* February 21, 2005). Concurs a Nigerian informant, "We [Nigerians] go into negotiations with the Chinese with our eyes closed—it's like taking candy [from] a baby."[46]

As a whole, the post-MFA era has seen a decline in prices and increased competitiveness within the sector. China has been the key beneficiary in this regard, as retailers and consumers have favored cheaper Chinese products. There is evidence that this trend has caused job losses in some African countries, though these may be offset as businesses retool and innovate. Take Lesotho. In 2004, its apparel sector employed around 50,000 workers and earned US$456 million in exports to the US market; in 2005, when the MFA lapsed, 10,000 workers lost their jobs as earnings dropped to US$391 million and factories closed. However, the government took the initiative and helped textile and clothing producers rebrand themselves as manufacturers of "ethical clothing" for the US market, facilitating a near-total recovery of jobs: "Rather than trying to compete with Asian clothing on cost, Lesotho's manufacturers are retooling to appeal to a niche market that values higher quality goods made in countries with good labor and human-rights practices. With the assistance of The Whitaker Group, Lesotho clothing can now be found in giant US retail chains like Target and The Gap, bearing the Product Red label created by rock star Bono" (*New Vision,* December 3, 2006). It seems indisputable that weaker African firms will continue to go under, in part because of the flood of Chinese imports. But China may also provide a model for lower-tech industrial development, inspiring manufacturing spinoffs or jump-starting local investment (Brautigam, 2007). Whether African entrepreneurs, enabled by their governments, seize opportunities to adopt it remains to be seen.

New FDIs in the textile and clothing sectors of economies that formerly benefited from preferential access are likely to diminish (though not to completely disappear). Those economies in Africa that profited most from preferential quotas on textiles and clothing are those most likely to suffer due to Chinese export expansion. However, as we have detailed, Africans themselves have played an equal if not more significant role in the decline of their clothing and textile industries; Chinese traders are simply making the most of it. To quote Moeletsi Mbeki, a South African political analyst (and brother of President Thabo Mbeki), African governments "have failed to develop manufacturing for a variety of reasons, and for the Chinese that's a huge opportunity. We are a very important market for China" (*New York Times,* August 21, 2007).

Moreover, while observers must be very careful not to make China a scapegoat for Africa's failings, they must also not place unrealistic expectations on the private Chinese entrepreneurs who are, after all, businesspeople motivated by profits (the overwhelming majority of them have no contact with the Chinese government beyond initial registration with local embassies).[47] Thus it is unrealistic to argue with Cephas Mukuka, assistant national executive secretary of the Federation of Free Trade Unions of Zambia that "little has been done by China to support the growth of local industries" and that "the Zambian government should come up with a policy to compel Chinese investors to help set up infrastructure to aid technology transfer in Zambia" even as China "commit[s] to long-term investment and set[s] up a university of science and technology in Zambia" (*Business Daily,* August 3, 2007).

It is clearly both an exaggeration and a simplification to claim that "the Chinese continue to be the worst businesspeople in the world," that "there [has been] no direct benefit from Chinese investors," or that "China is out to exploit Africa's material and human resources [by] coming here with finished goods and secondhand products, which have led to the collapse of the textile and clothing industries" (*Zimbabwe Standard,* May 13, 2007). However, ever-mindful of China's image, policymakers in Beijing will likely have to address these criticisms more forcefully to prevent the negative impressions of China's impact on Africa's manufacturing sectors, however unfair, from gaining ground across the continent.[48] In fact, according to Nina Sylvanus (2007: 4), "The biggest challenge China will have to face in the future is the increasing Sinophobic resentment" generated by Chinese traders whose products dominate local African markets. Hence the concern expressed by one Chinese diplomat that unscrupulous Chinese traders "give China a bad name,"[49]—especially as it is "very difficult to control them. If they are small-scale entrepreneurs, it is almost impossible to catch them, particularly as it seems a lot of what they bring into [Africa] is smuggled [or] actually brought in by [African] middlemen. But we realize it is important to stop them before it becomes a major issue." Given the immense endogenous and exogenous challenges facing Africa's manufacturing sectors and markets, this will not be an easy task to achieve.

▩ Notes

1. Interview with David Jabati, news editor, *Awareness Times,* Freetown, Sierra Leone, June 7, 2006.

2. Interview with Sanusi Deen, national chairman of the Sierra Leone Indigenous Business Association, Freetown, Sierra Leone, June 7, 2006.

3. Interview with Shu Zhan, Chinese ambassador to Eritrea, Asmara, Eritrea, June 29, 2006.

4. Interview with African Union official, Addis Ababa, Ethiopia, May 15, 2007.

5. Interview with African Union official, Addis Ababa, Ethiopia, May 16, 2007.

6. Interview with British diplomat, Addis Ababa, Ethiopia, May 15, 2007.

7. Interview with Moses Pakote, deputy director of Investor Services, Namibia Investment Centre, Ministry of Trade and Industry, Windhoek, Namibia, August 11, 2006.

8. Interviews with Chinese shopkeepers, Praia and Assomada, Cape Verde, November 5 and 6, 2007.

9. Interview with African Union official, Addis Ababa, Ethiopia, May 16, 2007.

10. Interview with African Union official, Addis Ababa, Ethiopia, May 15, 2007.

11. Interview with Ethiopian academic, Addis Ababa, Ethiopia, November 22, 2005.

12. Interview with Moses Pakote, deputy director of Investor Services, Namibia Investment Centre, Ministry of Trade and Industry, Windhoek, Namibia, August 11, 2006.

13. Interview with Western diplomat, Abuja, Nigeria, September 3, 2007.

14. Interview with Moses Pakote, deputy director of Investor Services, Namibia Investment Centre, Ministry of Trade and Industry, Windhoek, Namibia, August 11, 2006.

15. Interview with African Union official, Addis Ababa, Ethiopia, May 16, 2007.

16. Interview with Ethiopian academic, Addis Ababa, Ethiopia, November 22, 2005.

17. Interview with a journalist from the *Abuja Inquirer,* Abuja, Nigeria, September 3, 2007.

18. Interview with a representative from the House of Representatives, Abuja, Nigeria, September 3, 2007.

19. Interview with Western diplomat, Abuja, Nigeria, September 3, 2007.

20. Interview with an official from the Business Round Table, Abuja, Nigeria, September 6, 2007.

21. Interview with an official from the Business Round Table, Abuja, Nigeria, September 6, 2007.

22. Interview with Western diplomat, Abuja, Nigeria, September 3, 2007.

23. Interview with Chinese diplomat, Abuja, Nigeria, September 5, 2007.

24. Interview with Lucy Corkin, research manager, Centre for Chinese Studies, Stellenbosch, South Africa, July 31, 2006.

25. HS lines refer to the Harmonized Commodity Description and Coding System, known as the Harmonized System or simply HS, a multipurpose international product nomenclature developed by the World Customs Organization (WCO) and comprising about 5,000 commodity groups, each identified by a six digit code and arranged legally and backed up by established rules to achieve uniform classification.

26. Interview with David Jabati, news editor, *Awareness Times,* Freetown, Sierra Leone, June 7, 2006.

27. Interview with Saffie Koroma, National Accountability Group, Freetown, Sierra Leone, June 7, 2006.

28. Interview with Saffie Koroma, National Accountability Group, Freetown, Sierra Leone, June 7, 2006.

29. Interview with a journalist from the *Abuja Inquirer,* Abuja, Nigeria, September 3, 2007.

30. Interview with market trader, Victoria Park market, Freetown, Sierra Leone, June 8, 2006.

31. Interview with market trader, Wuse market, Abuja, Nigeria, September 4, 2007.

32. Interview with Cape Verdean hotel owner, Praia, Cape Verde, November 5, 2007.

33. Interview with Saffie Koroma, National Accountability Group, Freetown, Sierra Leone, June 7, 2006.

34. Interview with market trader, Kampala, Uganda, November 4, 2006.

35. Interview with DFID official, Freetown, Sierra Leone, June 7, 2006.

36. Interview with a journalist from the *Abuja Inquirer,* Abuja, Nigeria, September 3, 2007.

37. Interview with a journalist from the *Abuja Inquirer,* Abuja, Nigeria, September 3, 2007.

38. Interview with an official from the Business Round Table, Abuja, Nigeria, September 6, 2007.

39. Interview with African Union official, Addis Ababa, Ethiopia, May 15, 2007.

40. Interview with Western diplomat, Abuja, Nigeria, September 3, 2007.

41. Interview with African Union official, Addis Ababa, Ethiopia, May 15, 2007.

42. Interview with British diplomat, Addis Ababa, Ethiopia, May 15, 2007.

43. Interview with African Union official, Addis Ababa, Ethiopia, May 15, 2007.

44. Interview with Sanusi Deen, national chairman, Sierra Leone Indigenous Business Association, Freetown, Sierra Leone, June 7, 2006.

45. Interview with a journalist from the *Abuja Inquirer,* Abuja, Nigeria, September 3, 2007.

46. Interview with a representative from the House of Representatives, Abuja, Nigeria, September 3, 2007.

47. Interview with Chinese trader, Santa Maria, Cape Verde, November 7, 2007.

48. Interview with the acting head of the political-affairs section of the Chinese Embassy, Windhoek, Namibia, August 13, 2006.

49. Interview with Chinese diplomat, Abuja, Nigeria, September 5, 2007.

The Issue of Human Rights | 4

The growth in Sino-African relations has provoked criticisms of Beijing's perceived stance on governance and human rights on the continent (see Waging Peace, 2008). Human Rights Watch (2006) has alleged that "China's policies have not only propped up some of the continent's worst human-rights abusers but also weakened the leverage of others trying to promote greater respect for human rights." Similarly, Sariah Rees-Roberts, a press officer for Amnesty International, has argued that "China is having an adverse effect on human rights in other countries because by dealing with repressive regimes, such as [that] in Sudan, and putting its economic and trading interests ahead of concern for human rights, it's allowing these regimes to be provided with resources that they would not otherwise get so easily" (quoted in *UN Integrated Regional Information Networks,* June 27, 2006). Adds the Council on Foreign Relations,

> China's rise in Africa poses . . . challenges to the United States and its Western partners. [One] is China's protection of "rogue states" like Sudan and Zimbabwe in the face of egregious human-rights violations. [Another] is China's effect on patterns of Western influence: negative pressures—such as withholding aid or placing limitations on investments—to improve an African country's human-rights or governing practices provide less leverage if China is prepared to counterbalance that influence. (2006: 49–50)

Governmental and institutional leaders have joined in the criticism; in 2006, the then president of the World Bank, Paul Wolfowitz, was quoted as saying that Chinese banks were breaking the Equator Principles, a voluntary code of conduct that calls for lenders to ensure that the projects they fund meet environmental and social standards, including human rights (*Les Echos,* October 23, 2006). Hearings before a congressional subcommittee of the Committee on

International Relations of the US House of Representatives were replete with references to China's apparent stance vis-à-vis human rights in its diplomacy toward Africa. Typical among them was the comment that "the Chinese government's apparent 'see-no-evil' approach is dangerous to the stability of the region. In their quest to find markets for their goods and to extract natural resources from the region, the Chinese appear willing to overlook ghastly human-rights abuses and support authoritarian regimes in exchange for profitable contracts" (Krilla, 2005).

There is an explicit concern that China's perceived stance is threatening Western interests.[1] For instance, while major donor countries and institutions have embraced the notion that good governance and respect for human rights are an integral part of any foreign policy toward Africa, the sense that "[China's] diplomacy and economic outreach in Africa are not contingent upon this fundamental requirement. . . . [and therefore] may undermine important [US] development and diplomatic goals in Africa" (Bartholomew, 2005: 79) has grown, particularly after 2005, the so-called Year of Africa. In 2006, one British newspaper went so far as to state that "a year on from Live 8, China has trounced all hope of change in Africa by doing deals with its kleptocrats," adding that "China will deal with anyone, and pariah states are a gap in the market." Indeed, it went further, predicting serious implications for British foreign policy: "The Department for International Development is now trying to encourage good governance by cutting back aid to countries that persecute opposition leaders and supporters. The latest approach makes sense. But, sadly, the game is up: China makes it irrelevant" (*Times,* July 4, 2006). A 2007 editorial in the *New York Times* put it rather more bluntly:

> Misspent your country's wealth? Waged war against an ethnic minority? Or just tired of those pesky good governance requirements attached to foreign aid by most Western governments and multilateral institutions? If you run an African country and have some natural resources to put in long-term hock, you've got a friend in Beijing ready to write big checks with no embarrassing questions. That's nice for governments, but not so nice for their misgoverned people. (February 19, 2007)

African commentators have been equally critical. A selection of excerpts from African newspapers reveals the unease. From West Africa's *Public Agenda:* "[China] is sacrificing human-rights protection for natural resources. Unlike other western countries, which bar their companies from doing business with renegade regimes, Beijing insists on dealing with the continent's most brutal and corrupt leaders" (November 6, 2006). From *East African Business Week:* "Critics . . . point fingers at what they say are China's business dealings with pariah states in total disregard of the issue of human rights and accountability" (May 1, 2006). And from *The Namibian:*

Sino-African relations are essentially devoid of any political content, and this absence . . . complicates efforts at deepening and strengthening democracy and human rights . . . This self-interest in China's Africa policy empties it of moral content. . . . Certainly, this is . . . not a matter of concern for governments in power or China itself, but it is for the people of these countries who are inevitably victims of resource-rich undemocratic regimes whose wealth does not necessarily filter to the bottom. (January 19, 2007)

Hovering over such concerns is the specter of Chinese imperialism, as is evident in a Kenyan observer's comment that both "at home and abroad, China puts economic growth before human rights. It has vetoed UN attempts to issue a resolution critical of the repressive Sudanese government. China needs Africa's raw materials to fuel its economy. If African leaders do not act, they will be remembered for presiding over a time when Africa cast off Western imperialism to embrace an Eastern variety" (*East African Standard,* January 8, 2007).

In a nutshell, the criticisms—from both the West and Africa—are that Beijing will do business with any government, regardless of its human-rights or democratic record, and that it thereby undermines attempts to advance constitutional rights and champion broader issues of good governance on the continent. Both these criticisms and the arguable contradictions, fluctuations, and limitations of Beijing's stances on noninterference and the definition of human rights—as evidenced in its policies with respect to Zimbabwe—will all be discussed in this chapter. It is apposite, however, that we first turn to what constitutes the Chinese government's own understanding of human rights.

▓ Chinese Conceptions of Human Rights

According to Wan Ming (2001: 1), "Few issues in the relations between China and the West invoke as much passion as human rights." Although the concept of human rights is often central to criticisms of China's relations with Africa, its definition is a point of contention between Beijing and the West—one that has moved down the bilateral agenda—ever since then US president Bill Clinton delinked human rights and most-favored-nations trade status in May 1994. Subsequently, "although Western criticism of China's human rights remained, it gradually became ritualized and marginalized on Western diplomatic agendas in China" (Wan Ming, 2005: 288). Why and when the topic was resurrected with regard to Sino-African ties is in itself an interesting question, which undoubtedly relates to anxieties regarding how China's rise may affect Western, specifically US, interests (see, e.g., Mann, 2007; Peerenboom, 2007; cf. Lampton, 2007).

Negative focus is usually placed on China's transgressions of the norms adopted by the United Nations. However, it would be erroneous to regard what

Chinese sources call China's human rights outlook, which is grounded in native tradition, as one-dimensional—and thus, by inference, inimical to the international human-rights regime. As Albert Chen (2000: 2) points out, "When we turn to the Chinese tradition, we can, as in the case of the West, find . . . elements that have affinities with, or can contribute to, the modern conception of human rights as well as elements that contradict that conception. The former elements include the Confucian principle of benevolence as the basic norm governing relations between human beings [and] the idea of the equality of all human beings in terms of the capacity for moral cultivation and growth."

Traditionally, the dominant Chinese discourse on rights has focused on the obligations and responsibilities of citizens in building a rich and strong society. This emphasis has underpinned most official Chinese positions since 1949 and dominates Beijing policymakers' thinking on the subject today. Although it is evolving—after all, as Stephen Angle (2002) points out, individuals rather than abstract countries have dialogues—a certain amount of continuity in themes and values allows observers to talk of a Chinese human-rights discourse (see Weatherley, 2001). Very briefly summarized, China's discourse on human rights is characterized by a communitarian emphasis on solidarity and duty toward others, which coincides with the Confucian concern for promoting harmony. The perception within China by the leadership that the country is unstable also leads to Beijing's prioritization of social stability (Solinger, 2008). In short, this discourse is informed by pragmatic nationalism, with a strong emphasis on developmentalism. Then President Jiang Zemin's address to the Fifteenth National Congress of the Communist Party of China on September 12, 1997, laid out this position clearly:

> The fundamental task of socialism is to develop the productive forces. During the primary stage, it is all the more necessary to give first priority to concentrating on their development. Different contradictions exist in China's economy, politics, culture, social activities, and other areas, and class contradictions, due to international and domestic factors, will still exist within a certain scope for a long time to come. But the principal contradiction in society is the one between the growing material and cultural needs of the people and the backwardness of production. . . . Hence *we are destined to make economic development the central task of the entire Party and the whole country and make sure that all other work is subordinated to and serves this task* [emphasis added]. (*People's Daily,* September 13, 1997)

Jiang went on to note that "development is the absolute principle," but added that "it is of the utmost importance to balance reform, development, and stability and to maintain a stable political environment and public order. Without stability, nothing [can] be achieved" (*People's Daily,* September 13, 1997). Granted, "stability" can be interpreted in a variety of ways, depending on one's point of view.

If one accepts the Chinese discourse on human rights and the centrality of development, then one might argue that China has made considerable progress over the past few decades:

> It would be churlish of Western commentators to underestimate the enormous achievement, in the context of China's recent history, [that] is represented by the current economic development and material improvement in the day-to-day life of the Chinese population, albeit largely urban. . . . It has lifted over 150 million people out of poverty in less than a decade. By way of corroboration, according to figures from UNICEF, the UN, and UNESCO, China does better than India, a country with a similar population level, in infant mortality, life expectancy, and primary school enrollment. There are many more statistics indicating that although China is a lower-middle-income country, it outperforms a number of other countries in its class in relation to the basic economic, social, and cultural indicators. (Lee, 2007: 448)

Indeed, as Daniel Burstein and Arne de Keijzer (1999: 136) point out, "To the Chinese, the human rights to food, clothing, shelter, economic development, and security . . . are paramount over traditional Western-style individual political liberties. Judged by this standard, China in the last twenty years is a leader, not a laggard, in promoting the human rights of its people." Randall Peerenboom concurs:

> [The US State Department] reports for China invariably start with a description of the nature of the political regime, as if that were the most significant determinant for rights in the country. [For example,] the 2004 report on China begins: "The People's Republic of China . . . is an authoritarian state in which . . . the Chinese Communist Party . . . is the paramount source of power." Imagine if it began instead: "Human rights and other indicators of well-being across the board are highly correlated with wealth. China outperforms the average country in its lower-middle income category on every major indicator except civil and political rights (as is generally true for other East Asian countries)." (2007: 173)

In fact, adds Peerenboom, the rule of law, good governance, and the codification of most rights (including civil and political rights) correlate to relatively high levels of wealth. Thus a comparison of China to the developed world unsurprisingly reveals that the former has more departures from the rule of law, weaker state institutions, more corruption, and fewer individual freedoms than their Western counterparts. Peerenboom (2005) offers a variety of explanations for his view that the comparison is unfair and that China is held to higher (or even double) standards than other lower-middle-income countries. Among these are that the Western-dominated international human-rights community is biased toward democracies that promote liberal, civil, and political rights, holding nondemocratic countries to the same standards despite their differing needs and values. China is also singled out because of its potential threat to US domination; Beijing's growing economic and geopolitical muscle is seen to pose a normative challenge to the liberal human-rights regime insofar as China's elites could deploy it to defend and advance rights-based policies and ideals that clash with those of the West, predicated as they are on secular liberalism (Ikenberry, 2008). The idea that US hegemony might be challenged by Beijing reduces some commentators to near-apoplexy (e.g., Fingleton, 2008).

Ostensibly, then, it is in an ideological clash with the liberal West that China finds itself on the defense. With its strong emphasis on social stability, Beijing sees the notion that states must guarantee freedom and liberty for individuals as an abstraction at best and a danger at worst. A 2005 commentary in *Xinhua* on human rights put it thus: "Human rights [are] enjoyed by the collective in addition to [the individual]. The individuals' interests are upheld via the realization of collective interests. So China attaches importance to collective human rights as well as to individuals' human rights. This is in contrast to Western countries, where much emphasis is put on individuals' human rights while collective human rights are neglected" (*Xinhua,* December 12, 2005). This has become the position that Chinese officials generally take when discussing China's noninterference stance in Africa.[2] For instance, Foreign Minister Li Zhaoxing, when asked about China's investment in nations with records of human-rights abuses—notably Sudan and the Central African Republic—replied: "Do you know what the meaning of human rights is? The basic meaning of human rights is survival—and development" (quoted by *Associated Press,* January 8, 2007). A study by Robert Weil of Chinese students suggests that they share the official position of the elites, speaking as they did of "greater political democratization emerging in time from an expanding economy, in a mirror image of the United States' claim that all economic problems can ultimately be solved through the normal channels of politics. Both positions may be equally specious. But there is no fundamental reason why either claim should be privileged over the other as a basis for global human-rights standards, and China refuses to recognize any such arbitrary assertion" (1994: 104).

Importantly, China still adheres to the Five Principles of Mutual Coexistence (see Chapter 1). Though these principles originally prescribed relations only between China and India, by the 1970s they extended to relations with all states. It should be noted that a paper on China's Africa policy released by the Ministry of Foreign Affairs in 2006 expressly states, "China stands ready to develop friendly relations and cooperation with all countries on the basis of the Five Principles of Peaceful Coexistence" (Ministry of Foreign Affairs, 2006: 3). Noninterference and the importance of sovereignty—central to the Five Principles—are explicitly connected to the issue of human rights: "Human rights are something covered by the sovereignty of a country. A country's sovereignty is the foremost collective human right. . . . And sovereignty is the guarantor of human rights." Historical perspective underpins the statement, quoted in *Xinhua* that: "In the humiliating old days, China was bullied by foreign powers. Its sovereignty was trampled on, and [so were] the Chinese people's human rights. So the Chinese people know very well that sovereignty is a precondition to their enjoying human rights. In sum, there would be no human rights to speak of in the absence of sovereignty" (December 12, 2005). How remembrance of the past informs contemporary China's ideas of sovereignty and human rights is important to consider (Scott, 2007).

We should point out that the West has shown only recent interest in China's human rights record (Nathan, 1994). As China opened up to the global economy in the 1980s, Beijing began to involve itself in various international regimes vis-à-vis human rights:

> Perceived as undergoing a much-applauded modernization program with social as well as economic ramifications, Beijing was throughout the 1980s given favorable treatment by the Western media who saw/hoped that China was being remade as a Chinese imitation of the West's self-image. Western policymakers replicated this wishful aspiration, and . . . complaints over China's *laogai* (forced labor) system, public executions, and lack of democracy were eerily absent. (Taylor, 1998: 446)

The West appeared unconcerned that Beijing's contribution to human-rights progress was mostly rhetorical. Chinese praise for the Universal Declaration of Human Rights as "the first international instrument that systematically sets forth the specific contents regarding respect for and [the] protection of fundamental human rights"—despite China's transgressions thereof—underscores this point (*Xinhua* quoted in Zhang Yongjin, 1998: 188).

It was after Tiananmen Square that human rights came to the fore of China's international relations and that Africa's place in Beijing's foreign policy was reconsidered following a decade of neglect (Cooper, 1994; Taylor, 2006). Beijing was shocked by the level of Western criticism regarding Tiananmen and sought to counter it by attentively courting the developing world.[3] Anti-imperialist rhetoric was dusted off and employed in combination with an emphasis on state sovereignty and the advancement of different definitions of human rights and democracy. Beijing profoundly resented critiques of its human-rights record and perceived attempts by outsiders to interfere in China's affairs, which it linked to ulterior motives to halt China's modernization program, revealing deep-seated collective memories of colonial interference in China in the nineteenth century as well as a xenophobia that is arguably integral to Chinese political culture (see Liao Kuangsheng, 1990, and Lovell, 2007; but cf. Waley-Cohen, 2000).

At the time of the Tiananmen crisis, Deng Xiaoping commented, "I am Chinese and familiar with the history of foreign aggression against China. When I heard . . . Western countries . . . decided to impose sanctions on China, my immediate association was [of] 1900, when the allied forces of eight foreign powers invaded China" (Deng Xiaoping, 1994: 344). Observes Ming Wan (2005: 291), "In discussions with Chinese diplomats and officials . . . I sense a strong indignation toward the United States and an equally strong conviction that the US human-rights pressure was simply an excuse for keeping China weakened and subordinated, a humiliating situation that Chinese patriots should not allow to happen [again]." Indeed, the comment made by Deng Xiaoping in September 1989 that "there are many people in the world who hope [China] will develop, but there are also many who are out to get us" (Deng Xiaoping, 1994: 309) is typical. Such depths of feeling influence Beijing's foreign policy; they are often expressed in the context of Sino-African relations, usually with respect to China's subjugation and Africa's colonial experience and to assert the common history of China and Africa.

In sum, there remain two key elements to the PRC's foreign policy stance regarding human rights. The first involves the importance of the right to pursue economic prosperity. On a visit to China in April 1993, the Zambian foreign minister concurred with Beijing's assessment that for "developing countries, the most basic human rights are the rights to subsistence and to development' (*Xinhua*, April 10, 1993). He Wenping, director of the African Studies Section at CASS, has likewise averred that Beijing policymakers don't believe "human rights should stand above sovereignty. . . . We have a different view on this, and African countries share our view" (quoted in Mooney, 2005: 2). A Chinese commentary argues that such a position is in line with the UN's own: "The Universal Declaration of Human Rights is the first international document ever to put forward the principle of respecting and guaranteeing the most fundamental of human rights, reflecting the importance attached by the international community to the promotion of human rights and basic freedom. China's human-rights outlook is in keeping with the basic principles of the Universal Declaration of Human Rights" (*Xinhua*, December 12, 2005).

Indeed, Beijing's focus on economic and developmental rights does gel with some of the Declaration's articles, notably Article 25, which asserts that "everyone has the right to a standard of living adequate for the health and well-being of himself and of his family, including food, clothing, housing and medical care, and necessary social services." This fits comfortably with a focus on developmentalism. But it effectively deems other articles of the Declaration secondary; examples include Article 18, which states that "everyone has the right to freedom of thought, conscience, and religion"; Article 19, whereby "everyone has the right to freedom of opinion and expression"; and Article 20, which claims that "everyone has the right to freedom of peaceful assembly and association." It is a question of emphasis on economic as opposed to political rights; Beijing is little different from any other government in upholding some aspects of the Declaration while overlooking others.

As clear as Beijing's position on the Declaration is its insistence that China's human-rights regime is a work in progress.[4] A statement issued at the time of the PRC's signing of the International Convention on Civil and Political Rights is worth quoting at length:

> The Chinese Government believes that the principle of the universality of human rights must be respected, but the specific conditions of each country must also be taken into consideration in observing this principle. In such a large developing country with a population of 1.2 billion [as] China, it is essential to protect and promote the right to subsistence and the right to [the] development of its people. Over the past five decades, especially the past 20 years and more, since the introduction of reform and opening up, China has largely succeeded in meeting the basic needs of its people and improving their living standards significantly. It has thus ensured its people greater enjoyment of their economic, social, and cultural rights. China, which is a socialist country under the rule of law, attaches equal importance to the [people's] civil and political rights. It opposes any encroachment upon the citizens' lawful rights. Since 1978, the legislative body of China has made more than 300 laws and law-related decisions. As a result, China has a fairly complete set of laws for the protection of human rights. These progress [*sic*] and achievements that China has obtained have laid a solid foundation for China's signature and accession to more international legal instruments on human rights. (Ministry of Foreign Affairs, 2000)

Note that to date Beijing has not ratified this agreement, although it is widely expected to do so (Lee, 2007).

The second element of the PRC's philosophy of human rights concerns the principle of noninterference in others' domestic affairs and the norm of state sovereignty (see also Chapter 6). In Chinese diplomacy, as we have seen, sovereignty often trumps other norms—a fact that leads some critics to complain that China invokes sovereignty and noninterference selectively.[5] As far back as 1973, analysts like Jerome Cohen were denouncing as hypocritical "the PRC's enthusiastic participation in UN condemnations of the South African and Rhodesian governments for abuses against their respective peoples despite [its] earlier protests that UN condemnation of PRC conduct in Tibet constituted intervention in China's domestic affairs" (1973: 489). The PRC has also been accused of reserving the implicit right to condemn countries for any perceived ill-treatment of ethnic Chinese (particularly in Southeast Asia), in effect adhering to a race-based policy on so-called interference in other countries' affairs (Barabantseva, 2005; Sautman, 1997). Meanwhile, Beijing has made a point of blaming liberal democracy for many of Africa's woes, going directly against the view of the Western mainstream that it is a lack of democracy that partly accounts for Africa's maldevelopment.[6] During the high-water mark of the democratic swell in Africa in the late 1980s and early 1990s, when a number of African autocrats were being peacefully removed via the ballot box, Chinese commentaries dismissed the electoral process as an "obsession" and a "temptation" (*Xinhua,* July 1, 1992). Later, as the wave began to ebb, Chinese sources dubbed Africa's experiment with democratization a "disaster" (*Xinhua,* December 22, 1994), arguing that "multiparty politics fueled social turmoil, ethnic conflicts, and civil wars" (*Beijing Review,* July 29–August 4, 1996). Recently, Beijing has sought to downplay the importance of liberal democracy: "For a starving man, which should he choose, bread or ballot, if he is supposed to choose only one? The ballot is of course important. But he must feed himself with the bread before he can cast a ballot" (*Xinhua,* December 12, 2005). And on January 14, 2008, following postelection violence in Kenya, the *People's Daily* announced that

> transplanted Western democracy [can]not take hold in Africa. The African people have been living on the continent for generations; have forged special links among different ethnic groups; and have cultivated a unique African culture long before falling victim to Western colonialism. . . . The postelection crisis in Kenya is a product of democracy bequeathed by Western hegemony and a manifestation of values clashing when democracy is transplanted onto disagreeable land.

Opinions of this sort are welcomed by various African leaders for reasons linked to their states' modalities of governance, as detailed in Chapter 1. Although it is debatable whether stability generally "comes first in [a] country's development" (as the *People's Daily* put it), in the African context, "stability" usually means prioritizing elite interests, which has long proven problematic (Taylor, 2007b).

However, it is important to point out that the debate over the PRC's policies on human rights in Africa does not simply involve Beijing versus the West. A number of African leaders interested in the continent's welfare take positions that are arguably contrary to Beijing's, expressing concern for the possible "danger that China will serve to help rollback initiatives such as NEPAD, even if unintentionally," out of adherence to its stated principles.[7] A brief discussion of these fears is important for contextualizing China's behavior in Africa and illustrating that criticism of Beijing is not exclusively Western in origin.

▨ Africa's Emerging Norms

The PRC's policies arguably jar with Africa's increasing attempts to promote human rights and good governance, as crystallized in NEPAD. A select number of leaders from countries such as Nigeria and South Africa have been enthusiastically pushing NEPAD as a means to stimulate what has been termed the

African Renaissance. Launched in Abuja, Nigeria, in October 2001, NEPAD is ostensibly a development program to spur Africa's renewal (see Taylor, 2005).

NEPAD has a great deal to say on democracy and governance; in some ways it serves as a democratic charter for Africa. Per paragraph 43, "Democracy and state legitimacy have been redefined to include accountable government, a culture of human rights, and popular participation as central elements"; paragraph 45 asserts that "across the continent, democracy is spreading, backed by the African Union . . . which has shown a new resolve to deal with conflicts and censure deviation from the norm." As a result, says Paragraph 49, "African leaders will take joint responsibility for . . . promoting and protecting democracy and human rights in their respective countries and regions by developing clear standards of accountability, transparency, and participatory governance at the national and subnational levels." This pledge is particularly imperative because "African leaders have learned from their own experiences that peace, security, democracy, good governance, human rights, and sound economic management are conditions for sustainable development" (Paragraph 71). Further,

> development is impossible in the absence of true democracy, respect for human rights, peace, and good governance. With the New Partnership for Africa's Development, Africa undertakes to respect the global standards of democracy, [of] which core components include political pluralism; allowing for the existence of several political parties and workers' unions; [and] fair, open, free, and democratic elections periodically organized to enable the populace choose their leaders freely. (Paragraph 79)

Thus "The New Partnership for Africa's Development has, as one of its foundations, the expansion of democratic frontiers and the deepening of the culture of human rights. A democratic Africa will become one of the pillars of world democracy, human rights, and tolerance" (Paragraph 183). Compare such sentiments to the Chinese position that development essentially comes before issues such as political rights and democracy.

Hence the concern that although "in some countries China's involvement appears benign, in others its approach undercuts efforts by the African Union . . . and Western partners to make government and business more transparent and accountable" (*Africa Research Bulletin*, February 16–March 15, 2006: 16855). Conceivably, Beijing's involvement in Africa could lead to the reintroduction of practices that NEPAD officially rejects, even though Chinese leaders profess to fully support NEPAD. As one South African newspaper put it in 2006:

> Chinese aid is [as] likely to subsidize profligate and/or dictatorial governments as it is to advance the welfare of ordinary Africans. These develop-

ments threaten a project of particular importance to President Thabo Mbeki, and through him, to South Africa. One of the objectives of the New Partnership for Africa's Development . . . of which Mbeki is a coarchitect is to promote corruption-free, good governance in Africa, for its own sake as well as a means of securing sustained developmental assistance. . . . Aid that fails to advance democratic government, no matter whence it comes, is counterproductive. (*The Star,* July 4, 2006)

When Thabo Mbeki warned against neocolonization via China's expansion into Africa, a Nigerian newspaper article highlighted the apparent "hardening of his position on the subject" (*Daily Trust,* December 18, 2006). Beijing's support for the regime of Robert Mugabe in Zimbabwe is an interesting case study in this regard. It is also, however, an illustration of the limitations of Beijing's policies and the evolution in Chinese thinking.

▓ Zimbabwe: "Sold Down the River by China"?

Most criticism of the PRC's stance on human rights in Africa focuses on Sudan, particularly on Beijing's arms sales to and support of Khartoum, even at the United Nations (see Chapters 2 and 5, respectively). But Beijing's close links with Zimbabwe are equally noteworthy, if less spectacular. In 2006, one Zimbabwean critic asserted that "the Chinese government is wrong to insist on dealing with regimes whose survival depends on the absence of basic rights and freedoms. . . . Clearly, a lot of Africans trampled on by their governments feel they have been sold down the river by the Asian economic giant for its failure to insist on the observance of human rights and democracy" (*Financial Gazette,* November 8, 2006).

However, there is evidence that Beijing's policymakers are increasingly wary of associations between China and the southern African pariah state.[8] As with other facets of Sino-African policy, we can observe a maturing of China's stance. A look at Sino-Zimbabwean ties reveals the limitations of engaging with a regime such as Mugabe's.

The contemporary history of Sino-Zimbabwean ties has been covered extensively elsewhere (see, e.g., Taylor, 2006, Chapter 6). Suffice it to say that China supported Mugabe's Zimbabwe African National Union (ZANU) during the war of liberation against the white-minority regime to such an extent that, in the late 1970s, "China's most important link in southern Africa [was] with ZANU" (Legum, 1979: 15). Postindependence relations were kept at a relatively high level, and Mugabe's regime has always regarded Beijing as its "special friend and ally" (*Beijing Review,* August 29, 1983).

However, it is only in recent years that Chinese connections in Zimbabwe have attracted attention of a sort that is dialectically linked to Zimbabwe's collapsing economy and the human rights abuses perpetrated by Mugabe's government. Amid the casting of widespread blame on its so-called land-reform program for the country's ruin (Richardson, 2007), the regime has been fighting for survival and seeking allies. Initially, Harare turned to Tripoli as a source of petroleum and credit, but when Libya prioritized rapprochement with the West it was forced to look elsewhere. In 2003, Mugabe officially launched his Look East policy, suggesting that Malaysia was the key target. However, it rapidly became clear that his focus was on China. The policy emphasized Mugabe's heritage as a freedom fighter against Western oppression. In some quarters, this ploy worked, and Mugabe was able to shore up some domestic support while posturing as a significant international actor with new friends. Despite some material benefits, however, the strategy's success in redefining Zimbabwe has been limited (Youde, 2007).

In return for supplying Mugabe's regime with credit, equipment, and military supplies, "Chinese state-owned enterprises have assembled a portfolio of shares in some of Zimbabwe's prize assets" and "have stepped in where other developing nations (even Libya) have feared to tread" (Melville and Owen, 2005: 2). In fact, the Chinese have steadily become among the most important foreign investors in Zimbabwe, with more than thirty-five companies doing business there and a portfolio worth more than US$600 million (*Herald,* April 23, 2007). At the height of the land invasions, Wei Jianxing, a standing member of the Political Bureau of the CPC Central Committee, commented, "China fully supports the government of Zimbabwe's land-redistribution program" (*Herald,* June 14, 2002). Premier Wen Jiabao has likewise asserted that "China respects and supports efforts by Zimbabwe to bring about social justice through land reform" (*Herald,* December 17, 2003).

One theory for Chinese investment in Harare is that even as "Zimbabwe's deteriorating political situation and asset-hungry officials . . . deter most private investors, . . . the Chinese government can instruct managers of state enterprises to take the risk, rely on good intergovernmental relations to guarantee investment flow, and depend on state coffers to absorb any loss in the last resort" (Melville and Owen, 2005: 2). It is an unlikely one, however, given Beijing's declining capacity to direct Chinese investors in general and small-scale in particular. A Zimbabwean report frames the situation more accurately: "What could China want in Zimbabwe? We do not have oil; our population is small compared to those of larger African countries. Our location is not particularly strategic for an outsider. What the Chinese want is raw materials and opportunities for investment. They will be happy to have a share in mines, power production, anything that can turn them a profit for a comparatively small amount of investment" (*Sokwanele Special Report,* June 21, 2005). There is also the possibility that Chinese entrepreneurs position themselves in countries such as Botswana and Zimbabwe as a means to gain access to their neighbor South Africa's larger and more developed market.[9]

Chinese actors have been granted the rights to land confiscated from white Zimbabweans, including 100,000 hectares of irrigation land in the Mwenzi area (*The Age*, July 30, 2005). In 2005, it was reported that "settlers (newly established black residents) are being removed from those properties right now. Apparently this is what was agreed in Beijing, that the Chinese are going to take these properties over—and Chinese state farming organizations are actually going to run them" (*The Age*, July 30, 2005).

Meanwhile, Chinese vehicle manufacturers have been supplying transport to Zimbabwe. In 2005, Zimbabwe bought three passenger planes, six trainer jets, and almost 400 commuter buses. Chinese enterprises have also agreed to provide trains and rebuild Zimbabwe's rail network, while Beijing has pledged food relief for millions of Zimbabweans who face hunger as a result of the collapse of the country's agricultural sector. In the words of the Zimbabwean government mouthpiece at the height of Sino-Zimbabwean engagement, Harare and Beijing "struck a telepathic understanding" (*Herald*, August 4, 2005).

China's main import from Zimbabwe is tobacco, followed by asbestos, iron, and steel, as well as chrome and, notably, platinum. Zimbabwe's platinum deposits are second in size only to those of South Africa, and as of 2008 China is the leading consumer of platinum, garnering nearly 20 percent of world production. The Reserve Bank of Zimbabwe's governor, Gideon Gono, has advertised as much, announcing that he "would like to unveil to the Chinese people the vast investment opportunities that . . . abound in Zimbabwe, including our natural resource endowments" (*Herald*, May 25, 2005). Chinese corporations also have contracts for coke and coal concessions in Zimbabwe, supplying funds and equipment in turn. And the National Aero-Technology Import and Export Corporation (CATIC) and China North Industries Corporation (Norinco) have approved the financing of projects by Zimbabwe Electricity Supply Authority and Hwange Colliery Company, respectively (*Financial Gazette*, May 20, 2005). In return for the cooperation and contributions of Chinese corporations, Zimbabwe imports a whole range of cheap Chinese manufactured products. The fact that extractive industries such as mining and agriculture make up the bulk of Zimbabwean exports to China has led one opposition newspaper to argue that the country's economy is being subjected to new forms of dependency, this time on China (*Zimbabwe Independent*, October 8, 2004).

Like other African countries (see Chapter 3), Zimbabwe is being inundated with enormous quantities of Chinese-made clothing, shoes, and textiles, all of which sell at prices considerably lower than do those made in Zimbabwe. This fact is significant given that Zimbabwe has historically been Africa's second most industrialized country, following only South Africa, and long had its own manufacturing base. According to one commentary, Chinese manufacturers "need an outlet for the . . . [cheap] goods that cannot be sold in the developed world, where they sell [instead] their quality products" (*Sokwanele Special Report*, June 21, 2005). If this is the case, it is arguably at the expense of some Zimbabwean businesses, as much of what Chinese traders export to Zimbabwe is similar to that which local manufacturers produce; indeed, a 2004 estimate "brought to 30,000 the number of directly threatened jobs" by Chinese imports to Zimbabwe, "the affected industries [being] weaving, spinning, and clothing industries as well as manufacturers of shoes and producers of leather items" (*Zimbabwe Independent*, October 15, 2004).

Allegations that Zimbabwean traders are sometimes cast out of city centers in order to protect their Chinese rivals have also been made, with some merit. For instance, on May 19, 2005, Zimbabwean police began a campaign of forced evictions named Operation Murambatsvina—Shona for "get rid of the trash." Hundreds of thousands of families were branded as criminals and forcibly dumped in the countryside while their houses and small trading stalls were destroyed. The evictions began in Harare, Bulawayo, and Victoria Falls but spread all over the country. According to a report compiled by the Catholic Archdiocese of Bulawayo:

> Initially, we felt that that the real motivation behind Operation Murambatsvina was to punish those citizens that supported the MDC [Movement for Democratic Change] during the March 2005 elections. However, the motivation may go deeper than this. The failed land-reform process has driven many former farm workers and rural folk into towns where they are exposed to news and political opinions counter to those of traditional leaders and political councils in rural areas that have over the years been under the influence and favor of the Mugabe regime. The effect of moving hundreds of thousands of people into the countryside is to make them utterly reliant on government-controlled food aid for survival. (Ncube, Bate, and Tren, 2005: 8)

Still, the rumors that the action was also designed to protect Chinese merchants were rampant. One report, for instance, claimed that "the police, under direct orders from Didymus Mutasa, the head of the secret police (Zimbabwe's Central Intelligence Organization) brutally removed any competition to Chinese traders whose shops have sprung up around the capital over the past few years" (*Weekly Standard*, May 25, 2005). Morgan Tsvangirai, leader of the opposition group MDC, "accused Mugabe of ordering the crackdown in response to pressure from newly arrived Chinese businessmen to stop secondhand dealers undercutting their cheap imports. 'The country has been mortgaged to the Chinese,' Tsvangirai said in a statement. 'How can we violently remove Zimbabweans from our flea markets to make way for the Chinese? The majority of Zimbabweans depend on informal trade to feed, clothe, and educate their families'" (*Weekly Standard*, May 25, 2005). Here the very real dangers for the Chinese as allies of regimes such as Mugabe's become clear: they easily and swiftly serve as scapegoats for wider ills. In this case, an operation by Mugabe to punish people deemed to support the opposition is surreptitiously linked to Chinese interests.

▪ Mugabe's Support for Beijing

Given Chinese support, Mugabe's government has reciprocated at international forums. For instance, in 2004, China and Zimbabwe worked together at the UN Commission on Human Rights to prevent resolutions that would have censured both countries for human-rights abuses. For his part, Mugabe has been profoundly—and publicly—grateful for Beijing's backing. At the second Sino-African trade summit in Addis Ababa in December 2003, he "launched into a tirade against Britain and the USA, calling on African leaders to turn their backs on Western countries and to focus on better relations with China, which he said respected African countries" (*Cameroon Tribune,* December 17, 2003). In turn, at the height of Sino-Zimbabwean relations, Chinese official sources described Mugabe as "a man of strong convictions, a man of great achievements, a man devoted to preserving world peace, [and] a good friend of the Chinese people" (*Financial Times,* July 27, 2005).

Among the Zimbabwean people, however, China's position has remained controversial. "Only the Chinese," noted one editorial, "are prepared to assist [the Zimbabwe African National Union–Patriotic Front or ZANU-PF] to stay in power against the wishes of [Zimbabwe's] own people. . . . [The Chinese] have no compunctions about democracy or human rights, only a single-minded obsession with control. And since their own people do not enjoy democratic freedom of expression and participation, they have no check on what types of regimes they support elsewhere" (*Sokwanele Special Report,* June 21, 2005). Indeed, "not only is it China's protection from strong Western punitive measures that is attractive to African leaders but Beijing's investments[, which] come with no conditionality related to 'good governance'" (*Sunday Herald,* August 28, 2005).

▪ Rethinking Ties

Having noted all of the above, we should add that Beijing appears to be rethinking its relations with Mugabe. Its impetus is twofold, involving both international criticism that casts doubt on Beijing's claim to be a responsible power and the sheer economic irrationality of the Mugabe regime, which makes any investment, be it economic or political, perilous.[10]

Besides, Beijing is undoubtedly keen to refrain from stoking the fires of an anti-Chinese backlash. In Zimbabwe today, the term *zhing-zhong* has been coined by local Zimbabweans to describe cheap products—namely those made in China and sold by Chinese shopkeepers. The pejorative implies its referent is shoddy. Bumper stickers in Harare bearing the Ndebele-language slogan *"I Povo iyala! Ithi Lingathengi iZhing-Zhong!"* (The people say no. Do not buy zhing-zhong!) have been spotted. According to the chairman of the

Department of Political Science at the University of Zimbabwe, "The resentment of the Chinese is not only widespread, it's deeply rooted. It's affecting even other Chinese-looking people, like the Japanese" (*New York Times,* July 25, 2005). And it's now taking the form of accusations of neoimperialism:

> Mugabe fought the 2005 elections on the argument that Zimbabwe must not become a colony again. But it is questionable whether he has not in fact simply replaced Western colonialism with Chinese imperialism. Having ceded control of strategic state firms and [allowed] massive Chinese takeovers, including of railways, the electricity supply, Air Zimbabwe, and [the] Zimbabwe Broadcasting Corporation makes "win-win" economic cooperation between China and Zimbabwe appear doubtful. Given that Zimbabwe has no comparative advantage over China in any sector, this opening up of the economy is most likely to benefit the Chinese, perhaps even at the expense of Zimbabweans. (Karumbidza, 2007: 95)

Accusations of opportunistic exploitation by the Chinese are likewise surfacing:

> This week, Zimbos celebrated another great betrayal. Betrayal by our owners and by our best friends, the Chinese. A good friend does not take advantage of his friend's desperate situation to fleece them of the little they have. . . . Zimbabwe has just started taking delivery of tractors, lorries, and other farming equipment from a Chinese company. The equipment is reportedly worth "US$58 million." The money for the equipment is coming from the People's Republic of China. In return, the government of the Republic of Zimbabwe will, over the next two seasons, deliver to China 110,000 tons (110 million kg) of tobacco. That is the deal that our dear leaders celebrated their tails off over the past week. Common sense tells [us] that a good flue-cured tobacco crop can fetch up to US$2 per kg. The 110 million kg that Zimbabwe will give to China could, therefore, be worth anything up to US$220 million. Imagine a whole government being fooled to exchange tobacco worth US$220 million for poor-quality but overpriced farming equipment? And considering that this equipment is zhing-zhong . . . obviously the true value of the equipment could possibly be less than US$1 million. So what it means is that tobacco (or is it foreign currency?) worth US$220 million is exchanged for US$1 million worth of tired equipment. . . . Who said Zimbabwe will never be a colony again! (*Financial Gazette,* April 25, 2007)

It is very doubtful that Mugabe's government cares about popular opinion regarding the Chinese. However, the Chinese do, and their response only hastens the declining state of the Zimbabwean economy. Chinese companies have reportedly abandoned a number of projects in Zimbabwe due to nonpayment and the continuing political instability. Among those withdrawing are the National Aero-Technologies Import and Export Corporation; the China North Industries Corporation, which was involved in renovation projects at Zesa Holdings and Hwange Colliery Company; and the China International Water and

Electric Corporation (CIWEC), which was contracted to clear and install irrigation facilities at Nuanetsi Ranch and also "to clear 100,000 hectares of land for irrigation"—a project it "deserted . . . after clearing less than 5,000 hectares" (*Zimbabwe Independent,* May 12, 2006).

In short, it does appear that "China's relations with Zimbabwe, which include diplomatic support, trade deals, and close military ties, could be under strain as a result of [the] government's failure to service its debts" (*Zimbabwe Independent,* May 12, 2006). Indeed, there is now a fairly long list of failures by Mugabe's regime to maintain Chinese support. In July 2005, Mugabe visited China in a bid to negotiate an economic package that would rescue Zimbabwe. Nothing came out of that visit, and the claim by Zimbabwe's ambassador to China, Chris Mutsvangwa, that Mugabe was on the verge of securing a US$2 billion credit line from China "was . . . denied by the Chinese government" (*Zimbabwe Independent,* January 26, 2007). Although the Chinese have become important consumers of Zimbabwean tobacco, reported projects by several Chinese firms to finance tobacco farming have collapsed. A delegation from Air Zimbabwe, the Civil Aviation Authority, and the National Railways visited China in 2004 to secure investment promised by the National Aero-Technology Import and Export Corporation—which has, however, never come up with the goods. In fact, the latter has aborted several agreements it signed with the Zimbabwe Electricity Supply Authority to finance various power projects because Harare could not provide sufficient guarantees. Hence the rhetorical question in one Zimbabwean newspaper article: "Over the past couple of years Zimbabwe has signed many Memorandums of Understanding [MOU] with the Chinese. But how many of these have borne fruit?" (*Financial Gazette,* February 1, 2007).

In fact, Beijing has begun to go out of its way to snub Mugabe. In April 2006, President Hu Jintao visited Africa, touring Nigeria, Morocco, and Kenya, among other countries—but missed Zimbabwe. In early 2007, he returned to visit Cameroon, Liberia, Sudan, Zambia, Namibia, South Africa, and Mozambique, but again avoided Zimbabwe. In June 2006, Premier Wen Jiabao did likewise, visiting Egypt, Ghana, DRC, Angola, South Africa, and Tanzania but overlooking Zimbabwe. Noted the *Zimbabwe Independent:*

> No matter how the Zimbabwean government sees it, the Chinese move is clearly intended as a deliberate snub [of] Zimbabwe. It speaks volumes about the significance the Chinese attach to their relations with Zimbabwe. What is increasingly clear is that the Chinese view Zimbabwe with the same suspicion as does the West. The only difference is that the Chinese do not say it. . . . Relations [between Harare and Beijing] don't appear to be as intimate as we have been led to believe. (*Zimbabwe Independent,* January 26, 2007)

In August 2007, Liu Guijin, China's special envoy on African issues, confirmed as much, telling British Foreign Office minister Lord Malloch Brown that China "was dropping all assistance except humanitarian aid. The move follows a decision by China, a permanent member of the United Nations Security Council, to work more closely with the international community in bringing pressure to bear on 'rogue regimes'" (*Daily Telegraph,* August 31, 2007).

In sum, Beijing has backtracked from its relationship with a regime that is widely regarded as a pariah on the international stage (Taylor and Williams, 2002). Having taking advantage of Zimbabwe's situation, China finds itself accused of backing an autocratic administration and breaking international consensus—although the weak response of Mugabe's fellow African leaders to his depredations does bear notice (see Taylor, 2002b). Beijing and Chinese citizens operating in Zimbabwe have also attracted considerable criticism and hostility from Zimbabweans themselves. The PRC has learned the hard way about the ramifications of disregarding human-rights abuses and courting regimes such as Mugabe's. This is as true for China in Zimbabwe as it is for other states that court autocracies.

In fairness, Beijing embraced Harare early on in its recent exponential expansion of ties with Africa. Some policymakers in Beijing no doubt saw Zimbabwe's predicament in the early 2000s as a transitional crisis, and perhaps thought that Chinese stakes would be well positioned when the Zimbabwean economy recovered.[11] They were obviously mistaken; with annual inflation running at 1,063,572 percent based on prices of a basket of basic foodstuffs and unemployment standing at well over 80 percent, recovery is not going to happen anytime soon (*Scotsman,* June 20, 2008). In fact, the Chinese no longer appear to assume, any more than do "fence-sitting Western investors, that Zimbabwe can uphold bilateral investment protection agreements and manage its economy to international standards. They have witnessed, in Zimbabwe, instances of the arbitrary violation of that which is fundamental to market economy and business confidence" (*Financial Gazette,* February 1, 2007). After all, "unlike Western cooperation, the Chinese approach does not come shrouded in moral principles and universal values but is rooted on clear defined economic objectives"; thus Chinese "cooperation will only be sustained if Zimbabwe can deliver on what it promises it has to offer" (Friedrich-Ebert-Stiftung, 2004: 12). As of mid-2008, whether Mugabe's regime is in its last death throes or continues to stagger from one catastrophe to another, the prospects for *any* investor in Zimbabwe remains challenging.

Ultimately, Sino-Zimbabwean diplomacy constitutes a lesson for Beijing: win-win situations with regimes like Mugabe's are unlikely. In places where malgovernance is so acute, even opportunities for exploitation are limited and even counterproductive, particularly with regard to international reputation. If human-rights concerns did not dampen China's enthusiasm for Zimbabwe, cold hard economic facts—paradoxically brought about by said malgovernance—certainly have.

▓ Conclusion

From Beijing's perspective, China and Africa "support each other in international affairs, especially on major issues such as human rights, [to] safeguard the legitimate rights of developing countries" (Embassy of the People's Republic of China in the Republic of Zimbabwe, 2000b). The Beijing Declaration of the Forum on China-Africa Cooperation, in late 2006, makes it official: "Countries that vary from one another in social system, stages of development, historical and cultural background, and values, have the right to choose their own approaches and models in promoting and protecting human rights in their own countries. . . . Moreover, the politicization of human rights and the imposition of human-rights conditionalities on economic assistance should be vigorously opposed, as they constitute a violation of human rights" (quoted in *Xinhua,* October 19, 2006).

There is arguably some convergence between Chinese attitudes toward human rights and liberal democracy and those of the African elites. Many African leaders simply do not share the West's concerns.[12] They look at the economic and political inroads China has made into Africa very differently than Western critics who call China the "Patron of African Misgovernment" (*New York Times,* February 19, 2007).

However, while it is true that China's leaders and many of Africa's presidents share attitudes toward human rights and governance, the latter do not necessarily put economic rights over political rights or value national development the way the former do. National development for a broad-based productive economy is far less a concern to elites within most African political systems than is control of resources for their advantage and that of their clientelistic networks, as Chapter 1 made clear. In fact, development might stimulate opposition. As Bertrand Badie explains, "On the one hand, economic development is a goal that every head of state must pursue. . . . On the other hand, an overly active policy of development risks producing several negative results: it would valorize the competence of the technocratic elite relative to that of the fragile political elite, break up social spaces and favor the constitution of a civil society capable of counterbalancing the political system, and, indeed, neutralize neopatrimonial strategies" (Badie, 2000: 19). Beijing's "politics of development" are continually hidebound by the real possibility that "China's economic and political support could offer African politicians increasing leeway in misusing public funds or manipulating institutions to preserve their own power" (Lewis, 2006: 2; see also Lewis, 1996).

It is important to remember that the PRC's policy of noninterference in others' domestic affairs is not specific to Africa. It is in fact long-standing, rooted in the humiliations China endured in the nineteenth century to emerge as a mainstay of Beijing's foreign policy[13]—as Article 54 of China's first plenary session of the Chinese People's Political Consultative Conference makes explicit: "The principle of the foreign policy of the People's Republic of China is protection of the independence, freedom, integrity of territory, and sovereignty of the country." This principle underpins Beijing's interpretations of human rights and democracy in Africa or elsewhere. The emphasis on collective development, rather than individual civil and political liberty, as the paramount human right has to be understood. As David Shinn (2006b: 1) points out, 'If the West fails to take these different perceptions into account, it will never deal effectively with the challenges posed by China in Africa."

In this regard, much of the criticism heaped on China for its Africa policies vis-à-vis human rights and governance is rather misplaced; such policies are not particular to Africa. The problems start when the philosophies behind them converge with those of African leaders themselves, particularly the heads of neopatrimonial regimes and "quasi states" (Jackson, 1993) who are more than happy to have China as an ally.[14] It could be persuasively argued that the Chinese are, like all others, simply acting in a pragmatic and self-interested manner, according to their own understandings of particular concepts. Although justifiable disquiet surrounds those aspects of Chinese engagement in Africa that may undermine political and economic reform, much of Africa's predicament is complex, so erecting a scapegoat to blame makes little sense— beyond masking ulterior anxieties regarding China's African sojourn.[15] Here, we may level the charge of hypocrisy against the West, as do Daniel Burstein and Arne de Keijzer: "While the human rights situation in China is not good by American standards, it is not unlike that in Indonesia, India, or Saudi Arabia, for instance. Yet in most of these cases, the United States is able to have normal and even close relationships that are not overwhelmed by the human-rights agenda" (1999: 137). A 2006 editorial takes the point further:

> European and North American leaders in general, and French politicians in particular, tend to give their African counterparts lessons on democracy, respect for human rights, and governmental transparency—even if such lessons are also exercises in Western hypocrisy. France, for instance, maintains privileged relations with the corrupt regimes of oil-rich Gabon, ruled since 1968 by Omar Bongo, and of Congo-Brazzaville (Republic of the Congo). And the United States has been wooing African dictators such as Teodoro Obiang Nguema and José Eduardo dos Santos, who rule oil-rich, poverty-ridden Equatorial Guinea and Angola, respectively, both since 1979. (*Inter Press Service*, November 15, 2006)

Indeed, it is important to observe, with Peerenboom (2007), that many critiques of China's human-rights record are shaped by an interest in containing China's development and influence. Conversely, notes Zheng Yongnian (1999: 105), the Chinese suspect that certain "forces do not like to see a strong China with a rapid[ly] growing economy. Because they perceive China as their potential rival, they will use all possible means, including the Taiwan, Tibet and human-rights issues, to contain China's development."

By focusing narrowly on Beijing's approach to human rights in Africa to the neglect of other features of the relationship, international critics implicitly delegitimize China and, by extension, the actions of "the Chinese," whether at home or abroad.[16] For instance, Pretoria is as complicit in its engagement with Harare as Beijing, and South African entrepreneurs, like their Chinese counterparts, have exploited opportunities yielded by Zimbabwe's economic crisis (Solidarity Peace Trust, 2007). This is not to say that Beijing is or should be above criticism but only that context is required in order to avoid exoticizing, if not demonizing, China when discussing its engagements in Africa.

Before critiquing those aspects of Chinese involvement in sub-Saharan Africa that impact upon governance and human rights, analysts need to understand both the Chinese human-rights discourse and the nature of most African states. That said, there is a certain illogic to Beijing's position that needs reflection. Let us accept that different conceptions of human rights as well as different interpretations of the Universal Declaration exist. As we have seen, Beijing privileges rights to food, clothing, shelter, and economic development and has been quite active in asserting that its primary mission is to develop the productive forces of society, underlining the slogan that development is the absolute principle. From the perspective of Chinese policymakers, the liberal conception of human rights advocated by the West poses a potential threat to the stability essential to development.[17] That is certainly the message communicated by China's official Africa policies. So far so good.

But what if Sino-African diplomacy not only clashes with the advancement of "universal" (i.e., Western) norms regarding human rights but actually manages to undermine the very development that is ostensibly so essential to Beijing's own definition of rights? What if Beijing's diplomacy in Africa helps to consolidate governments that actively obstruct development insofar as it threatens elite control? The noninterference policy implicitly grants that Beijing will not interfere in the domestic affairs of the countries it assists. But if sovereignty is the guarantor of human rights, as the Chinese declare, on the one hand, and a means to effectively undermine development on the other, then there is a clear contradiction at the heart of the Chinese discourse on human rights. Surely in such cases Beijing is complicit not only in autocratic attempts to sabotage the nascent human-rights movement (one now supported by a number of African states) but also in problematizing its own concept of human rights as measured by development as well as its own interpretation of the linkage between human rights and sovereignty. As evidenced in Zimbabwe and elsewhere, support for abusive regimes can indirectly destabilize development plans; in lending such support, Beijing directly contradicts its own pronouncements on the meaning of human rights.

It is clear, for instance, that Mugabe's government not only tramples on the civil and political rights the West ostensibly holds dear but also subverts Zimbabweans' economic and social rights which China claims to prize. In such cases, to reiterate, the PRC resorts to a fundamentalist bottom line whereby sovereignty itself is the basis of human rights; it is up to each sovereign state to establish its own conception of the rights of its people—what they are in any given context and how they should be realized—without interference from outside forces. However, the reification of states and the attendant amalgamation of sovereignty and rights into a single principle of noninterference make little real sense in a milieu dominated by quasi states and neopatrimonial regimes; as one African informant put it, "'Non-interference' is an implicit green light to autocrats."[18] Furthermore, if Chinese actors, adhering to the principle of non-interference, actually make things worse for some in Africa, then the other great shibboleth of Chinese human-rights rhetoric—that basic socioeconomic rights are more important for the poor than abstract political rights—rings hollow.

Of course, the Chinese government can then reinvoke sovereignty by arguing that African states are free to deal with China or not, as they so desire.[19] But if Beijing's leaders genuinely believe that they will not repeat the crimes and misdemeanors of European colonizers in Africa, then engaging without damaging remains a big challenge: "China isn't the first outside industrial power to behave badly in Africa. But it should not be proud of following the West's sorry historical example" (*New York Times,* February 19, 2007).

That said, we should remember that "China" is changing, and so are its conceptions of human rights and sovereignty (see Chapter 6). China's official policies toward Africa are therefore likewise developing and maturing.[20] One of the reasons Beijing finds itself in such compromising positions with pariah regimes like Zimbabwe's and Sudan's is that, as relative latecomers to Africa, Chinese actors go where more established actors and corporations cannot or will not go. In other words, they sometimes end up in places impulsively, before the political environment is settled.[21]

Yet we should also note that relations with a regime such as Mugabe's are not typical of Sino-African diplomacy.[22] The realization among Beijing's policymakers that attempts to separate politics and business do not generally succeed, particularly in many of the African countries with which China engages, is growing. This shift in attitude and the attendant evolution of Beijing's foreign policies, however pragmatic, means the status quo on noninterference in domestic human-rights affairs is unlikely to continue, particularly if and when Chinese interests are endangered. Like all investors in Africa, the Chinese recognize that success requires security and stability, as well as economic rationality. Wherever human-rights abuses destabilize a polity, Chinese interests will be threatened.[23] By the same token, Beijing's focus on development is central; it sees a stable international order based on economic and political cooperation as key to a supportive environment in which to develop China.[24] Given that it is eager to be seen in turn as an unthreatening, responsible power, Beijing is concerned about the way China is perceived abroad; government officials and business leaders alike recognize that a bad national image is damaging to broad Chinese interests and power (Lampton, 2008). Thus Chinese policymakers are in future likely to think twice about any action that might undermine a stable environment or undercut Beijing's attempt to cast itself as a responsible player on the world stage.

▓ Notes

1. Interview with Western diplomat, Asmara, Eritrea, June 29, 2006.
2. Interview with Chinese diplomat, Abuja, Nigeria, September 5, 2007.
3. Interview with Wang Xue Xian, China's ambassador to South Africa, Stellenbosch, February 13, 1998.
4. Interview with Chinese diplomat, Addis Ababa, Ethiopia, May 15, 2007.
5. Interview with Western diplomat, Asmara, Eritrea, June 29, 2006.
6. Interview with Chinese diplomat, Abuja, Nigeria, September 5, 2007.
7. Interview with African Union official, Addis Ababa, Ethiopia, May 15, 2007.
8. Interview with the acting head of the Political Affairs Section, Chinese Embassy, Windhoek, Namibia, August 13, 2006.
9. Interview with Chinese trader, Gaborone, Botswana, September 26, 2004.
10. Interview with Chinese academic, Centre for African Studies, Peking University, Beijing, China, September 20, 2007.
11. Interview with government official, Gaborone, Botswana, September 25, 2004.
12. Interview with Ugandan academic, Mbarara, Uganda, November 2, 2006.
13. Interview with Shu Zhan, Chinese ambassador to Eritrea, Asmara, Eritrea, June 29, 2006.
14. Interview with Ugandan academic, Mbarara, Uganda, November 2, 2006.
15. Interview with Robin Sherborne, editor of *Insight,* Windhoek, Namibia, August 14, 2006.
16. Interview with Henning Melber, Namibian political economist, Windhoek, Namibia, August 14, 2006.
17. Interview with Chinese diplomat, Addis Ababa, Ethiopia, May 15, 2007.
18. Interview with African Union official, Addis Ababa, Ethiopia, May 15, 2007.
19. Interview with Shu Zhan, Chinese ambassador to Eritrea, Asmara, Eritrea, June 29, 2006.
20. Interview with He Wenping, CASS, Beijing, China, September 18, 2007.
21. Interview with British diplomat, Addis Ababa, Ethiopia, May 15, 2007.
22. Interview with Chinese diplomat, Abuja, Nigeria, September 5, 2007.
23. Interview with British diplomat, Addis Ababa, Ethiopia, May 15, 2007.
24. Interview with Shu Zhan, Chinese ambassador to Eritrea, Asmara, Eritrea, June 29, 2006.

The Arms Trade | 5

A s Chinese engagement with sub-Saharan Africa has increased, so has criticism aimed at Chinese enterprises that sell arms to African regimes
(Amnesty International, 2006a and 2006b). Because the continent has, since
the 1960s, been beset by conflict and unstable regimes, such critiques are quite
condemnatory. Furthermore, say critics, weapons sales constitute a diversion
of resources away from the development-oriented spending necessary to alleviate poverty on the continent.[1] Thus, they conclude, supplying weaponry to
Africa is inherently problematic if not immoral. Such censure is not specific
to the Chinese, of course—all arms suppliers face such criticism. This chapter
seeks to analyze the rationale behind China's arms sales to Africa and the effect that they have had on recipient countries as well as to provide analyses of
the supply-and-demand circumstances of Chinese arms sales to Africa, Beijing's attempts to control such transfers, and the evidence that Chinese policies on proliferation are evolving.

◼ China's Arms Industry

During the Maoist period, the PRC gave small arms and light weapons freely
to sympathetic governments and revolutionary organizations as part of a strategy to promote Maoism and Chinese interests (Taylor, 2006). Post-Mao, however, Beijing's arms exports became predicated on more commercial, less political bases, and the destinations of its arms exports became more diversified
(Hyer, 1992). By 1990, Chinese exports made up around 8 percent of the
world arms market, which Beijing was in not to sell small arms but rather
whole weapons packages. However, with the end of the Cold War and the poor
performance of Chinese arms in the Iran-Iraq War and the first Gulf War, the
reputation of Chinese-made weapons fell, and China's arms export industry

suffered a marked decline. Cheap but sophisticated Russian, Ukrainian, and Belarusian weapons systems that outcompeted Chinese products further weakened Beijing's stake in the arms market.

Indeed, Beijing's global arms exports have dropped dramatically from the peak years of the mid-1980s, when Chinese arms factories were supplying both sides in the Iran-Iraq War. In 1987, official Chinese arms sales reached US\$5.8 billion (Grimmet, 1994: 92). As the soon-to-be-discussed figures will show, however, Chinese arms sales in the 2000s are small not only in relation to the past but also compared to those of other exporters in the present. The problem for Chinese exporters is that Beijing's defense industries cannot construct state-of-the-art weapons systems, which is where the profits are to be made (Medeiros, 2004). Consequently, Chinese weapons manufacturers have to compete on the market on the basis of price rather than competence, such that relatively poor countries in the developing world are their main customers and that "promoting arms sales abroad has become a much less salient feature of . . . Chinese foreign policy" (Sutter, 2008: 147).

We must consider the domestic context of China's arms industry if we are to understand the supply-side equation. It is estimated that around 70 percent of China's SOEs are functioning at a loss; the state-owned arms industries are reputedly among the biggest money losers (Frankenstein, 1999: 197–199). Indeed, the then head of the State Commission of Science Technology and Industry for National Defense, Liu Jibin, stated that between 1993 and 2001, China's entire defense industry ran a net loss (*China Daily,* January 9, 2002). Its debt-ridden arms manufacturers are owed vast sums by other indebted SOEs, and there is very little chance they will ever be recouped, despite former premier Zhu Rongji's attempted reforms (see Brahm, 2002). Meanwhile, these SOEs often have a considerable number of employees reliant on the health care, housing, child care, and pensions they provide (see Wang Jifu, 2007). Such relics from the days of the *danwei* (work unit) system further contribute to the perilous state of much of China's arms industry, which is therefore desperate for funds and eager to source and exploit potential markets.

These circumstances are compounded by the dynamics of the industry's restructuring in the late 1990s (Johnston, 1996). Two issues in particular stand out. First, concern that the PLA was becoming too involved in the economy led to Premier Jiang Zemin's 1998 declaration that businesses were being officially delinked from the military (Gilley, 1998: 226–227). Like other SOEs, China's military-industrial enterprises operated on a "contract responsibility system"— that is, they paid the state both taxes and a segment of their profits. Profits that remained from the production of civilian goods went to production development and/or to military management. However, once the PLA was forced to stop openly operating civilian businesses, the search for profits narrowed to arms sales. Chinese aspirations to join the WTO drove such reform. Without income from their domestic business interests, the normally self-reliant PLA was compensated by an enlargement of the defense budget—but it also increased its income via arms sales (Xiaobing Li, 2007). Coordination between the activities of arms enterprises and broader Chinese foreign policy soon became an issue: "Using *guanxi* (personal gifts and rewards)—often the military export corporations are staffed by the children of senior Chinese leaders—the military often completed these transactions without the knowledge of the Ministry of Foreign Affairs" (Kornberg and Faust, 2005: 222). This will be discussed in more detail below.

Second, China's five old, centrally directed corporations—which were answerable to the State Council and were, for all intents and purposes, ministerial-level organizations—were replaced by ten defense-industrial enterprises or *jungong qiye*. These were set up as genuine conglomerates, and the government's role in their day-to-day business was significantly reduced. An eleventh company, producing defense electronics, was established in late 2002 (see Medeiros and Gill, 2000). The *jungong qiye* have the power to administer their own ventures and seek out markets; crucially, they are accountable for their profit-and-loss margins (*China Daily,* January 29, 2003). Indeed, a major objective of the restructuring process was to make defense enterprises more responsive to market forces by exposing them to competition. As a result, "the foreign exchange earned by weapon sales remains significant to China's defense industries . . . because they are allowed to retain part of the earnings (another portion goes to the Ministry of Finance)" (Byman and Cliff, 2000: 88). Of the ten arms enterprises, Norinco is probably the most well known for its exports to the developing world.

The restructuring of Beijing's arms industries reflects processes that have been underway since the Iran-Iraq War, which presented China with the occasion to develop its reputation as a dealer in cheap conventional weaponry. Unable to compete at the top end of the market, Chinese arms producers have exploited this niche in the market ever since, although not without problems.[2] In the words of one critical analysis, "When it comes to weapons, there is no doubt which end of the market [China's] sights are still set on. Some of the poorest and most unsavory regimes on earth, which either cannot afford or are not allowed to buy sophisticated Western arms, are turning to the world's newest superpower to buy guns, leg-irons, anti-riot equipment, and armored vehicles" (*BBC News,* June 16, 2006).

What's more, the Iran-Iraq War made clear that China was willing to provide weaponry to both belligerent sides—a policy it has continued in Africa, where it has been accused of arming both Eritrea and Ethiopia during their border war (to be discussed); to quote Samuel Kim, "China has no principles, only interests, driving its arms sales to the Third World" (Kim 1994: 146)—which, between 2002 and 2005, averaged about US$950 million per year (Grimmett, 2006: 11). Like most arms sales to the developing world, they consisted of low-priced weaponry and small arms rather than the spectacular armament typical of British and US megadeals.[3] However, small arms have proven a key element in the destabilization of African polities, contributing to crime and disorder as well as facilitating armed rebellions (Muggah and Batchelor, 2002).

The lack of transparency in China's arms industry and particularly its export policy makes any analysis of Beijing's weapons trade difficult. Indeed, the secrecy surrounding arms sales is such that Chinese companies are actually excluded from the list of arms-producing companies compiled by the Stockholm International Peace Research Institute (SIPRI), owing to a lack of comparable data; according to the British parliament, "The People's Republic of China does not publish details of its arms exports and last submitted data to the UN Register on Conventional Arms covering its exports in 1996. It is not therefore possible to provide figures on either the total number or value of Chinese arms exports to Africa" (House of Commons, 2007: 1447). Of course, China's "lack of transparency has been exploited by party-state actors to capture the benefits of the introduction of the market and use political power to attain economic benefit (and economic power)" (Breslin, 2007: 74); the small arms industry is probably no exception.

Lack of transparency poses particular problems for analysts of China's arms industry where energy sources (such as oil) are involved:

> It makes . . . the scope of activity hard to detect and the direct responsibility of Chinese state authorities hard to pin down. It is exceedingly difficult to establish conclusively that proliferation by a given Chinese company is linked to access to energy. Yet while an energy-for-arms link can neither be simply assumed nor easily proven, what gives cause for concern is that [a number of companies who are] "serial proliferators," besides having poor track records on proliferation, are [SOEs] at least nominally under the direct supervision of the State Council. (Calabrese, 2006: 60)

Although the restructuring of China's arms industry made defense companies more autonomous with respect to daily operations, they still remain under the direct regulation of the State Council. This fact raises some questions as to their behavior.

▩ The Problem of Proliferation

In response to arms proliferation, the PRC has exerted some effort to upgrade and improve the infrastructure for export controls, installing a nascent de jure system in place of the opaque administrative procedures and inexact bilateral commitments that marked policy until recently (see Davis, 2005). Until 2002, Beijing's conventional arms export controls followed the 1997 *Regulations on Export Control of Military Items*. In 2002, Beijing issued an amended set of conventional-arms regulations and a list of military products under export control per the decision of the State Council and the Central Military Commission (*Xin-*

hua, October 20, 2002). The list largely corresponds to that of the Wassenaar Arrangement, an agreement to promote transparency and greater responsibility in conventional arms transfers and the sale of dual-use goods and technology. However, critics assert that the guidelines use very broad categories and blurred classifications, giving quite a lot of slack to unprincipled arms-exporting factories, which could thereby "evade responsibility for certain transfers" (Srivastava, 2005). Notably, the 2002 policy on conventional-arms exports is predicated on Article 5 of the earlier policy, which states that "military-products export should proceed under the following principles: being useful to the self-defense capability of the recipient country; being not harmful to the peace, security, and stability of the relevant region or the world; and staying hands off the recipient country's internal affairs" (*Xinhua,* October 20, 2002).

However, these principles are in themselves contentious. To begin with, "the self-defense capability of the recipient country" inevitably translates as regime security; if the regime in question is autocratic or lacks legitimacy, the principle is inadequate for guaranteeing the security of the people in the recipient state especially if China will keeps its "hands off the recipient country's internal affairs" (however consistent that goal may be with Chinese diplomatic principle). For that matter, simply by supplying arms to a state, Chinese firms effectively and inextricably involve themselves in the internal affairs of the recipient country. Arms sales are not and can never be neutral; the noninterference policy of Chinese diplomacy thus puts Chinese arms exporters in a bind, as on the one hand they must pledge not to export arms to regions where security and stability are issues, while on the other hand they must officially disregard the domestic affairs of the recipient state.[4]

Furthermore, brokering and transshipment controls remain weak spots in China's regulatory system. The Chinese Ministry of Commerce does not recognize the role of brokers in export deals, although it is unclear whether Beijing forbids brokering activities or merely does not regulate them.[5] A problematic result is that "Chinese arms show up across the continent, from Liberia to Somalia. These seem to be mostly small arms [sold] to middlemen . . . who in turn sell to Africans, both governments and rebels" (Wilson, 2006). How the PRC's regulations on arms exports govern such sales is uncertain. Indeed, the "very limited use of postshipment verifications exacerbates the risk of Chinese exports' being put to unauthorized end-uses or being retransferred to unauthorized end-users without the Chinese government's knowledge" (Davis, 2005: 37). This risk has been realized in Africa (as we will see) as well as in the Middle East, where Chinese-made weaponry has turned up in the hands of the Taliban in Afghanistan and insurgents in Iraq, causing controversy among Western powers and prompting Beijing to issue strong protestations about its seriousness regarding arms-proliferation control.

In 2005, another White Paper titled *China's Endeavors for Arms Control, Disarmament and Non-Proliferation* was released (*Xinhua,* September 1,

2005). It was undoubtedly meant to address some of the concerns about Chinese arms exports, including as it did an expanded section covering the implementation and publication of export-control laws. However, it failed to allay concerns over "whether the current gaps between policy pronouncements and actual behavior simply mark[ed] a transition period to [Beijing's] new responsibilities or if this mixed record is symptomatic of its continued perception of nonproliferation as a 'selective, arbitrary tool' employed by Washington and its allies to maintain strategic and technological preeminence" (Srivastava, 2005: 1).

Granted, it is difficult to speak of the "Chinese arms industry" or what "China" does vis-à-vis arms sales; the restructuring of the defense enterprise in the late 1990s, combined with center-province tensions and rivalries, meant that the enforcement of laws designed to control the exports of individual arms factories was bound to become complicated. It is, for instance, unclear that all exports by Chinese companies—particularly those at the low end of the market, involving small arms and such—have the express approval of the state.[6] The judiciary in China is notoriously corrupt, particularly in the provinces, and the influence of well-placed insiders and/or bribes may lubricate export licenses:

> The divestiture of profitmaking enterprises from the PLA in the last five years, although nominally accomplished, may not have fully separated the enterprises from patronage and influence networks that may allow them to conduct trade beyond the oversight of China's export control apparatus. . . . Deng Xiaoping's son-in-law is the head of [one arms] company, and many of the company's managers are former military officers or individuals with close ties to high government officials. The persistent patronage networks of [such] companies . . . may impede export control implementation, and further reforms may be necessary to ensure that these entities are held fully accountable to Chinese export-control laws and regulations. (Davis, 2005: 36)

The abundance of agencies for overseeing weapons-export offenses also means that coherence in the application of law is confused. This incoherence is massively problematic for Sino-African diplomacy and international relations in general; there exists "a broad divide between the MFA on the one hand and China's defense-industrial community (including trading companies formerly linked to the PLA) on the other. The MFA gains little from arms exports and is often forced to deal with their negative consequences on China's broader diplomatic objectives" (Gill and Medeiros, 2000: 90). This divide is becoming an increasing concern for Beijing, threatening its aspiration to be taken as a responsible power.[7] For instance, in December 2006

> French defense minister Michèle Alliot-Marie told the upper house of France's parliament that there was a more sinister side to what she said was

Beijing's effort to gain a share of mineral wealth and win political influence [in Africa]. "It does not bother us that a big country comes to help Africa's development, which needs it, . . . provided that it happens in clear conditions . . . that encourage the development of democracy," she said. "We therefore draw its attention to the fact that too often we see Chinese arms intervening in conditions that are sometimes contrary to embargoes." (*Reuters,* December 14, 2006)

The scandal surrounding the April 2008 Chinese cargo ship carrying more than 70 tons of small arms, including 3 million rounds of ammunition for AK47s and 1,500 rocket-propelled grenades, for Zimbabwe's government is emblematic in this regard (*Guardian,* April 24, 2008). The refusal by dockers in Durban to offload the shipment stimulated international reactions that eventually led to the shipment being recalled to China by the arms company. Although Beijing initially defended the shipment as having been signed in 2007 and unconnected to the political situation in Zimbabwe, it was a hugely embarrassing moment in Chinese diplomacy. Even though there is no international arms embargo against Zimbabwe, the timing was awkward for Beijing's broader reputation, in the context of Mugabe's continued brutality and equally, as world attention was focused on China as the host of the Olympics.

▨ Arms Sales and Africa

To put China's arms sales to Africa in context: in 2005, the total value of conventional-arms sales worldwide, among both developing and developed nations, was US$44.2 billion. Of this, China's share was US$2.1 billion, dwarfed by the United States' US$12.8 billion worth of exports. One hundred percent of China's arms exports, however, goes to developing nations (as does Britain's). Trends suggest that China is focusing more and more on the developing world as a market, even as other exporting nations are cutting back or at least stabilizing their sales; between 1998 and 2005, Chinese arms sales to the developing world went from US$500 million to the aforementioned US$2.1 billion. In contrast, Germany's exports to the developing world fell from US$1.4 billion in 1998 to US$700 million, and the United States saw a significant decline, from US$9.4 billion in 2004 to US$6.2 billion in 2005 (Grimmett, 2006: 8). But China—despite global sales estimated at US$8.3 billion—is still a distant fifth in the ranks of arms suppliers to the developing world during the period 1998–2005, behind the United States (US$67 billion), Russia (US$38.8 billion), France (US$18.3 billion) and the United Kingdom (US$9.9 billion). Regardless, it is clear that Africa is an important market for Chinese arms. While just over half of China's arms exports go to other countries in Asia—52 percent—sales to Africa make up nearly 17 percent (compared to 0.44 percent from the United States). In fact, just over 15 percent of total arms imports into Africa come from China, behind France, which supplies nearly 23 percent, and Russia with 17.7 percent.

Weapons have factored into Sino-African relations since the beginning. Initially, they went primarily to African liberation movements, although in amounts dwarfed by the quantity sent by the Soviet Union and its allies (see Weinstein, 1975). After nations such as Zimbabwe secured their independence, Beijing often sought to cement ties via weapons supplies—although the amount, as well as the quality and technological sophistication, of these too compared unfavorably with shipments from Moscow.[8] Diplomacy via weaponry continues in the 2000s: "China's supply-side considerations include the desire to improve political ties with the recipient country, efforts to use the recipient state to balance against a strategic rival, and purely commercial considerations. [However,] no single determinant dominates either the demand or supply for weapons; which determinants are most prominent vary by the country involved" (Byman and Cliff, 2000: 7).

Using the methodology pioneered by SIPRI, we can see where the majority of Chinese arms sales to Africa go. SIPRI's Trend Indicator Values (TIVs), which correspond to the volume of arms transfers (not the financial value of the arms transferred) and which are useful for measuring trends in international arms transfers, highlight the key recipients of Chinese arms. Between 1990 and 2006, the foremost importers of Chinese arms were Egypt (with a TIV of 353), Algeria (160), Sudan (152), Tanzania (69), Nigeria (67), and Zimbabwe (49). Table 5.1 sketches out additional details to provide a summary of the main conventional-weapons sales from China to Africa in that time period.

Sales to Sudan and Zimbabwe are probably the most controversial.[9] The level of criticism over such exports is linked to China's noninterference policies, the consequences of which are beginning to play out.

▩ China's Arms Sales to Sudan

Khartoum has sourced weaponry from Chinese manufacturers since at least 1985, with transfers between 1985 and 1989 totaling US$50 million; as of the 2000s, "China, the largest shareholder in the Greater Nile consortium, is the key player in Sudan's arms" trade (Christian Aid, 2004: 8). Beijing's weapons-exporting policy has thus come under particular scrutiny in the context of the Sudanese civil war and the crisis in Darfur. In June 2001, the *Mideast Newsline* reported that Sudan had built three weapons factories with Chinese assistance in order to put a halt to rebel advances (June 17, 2001).

The Sudanese Air Force is equipped with US$100 million worth of Shenyang fighter planes, including a dozen supersonic F-7 jets. Beijing also reportedly authorized the sale of Chinese-made Scud missiles to Khartoum in 1996 in a deal underwritten by a US$200 million loan from the Malaysian

Table 5.1   Transfers of Major Conventional Weapons by China to Africa, 1990–2006

Destination	Number Ordered	Weapon Description	Year(s)
Algeria	1	Support ship	1990
	7	Patrol craft	1990–1991
	25	Anti-ship missiles	2000–2002
Egypt	1	Radar	1993
Eritrea	4	Y-12 transport aircraft	1994
Gabon	16	107mm rocket launchers	2004
	10	130mm rocket launchers	2004
	4	122mm rocket launchers	2004
Ghana	4	K-8 trainer/combat aircraft	2006
Kenya	6	Y-12 transport aircraft	1997
Mali	2	AS-365 Panther helicopter	2000
Mauritania	2	Y-12 transport aircraft	1995–1996
	1	Y-7 transport aircraft	1997
	1	Patrol craft	2002
Namibia	2	Y-12 transport aircraft	1997
	4	K-8 trainer/combat aircraft	2001
	12	F-7MG fighter aircraft	2006
Nigeria	12	F-7M fighter aircraft	2005
	20	Short-range air-to-air missile system	2005
Sierra Leone	1	Patrol craft	1997
Sudan	18	122mm towed gun	1991
	2	Y-8 transport aircraft	1991
	6	F-7M fighter aircraft	1995–1997
	3	A-5C fighter/ground attack	2003
	12	K-8 trainer/combat aircraft	2004
Tanzania	2	Patrol craft	1992
	2	Y-12 transport aircraft	1994
	2	Y-8 transport aircraft	2002
Tunisia	3	Patrol craft	1994
Zambia	3	Y-12 transport aircraft	1996
	8	K-8 trainer/combat aircraft	2000
	1	Y-7 transport aircraft	2006
	3	Y-12 transport aircraft	2006
Zimbabwe	2	F-7B fighter aircraft	1991
	1	Y-12 transport aircraft	1991
	6	K-8 trainer/combat aircraft	2005
	6	K-8 trainer/combat aircraft	2006

Source: Stockholm International Peace Research Institute, 2008.

government against future oil extraction. A former embassy official in Kuala Lumpur, Abdel Aziz Ahmed Khattab, claimed to have witnessed the deal, arranged by Sudan's state minister for external relations, Mustafa Osman Ismail. According to Khattab, the Malaysian national oil company was used as a cover to ship arms to Sudan:

> Arms deals agreed upon have been shipped by sea, in the name of the Malaysian National Petroleum Company and the Chinese National Petroleum

Company, under the guise of petroleum-exploration equipment. This is according to an agreement concluded between the government in Khartoum and these companies in Kuala Lumpur under which they provide weaponry and military equipment in exchange for being given concessions for oil explorations. (cited in Human Rights Watch, 1998a, n. 83)

Certainly, Khartoum has used hard currency generated by Chinese investment in Sudanese oil fields to finance its conflict in the southern part of the country, stoking criticism that "China has transferred military, security, and police equipment to armed forces and law-enforcement agencies in countries where these arms are used for persistent and systematic violations of human rights" (Amnesty International, 2006b). Ali Askouri (2007: 77) concurs: "[Although] China claims that it does not interfere in internal politics, the distribution of these [weapons] reveals that China is immersed in the internal politics of Sudan up to its neck. . . . Whoever happens to be in power is a friend of China as long as they will guarantee China access to resources."

Problematically, the vast majority of Sudan's oil is found in the Upper Nile, where the largely non-Muslim Dinka and Nuer people live. Oil has thus been an integral part of the long-standing internal dispute between Khartoum and the South (Johnson, 2003). Refugees International claimed that "China National Petroleum Corporation contribute[d] Chinese-made tanks, fighter planes, bombers, helicopters, machine guns and rocket-propelled grenades, firearms, and ammunition to the Sudanese military" (2006: 1), while Medecins Sans Frontieres reported in detail on activities south of Bentiu, the epicenter of oil development in Western Upper Nile:

According to [civilians from the road area], whose accounts were consistent, road clearing first began in 2000, often preceded by Antonov bombings and helicopter-gunship activity. Then the government of Sudan and Nuer troops, along with Chinese laborers, brought bulldozers to clear the site of the road and the surrounding area. After the bulldozers cleared a track, troops arrived in vehicles and burned all the *tukuls* [traditional dome-shaped houses] in the path alongside the road. Government garrisons were then established at thirty-minute intervals along the road. (Medecins Sans Frontieres, 2002: 3)

Human Rights Watch likewise reported that

weapons deliveries from China to Sudan since 1995 have included ammunition, tanks, helicopters, and fighter aircraft. China also became a major supplier of antipersonnel and antitank mines after 1980, according to a Sudanese government official. The SPLA in 1997 overran government garrison towns in the South, and in one town alone, Yei, a Human Rights Watch researcher, saw eight Chinese 122mm towed howitzers, five Chinese-made T-59 tanks, and one Chinese 37mm anti-aircraft gun abandoned by the government army. (Human Rights Watch, 1998b: 5)

The Sudanese government has been accused of pursuing a scorched-earth policy to protect its oil fields, leading to massive depopulation and displacement: "The Sudan Armed Forces were keen on laying waste to local communities in the South to ensure there would be nothing to threaten oil development. Along with its armed militias, Khartoum terrorized civilian populations with improvised Antonov bombers and helicopter gunships that became more readily available as oil revenues grew" (Patey, 2007: 1001). There is some evidence that airstrips built and maintained by Chinese workers in the oil areas were used during 2002 and 2003 as military bases from which the Sudanese government forces launched missions.[10] Many of the helicopter gunships in Khartoum's arsenal were obtained from China, often using projected receipts from oil extractions in the regions where fighting took place. Such activities have generated widespread opprobrium toward Beijing (see Chapter 2), and provoked China in turn to reconsider its involvement in Sudan.

▓ Zimbabwe

To return to another controversial Sino-African relationship, Beijing has provided arms and security equipment to Mugabe's regime, which it conceivably uses to defend itself from the Zimbabwean people. Deals have been shrouded in controversy as well. For instance, in 2000, Chinese small arms were exchanged for eight tons of ivory (*Financial Gazette,* July 20, 2000). A report released by one environmental NGO alleged that Chinese-made guns were delivered to Harare in exchange for ivory flown from Zimbabwe to China via Libya; the delivery was made "'just a few days after the international community had refused Zimbabwe's demand to sell ivory,' a senior Ecoterra [an environmental NGO] member said, referring to the Convention on International Trade in Wild Species of Fauna and Flora (CITES) conference in April [2000] in Nairobi" (*Reuters*, July 13, 2000). In 2004, it was reported that Mugabe's regime had again sold ivory, this time for US$1 million, as a means to pay for thousands of Chinese AK-47 rifles "in preparation for the next elections" (*Sunday Times,* July 9, 2004):

> According to wildlife experts monitoring the Zimbabwean government, the Chinese approached Mugabe after a referendum on constitutional change failed and it appeared that he would face additional pressures from the [MDC]. CITES has previously investigated rumors of the shipments but was assured by Zimbabwe's wildlife department that just over 23 tons of ivory were stored at its Harare headquarters, one ton less than when CITES inquired a year earlier. . . . Only a handful of trusted officials—all loyal to the ruling ZANU-PF party—have access to the stores. (*Zimbabwean*, June 26, 2007)

This was not a one-off deal:

Zimbabwe has been surreptitiously bartering tons of ivory with its ally, China, in return for military hardware amid reports the state has been systematically pillaging natural resources and poaching endangered elephants to enrich a few ruling elite. Details of the illicit operation emerged as the 171-member [CITES] relaxed its regulations in Geneva last week, allowing four African countries, including Zimbabwe, to put their ivory stocks on the market in a one-time sale. . . . Worth almost US$1 million, the sale was a serious breach of rules covering the ivory trade, and is being investigated by Interpol and CITES. . . . The Beijing government is officially opposed to the trade, but wildlife experts in Harare say that unofficially, Chinese demand is high. (*Zimbabwean*, June 26, 2007)

A US$240 million deal between Beijing and Zimbabwe in June 2004 involved twelve jet fighters and 100 military vehicles (*Vancouver Sun*, October 28, 2004), which the latter required to replace vehicles and aircraft that were no longer operational due to a lack of spare parts and maintenance issues resulting from Western sanctions. Interestingly, the order was covert, although it was eventually exposed; according to one report, "Chinese and Zimbabwean military ties are among the closest on the African continent. In April 2005, Zimbabwe's air force received six K-8 jet aircraft to be used for training jet-fighter pilots and for 'low-intensity' military operations, and the year before, a Chinese radar system was installed at Mugabe's US$13 million mansion in the Harare suburbs" (Eisenman, 2005: 2).

Since then, "rumors [have] abound[ed] that China has sold Zimbabwe's internal-security apparatus water cannons to subdue protesters and bugging equipment to monitor cell phone networks" (*New York Times*, July 25, 2005). In addition, Mugabe's government is reported to be pursuing legislation called the Interception of Communications Bill to monitor Internet use, with "reportedly obtaining Chinese expertise, equipment and technology in [the course of] its bid" (*BBC News*, August 31, 2006). It is true that in 2006 the Zimbabwean government began jamming a London-based opposition radio station that employed Zimbabwean journalists living in exile. The equipment it used was Chinese, leading Reporters Without Borders to comment, "Thanks to support from China, which exports its repressive expertise, Robert Mugabe's government has yet again just proved itself to be one of the most active predators of press freedom" (*Christian Science Monitor*, March 30, 2005). A Zimbabwean analyst explains: "Chinese 'noninterference' policy cannot be permanent. The Chinese are well aware of this themselves. Where deals are signed with unpopular dictatorial regimes that could later be revised by a new government, it becomes necessary for the Chinese to protect such regimes. This explains their arming of the ZANU-PF government" (Karumbidza, 2007: 88–89). Indeed, in 2006 Mugabe publicly "remind[ed] those who might harbor any plans of turning against the government: be warned, we have armed men and women who can pull the trigger. . . . The defense forces have benefited from government's

Look East policy, through which they have not only acquired new equipment but also learned new military strategies" (*Business Day,* August 16, 2006).

It could be argued that Beijing encouraged Mugabe to act with impunity: "Although the European Union and North American countries have imposed sanctions on Zimbabwe, including an arms embargo, the country has other sources of military and security equipment. China provides weapons[, and] Zimbabwe's cozy relationship with China has obstructed moves to address concerns at the United Nations Security Council, as Beijing simply exercises its veto" (Unendoro, 2007). As in the instance of Sudan, by allowing (or facilitating) arms sales to Harare, Beijing stands accused of supporting a regime that in turn stands widely held accused of human-rights abuses. It is difficult to see how this behavior does not undermine the region's peace, security, and stability according to the PRC's arms-exporting policy. The same goes for Chinese trade elsewhere in Africa.

■ Other African Customers

In the cases of Sudan and Zimbabwe, it might be argued that sovereign regimes under pressure invited Chinese arms companies to supply them with arms and equipment and on occasion this has been used to protect broader Chinese assets. This is not the case in Equatorial Guinea. Chinese specialists in heavy military equipment have been sent to Malabo presumably to offer weapons in exchange for oil. Over a three-month period ending in November 2000, Chinese trainers worked with the local army despite the fact that Equatorial Guinea has no heavy weaponry; thus the only guess one may make is that Chinese arms exporters want to introduce such weaponry to Equatorial Guinea in exchange for either oil concessions or hard currency. Equatorial Guinea appears the perfect customer, as climbing oil prices have granted the country extra finances. That China's military assistance might fuel some sort of arms race in the Gulf of Guinea is clearly of no concern (Wright, 2001: 92). China is, after all, the third-largest importer of oil from Equatorial Guinea, after the United States and Spain (*The Nation,* April 14, 2006); it also buys up to 60 percent of Equatorial Guinea's lumber exports.

In other parts of Africa, Chinese suppliers have played similar roles in the provision of weaponry, often during times of conflict. For instance, between 1998 and 2000, when Ethiopia and Eritrea were edging toward war, Chinese corporations dispatched nearly US$1 billion in weapons to both countries.[11] This war went on to claim as many as 100,000 lives. Earlier, in 1995, a Chinese ship carrying 152 tons of ammunition and light weapons was refused permission to unload in Tanzania: the cargo was destined for the Tutsi-dominated army of Burundi, and Tanzania was concerned that ethnic conflict there would be exacerbated by the arms shipment (*Agence France-Presse International*

News, May 3, 1995). It was not an isolated shipment, however. Human Rights Watch later released a report showing that at least thirteen covert shipments of weapons (three of which were in violation of regional or international arms embargoes) were delivered from China to Dar-es-Salaam, their final destinations mislabeled and the weapons disguised as agricultural equipment. Asks one critic, "If it [were] a legitimate transaction from one state to another—and not something more nefarious—why the need for the elaborate subterfuge?" (Pham, 2007: 1).

In DRC in 1997, Chinese exporters furnished Laurent Kabila with arms and have been supplying Kinshasa with weapons, frequently through Zimbabwean middlemen, ever since. Sierra Leone's brutal civil war may also have been fueled by extensive shipments of Chinese arms:

> Freetown concluded an agreement with China . . . in 1990. A former chief of staff of the Sierra Leone army, Brigadier-General . . . K.O. Conteh, remembers the Chinese shipment to have included about 1,000 AK-47-type rifles and ammunition. China provided more than just rifles. Conteh recalled that, in addition to the AK-47s, the consignment also included fifty machine guns, as well as a number of automatic grenade launchers and grenades. Retired Major-General Gottor concurred with this assessment, adding that the Chinese also provided ten twin-barreled, wheeled anti-aircraft guns and an assortment of 60mm, 82mm and 120mm mortars. He described the ammunition that accompanied the shipment as being a "huge amount." The shipment arrived in the first half of 1991. (Berman, 2000: 10)

Later, observers at a disarmament site, collecting weapons from the Revolutionary United Front (RUF) rebels, reported that "the weapons collected were from virtually every major arms-producing country [but included] Chinese-made AK-47s, 12.7mm machine guns, grenades ('mostly Chinese varieties'), anti-personnel mines, and Chinese 82mm mortars ('being the most common')" (Berman, 2000: 11).

Even in countries not torn apart by war, Chinese arms manufacturers have been accused of reckless arms sales—or at least of not being in control of their distribution. The Chinese parastatal Norinco has come under particular fire for its irresponsible arms vending, especially in South Africa where "Norinco 9mm pistols, which are cheaply manufactured in China, are commonly used in cases of robbery, rape, and other crimes" (*Mail and Guardian*, June 16, 2006). Amnesty International's 2006 report on Chinese arms sales was replete with examples of incidents involving Norinco pistols; Olajobi Makinwa, executive director of Amnesty International in South Africa, was quoted as saying that it was "quite difficult to get an estimate of the scale of Chinese weapons in the wrong hands," whether they were "legitimately imported and then subsequently diverted, lost, or stolen, ending up on the streets" or whether they were "smuggled into South Africa from China, directly or indirectly, by organized crime networks" (*Mail and Guardian,* June 16, 2006). Whatever the case, Beijing's reputation in Africa has been tarnished somewhat by its arms industry's apparent willingness to supply disreputable actors.

■ Conclusion

We should remember that African arms purchases are symptomatic of African problems surrounding the construction of states and the political cultures therein. The Sino-African arms trade cannot be blamed simply on irresponsible Chinese exporters; the demand-side equation is equally important. It is evident that "Beijing seeks to more effectively police illicit activities within its own borders at a time of rapid economic transformation, decentralization, and marketization of business, trade, and industrial sectors at home" (Gill, 2007: 98). However, its ability to do so is increasingly constrained by impulses associated with economic liberalization. In fact, "China's initial efforts at trade liberalization led to the massive proliferation of thousands of small- and medium-sized corporations trading with the outside world, which, in turn, vastly complicated Beijing's ability to implement and enforce its various commitments not to sell military equipment, materials, and technology" (Gill and Medeiros, 2000: 93); although "it might not be impossible for the central government to ensure compliance," with the law throughout China, observes Shaun Breslin, "it is a far from easy task" (2007: 101).

Indeed, a conflict of interest between central administrators and those in command at lower levels is apparent across China, not just in the arms industry (Davies and Ramia, 2008). Given that profit is now arguably central to most enterprises, this conflict can play itself out in quite unpredictable ways:

> The persistence of military-industrial ties and relationships between enterprise management and political elites . . . casts doubt on the full implementation of Chinese export-licensing requirements. Improvements appear to have been made in the regulation and oversight of China's military-industrial complex through government restructuring in 1998 and 1999. . . . Yet the Chinese government's ability to fully regulate trade by both private and public enterprises is tenuous. The Chinese state-owned defense-industrial conglomerate, Norinco—whose subsidiaries produce military, dual-use, and civilian goods—is a regular target of US proliferation-related sanctions, bringing into question the Chinese state's ability to bring such large and complex entities into the regulatory fold of its export control system. (Davis, 2005: 36)

This situation will need to be addressed by policymakers, as "enforcement is presently one of the weakest links in China's export control system. A wide disparity exists between the dictates of established Chinese law—which include adequate penalties for export-control violations—and the capacity of the

Chinese state to consistently implement its new export-control standards" (Davis, 2005: 37).

However, to return to Sudan and Zimbabwe, the central state is clearly heavily involved in arms manufacturers' relations with both Harare and Khartoum; the sorts of deals they have struck could not conceivably have occurred without Beijing's backing, tacit or otherwise. In other words, the weaponry sold to the Sudanese and Zimbabwean regimes is of a type that could not escape official notice. Of course, China is not the only nation that puts its own interests ahead of moral concerns. Nor is it the only one to turn a blind eye to abuses and/or to craft relationships with questionable regimes in exchange for access to resources. The issue is that the PRC itself claims to be different. The spokeswoman for the Foreign Ministry, Jiang Yu, answering questions about Hu Jintao's 2007 visit to Africa, asserted that

> the Chinese government consistently adopts a prudent and responsible attitude towards arms sale[s]. We have strict laws and regulations on it. China only exports military products to sovereign countries and requests the commitment of relevant countries not to transfer China's weapons to a third party. We strictly abide by relevant UN resolutions and do not export military products to the countries and regions on [the] UN arms-embargo list. China has only limited arms sale[s] to Africa, which is confined to conventional weapons in a very small amount. (*Xinhua,* January 31, 2007)

Whether this statement corresponds with some of the actions outlined in this chapter is debatable.

All that said, it is apparent that Beijing is becoming sensitive to the charge that its arms sales to Africa have had negative repercussions. Thus, in July 2007, China's special envoy to Sudan went public to claim that Beijing was actively trying to stop the use in Darfur of weapons it had sold to Sudan. "We will do our best to prevent the weapons from finding their way into the wrong hands and from doing the wrong things," Liu Guijin was quoted as saying. "I can assure you that China has applied strict criteria in exporting weapons to Sudan." Liu added that China was "only one of the countries that has sold weapons to Sudan, and it is not a major exporter in this regard" (*Guardian,* July 5, 2007).

As has been mentioned elsewhere, the PRC is on a steep learning curve in Africa, and its leaders are beginning to realize that their previous policy of doing whatever they wanted and simply waving off attendant criticism has unintended consequences. Allowing Africa, wittingly or unwittingly, to be flooded with arms has a certain blowback.[12] For instance, in April 2007, nine Chinese workers and sixty-five Ethiopians were killed by separatists at a Chinese oil exploration site in eastern Ethiopia (*Xinhua,* April 24, 2007). The Ogaden National Liberation Front (ONLF)—which has a policy of demanding that foreign oil- and gas-exploration companies stay out of the region—

claimed responsibility, stating that the Chinese workers had been killed in the crossfire. Similarly, in October 2007, JEM rebels in Darfur attacked the Chinese-run Defra oil field. The head of the rebel group in the Kordofan region, Mohamed Bahr Hamdeen, was quoted as saying, "We consider [all foreign oil companies] killers because they help the government buy the weapons [that it uses] to kill women and children. . . . The latest attack is a message to the Chinese companies in particular." The rebels then gave Chinese and other oil companies a week to leave the country (*Associated Press,* October 25, 2007). Added JEM commander Abdel Aziz el-Nur Ashr, "This is a message to China and Chinese oil companies to stop helping the government with [its] war in Darfur" (*Reuters,* October 24, 2007).

Two aspects of these incidents are noteworthy. The first is the general point that although "Africa's leaders may be happy to take the Chinese yuan, its resentful people are accusing China of being modern colonialists" (*Independent,* April 26, 2007). This sort of discourse has become common in some parts of Africa and is certainly not helped by portrayals of China as an irresponsible arms dealer. The second is even more important for Chinese policymakers to come to grips with, and that is the unpredictability of African politics and the potential—albeit unintentional—repercussions of selling arms to reckless regimes.[13] As we have seen, Chinese manufacturers were enthusiastic suppliers of weapons worth millions of dollars to both Ethiopia and Eritrea. Yet the Eritrean government allegedly supports the ONLF and supplies the organization with weapons and training. It would be tragically ironic to discover that the slain Chinese oil workers were killed by Chinese-made weapons in the hands of insurgents engaged in an effective proxy war between Asmara and Addis Ababa. Likewise, now that it is seen as Khartoum's closest ally, Beijing, and hence its interests, are now in the line of sight of the rebels in Darfur. As of 2008, peace is being maintained in south Sudan, but if war were to break out again, Chinese assets would likely be in jeopardy. The attempt to separate economics from politics is not tenable as the case of Chinese arms sales to Africa clearly illustrates.[14]

To reiterate, Beijing proposes three guiding principles for its international arms-transfer policy. First, exports should boost the legitimate self-defense needs of their recipient. Second, they should not damage regional and/or international peace and stability. And third, China should not interfere in the domestic affairs of recipients. The inherent problem with such a policy, however, is that it is often difficult to determine who or what constitutes a legitimate government in Africa.[15] In many African countries, power is fundamentally dependent upon capturing the state by force—or being linked favorably to those who have. Therefore, in making arms sales, Beijing is often dealing with governments that are little more than glorified kleptocracies and quasi states whose principal aim is ensuring the survival and enrichment of the elite.[16] For instance, although Mugabe's government may indeed be officially recognized at the United Nations, can Chinese policymakers honestly state that its self-defense needs are legitimate? And as Zimbabwe's decline continues, are Chinese arms sales to Mugabe not damaging to the stability of southern Africa?[17] As one commentator noted, "China's policy on arms trade is characterized by a substantial gap between discourse and deeds. Not [that] the illicit export of Chinese arms is the key problem[;] rather, the officially monitored trade [operates under] very lax formulation of requirements and the careless interpretation of 'regional peace'" (Holslag, 2007a: 9). Finally, is it credible for Beijing to claim that humanitarian abuses and violations of human rights in places like Zimbabwe and Sudan are simply "domestic affairs" that cannot and should not be addressed?[18] As we discussed in Chapter 4, Beijing does appear to be shifting its stance on such issues.

At the same time, Beijing's capacity to monitor the increasing volume of exports and to uncover export control violations is diminishing, "especially given its heavy dependence on foreign intelligence to alert it of illicit activities. . . . Complicating matters are the nation's continuing struggle against corruption and its lack of an independent judiciary. Furthermore, the Chinese government's very limited use of postshipment verifications exacerbates the risk of Chinese exports' being put to unauthorized end-uses or being retransferred to unauthorized end-users without the Chinese government's knowledge" (Davis, 2005: 37). Thus, "even when the culprits are identified, China's opaque system makes it hard to determine whether these activities are instigated by companies operating outside the control of the central government, rogue elements in China's military and intelligence services, or decisionmakers in Beijing" (Kleine-Ahlbrandt and Small, 2008: 52). For instance, ultimate responsibility for the aborted arms shipment to Zimbabwe in 2008 has still to be ascertained.

It bears repeating that China is hardly the only arms-exporting country guilty of weapons sales to repressive African countries. Arms exports from China pale in significance to those of the United States, and are even smaller than those from Russia, France, or Britain. Indeed, under New Labour, British arms sales to Africa quadrupled, and many of the customers were authoritarian states with poor human-rights records.[19] It should also be noted that China supported the October 2006 draft UN resolution on the illicit trade in small arms and light weapons while the United States opposed it. Yet civilians in many of these Western countries have actively petitioned their governments to set arms-export regulations on autocracies. Such civil movements are largely nonexistent in China and consequently there is little domestic pressure upon Beijing. In addition, China has refused to sign any multilateral agreements governing arms sales, stymieing effective regulation and control. That China does not publish information about its arms exports—it last submitted data to the UN Register on Conventional Arms in 1996—ensures its policies remain highly opaque.[20]

Although China did announce in September 2007 that it would begin reporting its armed-forces budget as well as its holdings and sales of conventional arms, it "customarily places heavy secrecy on everything involving the military. . . . So the usefulness of any new information [its leaders] give depends on how far they want to go" (*Agence France-Presse,* September 3, 2007). Nevertheless, Beijing's desire to be recognized as a responsible stakeholder in the international arena, one that is qualitatively distinct from the former colonial powers of the West, has made it sensitive to external criticism and pressure; thus the international community has an opportunity to influence its behavior and shape its ever-maturing policy toward Africa.[21] Still, outside commentators must be cognizant of China's "ability, and ours, to differentiate between acts of companies and state acts, so that we are both identifying bad actors, not raising every issue to the level of state-to-state action" (Nealer, 2004: 246).

As of 2008, "Beijing still has considerable work to do to improve the system and prevent Chinese companies and individuals from proliferating [arms]" (Gill, 2007: 102). However, there is evidence that Beijing is increasingly focusing on enforcement, "taking steps to improve its capacity to uncover export-control violations and interdict illicit transfers" (Davis, 2005: 37). Beijing's growing integration into the global economy, combined with the rising threat of violence against Chinese interests in volatile regions, has led Chinese policymakers to realize that nonproliferation is vital to China's security, domestically and overseas.[22] In the long run, they now see, Chinese interests are best served by a stable and conflict-free Africa.

▓ Notes

1. Interview with David Jabati, news editor, *Awareness Times,* Freetown, Sierra Leone, June 7, 2006.
2. Interview with military attaché, Western embassy, Addis Ababa, Ethiopia, May 15, 2007.
3. Interview with military attaché, Western embassy, Addis Ababa, Ethiopia, May 15, 2007.
4. Interview with military attaché, Western embassy, Addis Ababa, Ethiopia, May 15, 2007.
5. Interview with Western diplomat, Asmara, Eritrea, June 29, 2006.
6. Interview with military attaché, Western embassy, Addis Ababa, Ethiopia, May 15, 2007.
7. Interview with Chinese academic, School of International Studies, Peking University, Beijing, China, September 20, 2007.
8. Interview with the acting head of the Political Affairs Section, Chinese Embassy, Windhoek, Namibia, August 13, 2006.
9. Interview with Pentagon official, Washington, DC, United States, April 5, 2007.
10. Interview with British diplomat, Addis Ababa, Ethiopia, May 15, 2007.

11. Interview with Western diplomat, Asmara, Eritrea, June 29, 2006.

12. Interview with military attaché, Western embassy, Addis Ababa, Ethiopia, May 15, 2007.

13. Interview with Western diplomat, Asmara, Eritrea, June 29, 2006.

14. Interview with military attaché, Western embassy, Addis Ababa, Ethiopia, May 15, 2007.

15. Interview with Henning Melber, Namibian political economist, Windhoek, Namibia, August 14, 2006.

16. Interview with African Union official, Addis Ababa, Ethiopia, May 16, 2007.

17. Interview with Robin Sherborne, editor of *Insight,* Windhoek, Namibia, August 14, 2006.

18. Interview with government official, Gaborone, Botswana, September 25, 2004.

19. Interview with military attaché, Western embassy, Addis Ababa, Ethiopia, May 15, 2007.

20. Interview with military attaché, Western embassy, Addis Ababa, Ethiopia, May 15, 2007.

21. Interview with British diplomat, Addis Ababa, Ethiopia, May 15, 2007.

22. Interview with the acting head of the Political Affairs Section, Chinese Embassy, Windhoek, Namibia, August 13, 2006.

Peacekeeping | 6

A paradox of Chinese diplomacy in Africa is that even as Chinese arms exporters have been supplying weapons to some of the parts of the continent most in need of peacekeepers, Beijing has been contributing an increasing number of troops and support personnel to United Nations peacekeeping operations (UNPKOs). Since 1990, China has contributed about 7,500 peacekeepers to UNPKOs, according to the Peacekeeping Affairs Office of the Ministry of Defense. In mid-2008, 1,977 Chinese peacekeepers were serving on UN missions in countries such as Côte d'Ivoire, Liberia, Lebanon, and Sudan. It should be noted that the number of Chinese peacekeepers worldwide is much smaller than the number Pakistan supplies the United Nations—10,623 as of mid-2008—or that supplied by Bangladesh, which has 9,037 participants in many of the UN's twenty-two missions worldwide (United Nations Department of Peacekeeping Operations, 2008). However, compare China's contribution to that of the United States, which in June 2008 engaged only fourteen soldiers, sixteen military observers, and 259 police officers in UN peace operations.

In fact, China contributes more personnel to peace operations than most other permanent members of the UNSC, which is supposed to bear special responsibilities for international peace and security. As of June 2008, in contrast to the 1,977 military and police individuals China was contributing to UN operations, the United Kingdom sent 358, the United States 289, and Russia 299. Only France, with 2,090 uniformed personnel serving under the UN beat China (United Nations Department of Peacekeeping Operations, 2008); hence the boast by Wang Guangya, China's UN ambassador, that "China is filling a vacuum left by the West. 'The major powers are withdrawing from the peacekeeping role,' he said. 'That role is being played more by small countries. China felt it is the right time for us to fill this vacuum'" (*Washington Post,* November 24, 2006). Meanwhile, the other permanent members do little more than determine which UNSC Resolutions get passed and which do not.

Granted, they pay quite a bit of the UN budget, but they generally do not put their own troops on the ground.

The ambiguities and contradictions in Beijing's own involvement in peace operations can be explained by its stance on state sovereignty and intervention. The most remarkable feature of China's "flurry of UN peacekeeping" efforts in the post–Cold War era has been its focus on the "domestic political scene" of the countries where the Chinese contribute to peace operations (James, 1993: 359). This has at times put Beijing in a difficult position, something we will discuss, after a brief detour to define the terms "intervention" and "interference," both deployed frequently but imprecisely by Beijing in its commentaries on peace operations.

While the verb "to interfere" simply means to obstruct, get in the way, or impede, since the end of the Cold War, the meaning of the verb "to intervene" has undergone a prolonged transformation, at least in the context of peacekeeping (Ramsbotham, 1997). Alex Bellamy and Paul Williams (2004) propose a five-tier typology of intervention: traditional peacekeeping, as exemplified by the UN Peacekeeping Force in Cyprus (UNFICYP); transition management, as represented by the UN Observer Mission in El Salvador (ONUSAL); wider peacekeeping, à la the UN Assistance Mission for Rwanda (UNAMIR); peace enforcement, such as we see in Haiti; and peace support, undertaken by groups like the International Security Assistance Force (ISAF) in Afghanistan. Very few of the African operations have involved traditional peacekeeping or peace enforcement, but are rather managing transitions, wider peacekeeping, or peace support missions. In 1967, Oran Young defined an intervention as "any action taken by an actor that is not direct party to the crisis, that is designed to reduce or remove one or more of the problems of the bargaining relationship and, therefore, to facilitate the termination of the crisis itself" (34). The majority of peacekeeping literature uses it to refer to military action by outsiders without the host government's consent (Bellamy, Williams, and Griffin, 2004). And Robert Jackson (1993: 581) has defined it as "dictatorial interference by a sovereign state, a group of such states, or an international organization, involving the threat or use of force or some other means of coercion, in the domestic jurisdiction of an independent state against the will or wishes of the government of the targeted country." However, "no commonly legal accepted definition of humanitarian intervention has emerged [that] could serve as a guideline to allow intervention in cases where harsh measures are called for and [not] where it is inappropriate and counterproductive to international peace and human security" (Schnabel, 2002: 16). What is more, the UNSC has yet to authorize intervention against a functioning state without the latter's say-so (Bellamy, 2005: 38), although unilateral "intervention by invitation" (Byers, 2003: 14) is consistent with Article 2 of the UN Charter.

Within Chinese circles, there seems to be some confusion between *gan yu* (intervention) and *gan she* (interference). For most Western observers, intervention amounts to a Chapter VII episode (where the UNSC authorizes the use of military forces under a UN mandate to maintain or restore peace and security) or its functional equivalent, which might be sanctions and embargoes, or international criminal prosecutions; "less intrusive levels of outside encroachment that fall short of the three kinds of coercion in the internal affairs of a state do not amount to intervention" (Weiss, 2003: 271). For Chinese analysts, however, "there is a very pejorative connotation attached to 'interference' and a more positive one to 'intervention', especially in cases where the [latter] signifies that an operation has been authorized by the UN Security Council" (Weiss, 2003: 271). Thus "China, on various occasions, has strongly denounced NATO's bombing of Yugoslavia since the outbreak of the Kosovo crisis, [calling] it interference in another country's internal affairs under the disguise of human-rights protection" (Chu Shulong, 2002: 16). The bombing of Kosovo by the North Atlantic Treaty Organization (NATO) was quite clearly an intervention according to the generally accepted definition, but because it did not have UN backing, it could not be termed as such by the Chinese, who hence simply called it interference. But linguistic differences notwithstanding, it remains the case that,

> in terms of legitimacy, different approaches arise from giving weight to sovereignty, on the one hand, thus stressing the inviolability of frontiers, and from giving weight, on the other hand, to human rights, thus sanctioning forcible border-crossings to prevent massive state abuse. On the ethical side, appeals to the supreme importance of international order confront no less urgent demands for the protection of civilians against abuses committed or sanctioned by states. (Badescu, 2007: 51)

We will now turn to China's stance on such issues.

▓ China, State Sovereignty, and Peace Operations

One of the consequences of China's emergence as an economic giant since the end of the Maoist era is increasing scrutiny by the international community. Indeed, anxieties that Beijing is a revisionist power set on reconfiguring the globe are regularly aired, particularly with regard to the implications of its rise for the United States (Lampton, 2008; Wang Sheng-wei, 2008). Though there is some uncertainty in the West as to the meanings of both the terms "revisionist" and "status quo" in terms of China (Johnston, 2003), it seems clear that Beijing is dedicated to the status quo and defensive of traditional beliefs about sovereignty, even in the event of threats to Chinese interests. Certainly the belief that nonintervention in the domestic affairs of states is vital for preserving international peace and stability à la the Peace of Westphalia continues to underpin Beijing's international relations, having been enshrined in its Five Principles of

Peaceful Coexistence and revisited only reluctantly in recent years (Kang, 2008).

Some Chinese scholars go so far as to dismiss out of hand the very notion of humanitarian intervention—Cheng Xiaoxia of the Law School at Renmin University, Beijing, for example, who asserts that "'intervention' violates the UN Charter, so it is ridiculous to connect 'intervention' with 'humanitarianism.' 'Intervention' is a kind of coercive and arbitrary behavior and has nothing to do whatsoever with 'humanitarianism'" (Cheng Xiaoxia, 2003: 140–141). In fact, intervention is allowed under Chapter VII with UNSC authorization; it is intervention without UNSC authorization that is in dispute. At any rate, such hard-line positions are untenable in the postmillennium, being out of touch with international realities that have shifted the debate from the sanctity of state sovereignty to that of individual sovereignty (see Boutros-Ghali, 1992; Deng et al., 1996; Annan, 1999). The post-Westphalian idea of sovereignty presumes that liberal-democratic societies are best placed to secure international harmony, concomitantly implying that they are inherently involved with other sovereign states and may intercede without compunction if the sovereignty of individuals are being transgressed (see Bellamy, Williams, and Griffin, 2004).

To reiterate, by contrast, China has traditionally maintained that the principles of state sovereignty and noninterference must serve as the bases for international relations between states—though we should now emphasize that its position is shifting, as its growing involvement in peace operations demonstrates. As we have suggested, China's valorization of sovereignty springs from its experiences in the nineteenth and early twentieth centuries. This Century of Humiliation, in popular Chinese parlance, lasted from the First Opium War in 1839 to the triumph of the CPC in 1949—when, per Mao Zedong, the Chinese people stood up *(Zhongguo renmin zhancilai le)*—and the thought of it still rankles today (Scott, 2007): "To every Chinese leader or schoolchild, modern Chinese history of the last 150 years is a history of humiliation, a history of being invaded, a history of losing sovereignty and independence" (Chu Shulong, 2003: 183). Thus China guards its sovereignty as a correlative of "regaining" its "rightful place" in international affairs (Elegant, 1963): "The attainment of . . . great-power aspirations . . . draws upon strong emotions, linked to nationalist sentiments, traditional cultural ethnocentrism, and a deeply rooted sense of injustice at the hands of . . . (especially) Western countries" (Swaine, 1995: 84). The Century of Humiliation thus constitutes a key motif in Chinese discussions regarding sovereignty and intervention:

> Chinese historical textbooks continue to teach Chinese people that in the 100 years between 1840 [and 1949] almost every "imperialist state" . . . invaded China and bullied the Chinese people. And the Chinese believe those countries would . . . do the same [today] if China did not stand strongly against such intention[s]. This is the meaning when Chinese leaders repeatedly say

that national sovereignty and independence are more valuable to developing countries like China. (Chu Shulong, 2003: 183–184)

In addition, China has traditionally emphasized the right of states to resolve issues among themselves, in keeping with its resistance to outside involvement in affairs it perceives as strictly domestic, such as those of Tibet and Taiwan.[1] As Pang Zhongying (2005: 88) notes, "Central to Chinese concerns is the changing nature and context of peace operations—with the potential for mission creep and the move to 'coalitions of the willing'—and the implications [these] would have for international involvement in China's key internal affairs relating, for example, to Taiwan, Tibet, and Xinjiang." Beijing has scrupulously avoided establishing international precedents that could later be used to justify interference in China's so-called domestic issues, even at the risk of inviting occasional cynicism from non-Chinese observers such as Adam Garfinkle, former speechwriter for Colin Powell, who provocatively stated at a conference on sovereignty and intervention held in China that "when Chinese officials and scholars state their concerns about sovereignty, they are motivated not by legal abstractions but by the debatable nature of their own claims to sovereignty over specific territories added to China during the Manchu Qing dynasty" (Garfinkle, 2003: 248–249).

However, we should emphasize that the rhetoric contained in official Chinese pronouncements "has led many observers to reach the premature conclusion that Beijing opposes all forms of intervention and is wedded to an antiquated approach to sovereignty" (Carlson, 2006: 218). In fact, it is possible to discern a subtle shift in China's position regarding state sovereignty.[2] Consider, for instance, the evolution of four of its official guidelines on legitimate intervention. These state that intervening bodies must first proceed with respect for the concerned state's sovereignty. Second, they must gain the authorization of the United Nations. Third, they must secure an invitation from the concerned state. Finally, they should use force only when all other options have proven ineffective (Carlson, 2004). This set of necessary conditions demonstrates that Beijing has softened its hard-line stance on state sovereignty and noninterference.

However, the Westphalian notion that interference requires an invitation holds even in the event that the host government has embarked on widespread and systematic killing or territorial cleansing. By implication, such governments can veto intervention. In the past, when foreign troops intervened in the affairs of a state at the behest of its government, China based its opinion of the legality of the action on whether the official request corresponded to the genuine desires of "the people" as it saw them. This qualification, of course, permitted China to decide legality on the basis of political expediency (see Cohen, 1973). China has now effectively abandoned this position and currently focuses on a legalistic interpretation of state sovereignty in the face of intervention. The will of the people is not part and parcel of China's diplomacy or decisionmaking process in this regard.

Perhaps to avoid such potential conundrums, China has become quite adept at pursuing a strategy of nonparticipation or abstention from Security Council debates and votes on peace operations (Morphet, 2000). It can in fact be argued that abstention is an expedient strategy for China, since it precludes both criticism from the West regarding obstructionist opposition to contentious peace operations *and* criticism from the developing world, allowing China either to disassociate itself from controversial operations or to remain in accordance with its doctrine of noninterference even with respect to popular peace operations.[3] In Samuel Kim's words, "China's voting behavior, particular its abstention on Chapter VII enforcement resolutions, is neither positive engagement nor destructive obstruction but [a matter] of pursuing the maxi-mini strategy in a situation-specific and self-serving way" (2003: 69). Such behavior has worked to a certain extent, allowing Beijing to say it wishes to play a more significant role within the United Nations while avoiding many of the obligations thereof.

The changing nature of UNPKOs has itself made abstention an important tool of Chinese diplomacy. Under Chapter VII, the Security Council is allowed to take coercive action, including military force, against a state (Article 42) if the Council concludes that it has made "any threat to the peace, breach of the peace, or act of aggression" (Article 39). The notion of state sovereignty "shall not prejudice the application of enforcement measures under Chapter VII," per Chapter I, Article 2. This article is a problem for Beijing, which has had to face several similarly thorny issues in the era following the Brahimi Report, which was issued in 2000 by a high-level panel chaired by former Algerian foreign minister Lakhdar Brahimi and reviewed all facets of UN peacekeeping operations. The report made four significant proposals:

1. Peacekeepers need to be expressly mandated to be able to use force more advantageously to defend themselves, their mission, *and* civilians under threat of attack.
2. The UN should never mandate a peace operation prior to marshalling the necessary resources to execute the mission.
3. There needs to be improved discussion between the Security Council and the contributing countries to any peace operation.
4. A diversified approach to peacebuilding, including the training of local police, strengthening the legal machinery in postconflict states, disarmament, demobilization, and reintegration of former soldiers and the advancement of human rights—basically the construction of liberal-democratic states under the rubric of what might be termed the liberal peace. (United Nations Secretary-General, 2000)

Post-Brahimi, peace support emerged as a novel type of peacekeeping (Bellamy and Williams, 2004). The Brahimi Report effectively codified changes that had been occurring since the end of the Cold War. While providing a new framework and approach, it fundamentally reflected events and debates that had been going on since at least 1990. Importantly, it was understood that this framework amounted to clear authorization for the deployment of military force to pressurize warring sides to abide by established peace agreements, although UN peace operations (also known as blue-helmet operations) still only deploy with host-government consent.[4] While the Brahimi Report did not legitimize intervention and indeed confined itself to talking about peace operations, it nonetheless dictated that blue-helmet troops deployed in peace operations could not stand by in the face of civilian massacres. But even this concession raised ire among the Chinese, as the argument of one scholar illustrates:

> Will the out-of-control "humanitarian intervention" become a reprint of the globalization of colonialism in the twenty-first century? . . . [The colonialists] didn't take into account [the] rights and ideas of people of the colonies in Asia, Africa, and Latin America at all. And today, it is these former colonial countries that [have] their hedge of sovereignty being breached in the process of the generalizing of "humanitarian intervention." (Qin Xiaocheng, 2003: 169)

But ultimately, the Brahimi Report represented (and reflected) a shift from traditional peacekeeping actions to peace-support missions as the UN took a more active role in upholding international peace and security as well as in member-states' affairs. For the Chinese, traditional peacekeeping "is organized and deployed directly by the UN with the consent of all parties" (Zhang Li, 2003: 209). "All parties" in this context refers to state actors. In contrast, the Brahimi Report urged consent from the host government but not necessarily from all the parties involved, a provision Beijing felt comfortable with, as the 2002 Chinese Defense White Paper illustrates: "China supports the active measures taken by the UN Secretariat in this regard and welcomes the progress made by the UN General Assembly and the Security Council in deliberating the Brahimi Report on Reforming the UN's Peacekeeping Operations" (Information Office of the State Council, 2002). This move has had implications for the evolution of China's peacekeeping commitments in Africa and elsewhere.

▓ The Evolution of China's Involvement in Peace Operations

According to He Yin (2007), there have been four phases in the evolution of Beijing's attitude toward peace operations. The first phase, lasting from 1971 to 1980, was characterized by inactivity if not outright hostility with respect to such missions. The second phase reflected a gradual change in attitude from

1981 to 1987. The third period, from 1988 to 1989, saw China cooperate in some UN peace operations while issuing a fair number of challenges toward others. And the fourth period, from 1999 onwards, is marked by greater and greater Chinese participation in operations, despite some remaining reservations on certain issues.

In the first phase, China avoided playing any role in UN peacekeeping missions and did not even contribute to their costs (Morphet, 2000). We should remember, however, that China was the object of the first US-led enforcement mission sanctioned by the Security Council in 1951. Thereafter Beijing saw all UN interventions as superpower chicanery aimed at weaker states within the international system (Zhang Yongjin, 1998). This suspicion—compounded by the memory of the Korean War—lasted well past the era of Mao. Indeed, in 1990, then Foreign Minister Qian Qichen stated that Beijing's reluctance to support the enforcement mission in Iraq sprang from the fact that "the Chinese people still clearly remember that the Korean War was launched in the name of the United Nations" (quoted in Kim, 1995: 423). Consequently, "most of such UN actions were seen as interference in countries' internal affairs and as the undesirable result of US-Soviet hegemonic power competition" (Wang Jianwei, 1999: 70). What is more, the PRC was emerging from the Cultural Revolution at the time, so issues of Chinese diplomatic capacity within the UN system cannot be underestimated (Barnouin and Changgen Yu, 1998; see also MacFarquahar and Schoenhals, 2006; Clark, 2008).

Conversely, upon joining the United Nations, China was often accused of free riding off of the international community and avoiding its global responsibilities as a permanent member of the Security Council. Indeed, China was charged with being a group of one, uninterested in contributing to world order but reaping all the benefits thereof (Kim, 1995); it was not until the 1980s that Beijing's overall attitude toward the UN began to evolve.[5] Interestingly, however, when China did begin to play a more active role, some in the West feared that it would represent the more conservative, old-fashioned opposition to those in favor of the evolving form of peacekeeping that was more forceful and involved potential interference in the domestic affairs of recipient nations (Morphet, 2000). While the traditional peacekeeping initially favored by China may still have its place after Brahimi—for example, in conflicts like the Ethiopian-Eritrean border war—it would not really work in contemporary civil wars, as exemplified by Darfur. Given that Chinese foreign policy has long been predicated on the Five Principles of Peaceful Coexistence, which includes a strong normative commitment to noninterference, Beijing's increasing willingness to play an active role in peacekeeping missions is indeed intriguing. It has certainly begun to shape an aspect of China's Africa policy hitherto ignored by most commentators.

Initially, upon entering the United Nations in 1971, China maintained its vehement opposition to all peacekeeping operations, refusing to take part in

Security Council votes on resolutions pertaining to peace operations and going so far as to refuse to pay the yearly peacekeeping contributions expected of it as a member of the Security Council (Morphet, 2000). Contributing troops to peace operations was certainly out of the question: "Based upon Mao's theory of just war, China viewed peacekeeping as an act of superpower 'power politics,' a pretext deployed to justify US or Soviet intervention in the affairs of small states" (Taylor Fravel, 1996: 1104).

To trace the evolution in Chinese thinking more specifically, in 1981, as China's modernization project was continuing apace, China voted in favor of such peacekeeping resolutions as an extension of the UN mission in Cyprus and also began to disburse its annual peacekeeping contribution. It thereafter supported every resolution on UN peace operations from 1981 to 1990 (Morphet, 2000). This policy change sprang from the adoption of an "independent foreign policy of peace" *(duli zizhu de heping waijiao zhengce)* which the CPC inscribed into the PRC's revised constitution at the Twelfth National Congress in 1982 and reflected policymakers' awareness that China needed a stable and peaceful world in which to realize its plans for economic development and modernization (see Kapur, 1985). "'Peace' mean[t] that China began to formulate its foreign policy from the viewpoint of whether it [was] beneficial to international and regional peace instead of [to the pursuit of] military superiority, while 'independence' mean[t] that China began to formulate its foreign policy according to its national interests and the common interests of peoples of all the countries in the world" (Xia Liping, 2001: 18). This included maintaining "equidistant" relations with the United States and the Soviet Union as well as a "more positive [attitude toward] UN affairs" in general (Pang Zhongying, 2005: 90).

Equally, the policy allowed China to pose as a counterbalance to the superpowers in the name of the developing world, where peace operations were most likely to take place: "China in the early 1980s sought to distance itself from its alliance with the United States by emphasizing its role as the self-proclaimed leader of the developing world, which required a more cooperative attitude toward the UN and peacekeeping operations, since these institutions were important to many developing states" (Taylor Fravel, 1996: 1104). At the same time, however, Beijing was still "stak[ing] out a particularly narrow interpretation of the international community's right to intervene . . . predicated upon an interpretation of sovereignty as a virtually sacred right of states" (Carlson, 2006: 221).

Yet as the 1990s developed, Beijing reluctantly began to accept the development of trends in international politics that militated against this hard-line stance. According to a *China Daily* article by Wu Miaofa of the China Institute of International Studies, (May 29, 2007), China changed its tack for three key reasons. First, Beijing became conscious of the fact that UN peacekeeping operations were "an important means of maintaining international peace and security," for although "many of the long-standing conflicts [could not] be permanently resolved by peacekeeping efforts alone . . . peacekeeping [could] alleviate crises and provide strong support for developing countries suffering from a lack of allies as well as their own weaknesses." Second, a Chinese analysis of peacekeeping operations "carried out from 1948 to 2000 showed that a total of 54 missions concerning 52 countries mostly involved developing nations." Since "some developing countries also joined peacekeeping operations, including seven African, six Asian, and six Latin American nations," and since "quite a few commanders of peacekeeping troops were from developing countries," China was, in Wu's view, motivated to change its policy by its self-image as the de facto leader of the developing world. Finally:

> As one of the permanent members of the UN Security Council, China reassessed its position in the international system and concluded: despite undesirable aspects, the current international order [could] drive the growth of productivity; it remain[ed] a long-term task to build a new international political and economic order; [and thus] China should join other developing countries in pushing the international political and economic order in a more sensible direction. This includeed using the UN peacekeeping mechanism.

Drew Thompson (2005: 7–8) likewise avers that "China's economic growth and military-modernization process has caused concern about China's 'rise,' resulting in efforts to reassure neighbors that China strives to be a 'responsible power.' Actively participating in United Nations peacekeeping missions furthers China's image as a status quo nation that seeks to contribute to international stability through diplomatic and security measures." As China's economic and political clout continue to grow, Chinese policymakers are also gaining confidence, which enables them to commit to selective involvement in international affairs despite the traditional reluctance to do so in favor of maintaining a low profile *(tao guang yang hui)*, a goal formulated by Deng Xiaoping in order to focus Chinese efforts on domestic development. Although *tao guang yang hui* literally means "hide brightness, nourish obscurity," it can be translated as advice to conceal one's capacities and bide one's time—which has obviously sinister connotations. However, "the new Chinese diplomacy is changing from *tao guang yang hui* to *you suo zuo wei* (do something right), and it is the opportunity for asserting a new role for China in both the domestic and diplomatic arenas" (Wang Fei-ling, 2005: 478). Either way, involvement in international affairs is increasingly central to Chinese foreign policy, and peacekeeping is no exception.[6]

The Chinese are also interested in gaining experience by participating in the UN and its peace operations (He Yin, 2007). In fact, Drew Thompson (2005) identifies several important benefits China derives from taking part in UN peace operations. First, participation enhances Beijing's authority not only in regions where Chinese peacekeepers operate but also on the UNSC and among other voting members of the UN as well, not least those representing Africa—who are thus all the more likely to continue providing useful support in times of difficulty. Second, China's reputation as a responsible world power is enhanced by involvement in peace operations; as "the most self-conscious rising power in history . . . [China] is desperate to be seen as a benign force" (*Christian Science Monitor,* June 27, 2007). Third, by participating in peace operations, China increases its strategic presence in regions, particularly within Africa, whose resources may prove crucial for meeting China's energy needs.

Furthermore, by participating in peace operations, China restricts Taiwan's ability to practice "dollar diplomacy" and secure diplomatic recognition.[7] We should note here that China deployed peacekeepers and sent a generous aid package to Liberia soon after Monrovia switched its relations from Taipei to Beijing (Thompson, 2005: 8). What's more, as we have suggested, China is also filling a prominent vacuum left by Western members of the UNSC who contribute financially to peace operations but generally shy away from committing significant troop numbers. As Bonny Ling (2007: 48) notes, "This has undoubtedly enhanced China's strategic positioning at the UN, especially since peacekeeping is the single most high-profile element of any UN activities on the ground."

China took part in its first UNPKO in 1988, having joined the UN Special Committee on Peacekeeping Operations (UNSCPO) shortly after UN peacekeeping forces had received the Nobel Prize for Peace (Staehle, 2006). The following year it sent nonmilitary personnel to observe Namibia's general elections, and in 1990, it sent five military observers to join the United Nations Truce Supervision Organization (UNTSO) in the Middle East. Later, in 1993, Beijing approved the UN Transitional Authority in Cambodia (UNTAC), not only financing a good part of the operation but also sending in a military unit. These moves represented a "significant departure from [China's] past behavior in multilateral diplomacy for collective security purposes" (Wang Jianwei, 1999: 76). In fact, "since the early 1990s, the Chinese . . . [have] consistently finessed the meaning of these principles [regarding sovereignty] in order to create a rhetorical space for [their] acquiescence in various 'Western'-sponsored UN operations" (Carlson, 2006: 218) as a way to break out of the temporary diplomatic isolation encountered after Tiananmen Square in 1989 (Roy, 1998: 147–148).

Nevertheless, China remained cautious in its attitude toward peacekeeping, restating its opposition to the use of force whenever it overrode the sovereignty of a state. Beginning in the mid-1990s, "Beijing saw problems as the lines between peacekeeping and peacemaking became fuzzier; as expansion was accompanied by civilian missions concerned with human rights, refugees, and inspections; and as these missions had less-than-complete support from host nations" (Gill, 2007: 116); in the words of one Western academic, it "seemed that an era might be dawning in which Western governments, freed from the constraints of the Cold War, would use their armies to save strangers in places far from home" (Wheeler, 2000: 172). Consequently, China's "involvement in UNTAC was not repeated in subsequent missions. This was partly due to [its] attitude toward the principles of state sovereignty and its concern about the use of force in peacekeeping operations. These issues only served to highlight the emerging contradictions and ambiguities with regard to China's position on the nature of peace operations" (Pang Zhongying, 2005: 91).

As a result, China opposed features of Operation Provide Comfort in Iraqi Kurdistan, UN Protection Force (UNPROFOR) in Yugoslavia, Operation Turquoise in Rwanda, and Operation Restore Democracy in Haiti—all by abstaining on the Security Council resolutions to authorize or expanding them (Carlson, 2006: 224). China was clearly taking a rearguard action against contemporary peace operations insofar as they involved military enforcement, while supporting traditional peacekeeping operations. It was, for all intents and purposes, a stance against "mission creep," which China believed meant that "the United Nations was becoming an instrument of 'hegemonism'" (Gill, 2007: 116).

In the run-up to the first Gulf War (1990–1991), Beijing was supportive of Chapter VII resolutions concerning Iraq, though it expended a great deal of energy working to take out recommendations specifying military force (Staehle, 2006). When the UN did approve Resolution 678, entailing the deployment of all necessary means including military force, China abstained. However, as part of its effort to rebuild its international image post-1989, Beijing continued to support traditional peacekeeping missions such as the 1994 UN Operation in Mozambique (ONUMOZ), which it saw as demonstrating the efficacy of traditional peacekeeping; as a Chinese commentary put it: "The experience of ONUMOZ has proved that as long as the two parties to the conflict are sincere about resolving their problems through negotiations and unswervingly implement the agreements reached by the parties, it is highly possible for them, with the help of the international community, to end yesterday's suffering and open up a new vista" (quoted in Choedon, 2005: 43).

However, China had more difficulty determining what to do when said parties resisted the implementation of peace agreements.[8] For instance, although Beijing was an active supporter of the UN Transitional Authority in Cambodia (UNTAC) in 1992—voting in favor of administrating elections, overseeing the government, operating a disarmament program, and probing human rights abuses (all of which constitute interference in the domestic affairs of a state, by any measure)—it refused to sanction peace-enforcement operations after the Khmer Rouge pulled out of the peace process (Staehle, 2006). Granted, China was one of the Khmer Rouge's main backers (Chong, 2002). However, to quote Gary Rawnsley (2006: 10), China has in general opposed deviation from Chapter I (Article 4 of which opposes the use of force "against the territorial integrity or political independence of any state") and Chapter VI of the UN Charter that requires from peacekeeping operations impartiality of the peacekeeping forces, the consent of the parties involved in the dispute, the use of means other than force to keep the peace, and the prior agreement to a ceasefire between the parties concerned. These remain the legal basis for China's support for peacekeeping operations, and, naturally, their violation forms the basis for Chinese opposition.

Yet it should be noted that one of China's first peacekeeping roles in Africa involved support of the United Task Force (UNITAF) and its UN Operation in Somalia (UNOSOM). UNOSOM was organized to monitor the ceasefire between warlords, despite the fact that they were still engaging in violence and that humanitarian assistance was under threat from looting and abuse by their militias.

It was the interception of humanitarian aid that led to the authorization of the UNITAF mission under Chapter VII. China supported UNITAF but made clear that it considered the situation exceptional, as anarchy was raging in the absence of any government in Mogadishu—a key point as far as it was concerned. Beijing's position was influenced by the fact that it "did not want to be perceived as obstructionist by casting vetoes on Somalia-related UNSC resolutions and hindering humanitarian assistance. This was especially true since it already had a bad image abroad, especially in the West, following the 1989 Tiananmen incident" (He Wenping, 2007: 29).

Once UNITAF had completed its mission, Beijing supported UNOSOM II, again under Chapter VII and again on the grounds that Somalia constituted a temporary exception and that normal peacekeeping operations should be resumed as soon as possible. However, once fighting between UN troops and Somali militias began—culminating in the infamous Black Hawk Down incident—China backtracked. For instance, the *Beijing Review* asserted that "the torturous experience in Somalia has taught the lesson that peacekeeping must be limited to peacekeeping. The internal affairs of one country can be solved only by the people of that country. The efforts of the international community can only be helpful or supplementary" (quoted in Taylor Fravel, 1996: 1114). Assistant Minister of Foreign Affairs Li Zhaoxing likewise stated that "the fundamental and effective way to settle the Somali question is by peaceful means. Resort to coercive military actions will only serve to complicate matters" (quoted in Taylor Fravel, 1996: 1113–1114).

Crucially, the Mogadishu debacle resulted in a de facto refusal by Washington to get involved in efforts to stop the 1994 genocide in Rwanda. While the United States and other Western powers have been (rightly) lambasted for resisting calls to intervene (see Melvern, 2000), criticism of China, which was equally resistant to getting involved, has been muted.[9] In fact, it was only in

June 1994 that a multinational force was authorized under Chapter VII to stabilize the situation (although the French actually started deploying before the Resolution was passed). The United Nations Assistance Mission for Rwanda (UNAMIR) did not reach the military numbers it required to deploy until much later. China abstained from the vote, even though the resolution authorizing the Chapter VII mandate emphasized the temporary and unique nature of the mission, on the grounds that the mission did not have the approval of all parties involved in the fighting—granting the *genocidaires* an implicit veto on the vote to stop their butchering.

In May 1997, China agreed in principle to contribute to the UN Department of Peacekeeping Operations (DPKO). However, that same year, it was active in warning against the intrusion into the domestic affairs of African countries under the guise of peace operations; it backed the establishment of the United Nations Observer Mission in Angola (MONUA) but expressed concern that the military element of the mission might get drawn into issues that should by rights concern other UN departments. Wang Xue Xian, China's UNSC representative, stated at the time that "as a principle, the Security Council should not get involved in those activities which fall under the terms of reference of other United Nations bodies" and that "China had reservations on certain elements of the draft resolution and on aspects of the observer mission's mandate" (quoted in United Nations Security Council, 1997). China had similar concerns with the United Nations Mission in the Central African Republic (MINURCA), which aimed to stabilize and restructure the republic's military. In a vote to extend MINURCA's mandate, China's UNSC representative, Lin Chengxun, while supportive, observed that although "the mission had played a great role and . . . demonstrated that the Security Council could do concrete work for African countries and people . . . reforms, especially the restructuring of the armed forces, [are] the internal affairs of a country. Therefore, the Council should not intervene too much in that area" (quoted in United Nations Security Council, 1999).

The events in Kosovo in 1998 and 1999 particularly worried Beijing as NATO's air campaign served to flag for Chinese policymakers the dangers of non-UN-mandated interferences in domestic affairs. Beijing was absolutely against the NATO campaign, deeming the whole exercise deeply problematic if not ominous. Indeed, after the Chinese embassy in Belgrade was hit by NATO missiles on May, 7, 1999, indignant, anti-Western nationalism proved difficult to contain (Gries, 2001; Zhao Dingxin, 2002; Xiao Gongqin, 2003); "the view from China's capital was that the United States—the main organizer and contributor of the coalition—was bent on enforcing its vision of proper global order on the rest of the world, even if the attainment of this goal required armed aggression" (Dreyer, 2000: 3). Yet the Kosovo campaign may have served as a positive catalyst for changes in China's policies, as "the shock of [it] and especially the embassy bombing compelled Chinese strategists to seek new ways to ensure Chinese influence over the methods and processes of international intervention" (Gill and Reilly, 2000: 48).

This shift helps explain China's support for a 1999 mandate for the UN Mission in Sierra Leone (UNAMSIL) to implement a Disarmament, Demobilization, and Reintegration (DDR) program, support elections, and smooth the transfer of aid to the country (Staehle, 2006: 41). UNAMSIL was authorized under Chapter VII to ensure the safety of its personnel and to defend civilians but acknowledged the rights and responsibilities of the government of Sierra Leone, which in turn fully supported the mission. Thus China was likewise more than willing to support it. Protecting the distribution of humanitarian aid and patrolling strategic locations within Sierra Leone were clearly compatible with China's stance on peacekeeping. China also supported the UN Transitional Administration in East Timor (UNTAET) in 1999 "once [its] prerequisite of Indonesian acquiescence was fulfilled. . . . China sent election observers, voted for sending in a multinational non-UN force to quell the violence, and then contributed civilian police for the first time in a UN role" (Gill and Reilly, 2000: 48).

In subsequent missions, China collaborated on peace-support operations in DRC, Liberia, Côte d'Ivoire, Burundi, and Sudan (as we will see), since they all explicitly limited military force to the defense of UN personnel and civilians in impending danger and "interference" in domestic affairs was not an issue. In short, China agreed to peace-support operations with elements of peace enforcement, provided they were carefully restricted.

However, as the UNSC has adopted an increasingly broad interpretation of what constitutes a threat under Chapter VII, China's position has become increasingly complicated.[10] Beijing still insists on securing the blessing of the host country before authorizing operations based on human-rights infringements. Thus China unambiguously supports the UN Organization Mission in Democratic Republic of Congo (MONUC), which was created with Kinshasa's approval after the signing of the Lusaka Ceasefire Agreement in 1999. MONUC is authorized under Chapter VII to take the necessary measures to improve security in North and South Kivu and the Ituri district, where the UNSC has identified serious human-rights abuses. Importantly for China, the Congolese government was a key signatory of the original agreement for the cessation of hostilities in DRC and hence a willing host nation of MONUC—however limited in practical terms its reach may have been in the areas in question. China's position relied on the literal definition of "host nation" *(dangshi guo)* used in its Defense White Paper of 2002 (a revision of the 1998 White Paper), namely "the state that is a party" (Information Office of the State Council, 2002). This definition suggests that the consent of all parties to UN involvement is not absolutely necessary, a qualification that is important "where state authority is either highly disputed or effectively nonexistent," as in the case of DRC (Gill and Reilly, 2000: 44).

In stark contrast is the case of Darfur, where Beijing opposed initial efforts to involve outsiders in improving the security conditions. Thus, whereas the UN Mission in Sudan (UNMIS) had functioned in southern Sudan since early 2005, it took considerable efforts—often in the teeth of Chinese opposition—for a mission to be sent to operate in Darfur. Initially, only a somewhat lackluster effort by the African Union was allowed by Khartoum, with Beijing continually backing up the Sudanese refusal to allow a more intrusive and fully international mission. This continued even after it became clear that the African Union's ability to defend Darfurians was negligible, as Beijing continued to insist it would back peace-support operations only with an invitation from the host country.[11] To return to a key motive for such a view, Gary Rawnsley (2006: 12) observes that "too much leeway in peacekeeping raises the specter of interference in China's internal affairs. China remains suspicious that the norms of international governance and multilateral activity are designed for the fulfillment of a Western, and specifically [US-led], agenda. Hence, China is willing to play the game by the rules, but only when the rules do not threaten Chinese interests." Other scholars agree: "The debates in Beijing have moved on from how to defend the principle of noninterference to the conditions under which intervention is justified. But there are important limitations. China has not undergone an underlying shift in values. Its economic interests remain paramount, and it still does not share Washington's views about human rights or democracy" (Kleine-Ahlbrandt and Small, 2008: 39). Therefore, Beijing has consistently "tried to influence the process of decisionmaking regarding UN operations" (Pang Zhongying, 2005: 92).

However, since late 2006 Beijing began to exhibit an increased willingness to engage with the international community on Darfur and started to apply pressure on Khartoum to modify its behavior and engage in a political process for the peaceful resolution of the Darfur conflict. This change in policy by Beijing was mainly due to overwhelming international criticism of China's role in Sudan and the increasing reputational costs that Beijing was experiencing by being closely associated with Khartoum. Subsequently, Beijing voted for UNSC Resolution 1769 that created a hybrid United Nations African Mission in Darfur (UNAMID). While it was the case that China at times went along with the Sudanese government's opposition to its full implementation, by mid-June 2008, Hu Jintao strongly urged Sudan to cooperate in allowing the deployment of peacekeeping forces into Darfur as part of UNAMID, clearly indicating that the limits of Chinese patience had been reached. Indeed, in a meeting with Sudan's vice-president, Ali Uthman Muhammad Taha, Hu was reported to have used unusually frank language in calling on Khartoum to try harder to settle the conflict in Darfur. This was in the context whereby 26,000 peacekeepers were supposed to have been deployed in Darfur, but no more than half that number had arrived on the ground by mid-2008, mainly due to intransigence by Khartoum. According to one report: "Hu's comments and their prominent publication . . . are part of an increasingly open Chinese diplomatic campaign to persuade Sudanese leaders to cooperate more with international efforts to end the fighting in Darfur. . . . China has come under criticism from human rights activists for failing to pressure Khartoum forcefully enough [and] the official portrayal of [the] meeting was seen as a departure from China's usual style of quiet diplomacy and ritual proclamations of friendship" (*Washington Post*, June 13, 2008).

China's Contributions to Ongoing Peace Operations

In mid-2008, Chinese personnel were taking part in seven UN-mandated peace operations in Africa, with 1,453 Chinese personnel deployed on the continent. We will now detail the exact nature of these missions and of Chinese actors' roles therein.

The United Nations Mission for the Referendum in Western Sahara (MINURSO)

This was established by Security Council Resolution 690 in April 1991 to supervise the ceasefire between the government of Morocco and the Frente Popular de Liberación de Saguía el Hamra y Río de Oro (also known as the Frente Polisario). The mandate includes the duty to carry out a referendum on Western Sahara's future, the choice being between independence and integration with Morocco. The mission has an authorized strength of 230 military personnel; in June 2008 China was contributing 14 military observers.

The United Nations Organization Mission in Democratic Republic of Congo (MONUC)

Democratic Republic of Congo and five other regional states signed the Lusaka Ceasefire Agreement in July 1999. MONUC was set up by the UNSC in November 1999 and incorporated UN personnel authorized by previous resolutions. MONUC's mission is to perform disarmament, demobilization, repatriation, resettlement, and reintegration (DDRRR). It has an authorized maximum strength of 16,700 military personnel and 475 police, although the UNSC allowed a temporary increase during the Congolese elections of 2007. As of June 2008, MONUC had a total of 18,428 uniformed personnel; China contributed 218 soldiers and sixteen military observers.

The United Nations–African Union Mission in Darfur (UNAMID)

A joint AU/UN hybrid operation in Darfur was authorized by UNSC resolution 1769 at the end of July 2007. The UNSC authorized UNAMID to take necessary action to support the Darfur Peace Agreement under the provisions of Chapter VII. The UNSC decided that UNAMID should start implementing its mandated tasks no later than the end of 2007. In mid-2008 the mission had 9,563 uniformed personnel; China contributed 147 troops.

The United Nations Mission in Ethiopia and Eritrea (UNMEE)

Following two years of border skirmishes and proximity talks led by Algeria and the Organization of African Unity in June 2000, Ethiopia and Eritrea signed an agreement to cease hostilities. The UNSC set up UNMEE in July 2000 to maintain contact with the parties and institute a mechanism for monitoring the ceasefire. In September 2000, the Security Council authorized deployment of up to 4,200 military personnel to aid in the parties' adherence to various security commitments. UNMEE has an authorized maximum strength of 4,200 military personnel, although in mid-2008 it had an actual strength of only 328 military personnel, including 244 troops and 88 military observers, of which 2 were Chinese.

The United Nations Mission in Liberia (UNMIL)

This was established by Security Council Resolution 1509 (2003) in September 2003 to support the implementation of a Comprehensive Peace Agreement (CPA); protect UN staff, facilities, and civilians; and support humanitarian and human-rights activities. The mandate also includes a mission to support national-security reform, from national police training to the development of a restructured military. In mid-2008 its strength totaled 12,934 uniformed personnel; China's peacekeeping contingent was 580.

The United Nations Mission in Sudan (UNMIS)

This was established by the UNSC via Resolution 1590 in March 2005 to support implementation of the Comprehensive Peace Agreement (CPA) signed in January 2005. The mandate also includes the performance of functions relating to humanitarian assistance and the protection and promotion of human rights. In June 2008, UNMIS had a deployed strength of 9,924 uniformed personnel, of which China contributed 444 troops, as well as eight police officers and fourteen military observers.

The United Nations Operation in Côte d'Ivoire (UNOCI)

The mission was authorized on February 27, 2004, by resolution 1528. Its aim is to facilitate the implementation of a peace agreement, signed in January 2003, between the Ivorian government (who control the south of the country), and the New Forces (who control the north) to end the Ivorian civil war. The UNOCI mission aims to establish a "zone of confidence" in the center of Côte d'Ivoire, separating the two belligerent parties. In mid-2008 there were 9,174 uniformed personnel deployed by the UN of which ten were Chinese military observers.

▨ Conclusion

China has long been circumspect about intervening in other countries' affairs even when sanctioned by the United Nations and remains suspicious that the UNSC authorizes Chapter VII mandates too readily.[12] However, as Beijing has emerged as an economic superpower it has been compelled to embark on a change of direction in some aspects of its foreign policy. One such shift is from an absolute refusal to support peace operations under any circumstances to a permanent commitment to doing so. China is now a major contributor of UN peacekeepers, most of whom are in Africa (three-quarters of all Chinese personnel deployed under the UN serve in Africa). It also maintains two training facilities for peacekeeping personnel—one in Nanjing, in Jiangsu province, and the other in Langfang, in Hebei. And in August 2007 it was announced that Major-General Zhao Jingmin would be appointed force commander for MINURSO, making him the first Chinese national to head a UN mission (*Xinhua,* August 28, 2007).

In many ways, Beijing has had international leadership pushed upon it.[13] As China's economy has exponentially expanded and its trade profile has increased across the globe, expectations that Beijing would (and should) play a greater role in international relations has been almost axiomatic (Lanteigne, 2005). Furthermore, in considering questions of domestic security, "China has gradually realized that peacekeeping missions can help to secure a peaceful international environment, which works in China's national interest as the country begins to build a sound external environment for its long-term economic growth and social development" (Pang Zhongying, 2005: 97). Dennis Blasko (2006: 180) further makes the point that there may be a domestic dimension to China's interest in sending troops overseas on peacekeeping missions:

> The Chinese media has paid a lot of attention to both the PLA's and to the civilian police's role in UN missions. This positive image may be useful in appealing to Chinese civilians who want to see their military and police force

> engaged in socially beneficial functions and their country taking an active role as a responsible member of the international community. As such, these missions may be a positive factor in promoting overall civilian support to the armed forces and [the] civilian police force.

Although as of 2008, nearly twenty years have passed since Tiananmen Square, the government's desire to rebuild civil-military relations and restore the Chinese public's confidence in the PLA should not be discounted, especially in light of the rise in Chinese national pride that has grown with the economy (Chen Zhimin, 2005) and generated demand that China play a more energetic role abroad.

China's increased profile, particularly in Africa, has led to criticism—including charges of neocolonialism—that Beijing's foreign policy makers are attempting to counteract. Acutely aware of its global reputation, China is taking part in peace operations as one way to project a more benign and even positive image. As Dai Shao'an, vice-director of the Peacekeeping Affairs Office of the Ministry of Defense, has put it, "wherever they go or whatever they do, [Chinese peacekeepers] always bear in mind that they are messengers of peace, representing China. . . . To win hearts and minds, you need to devote your own hearts and minds, and that is exactly what our peacekeepers are doing" (*China Daily,* July 24, 2007). A Chinese academic agrees that "active participation [in peace operations] is a demonstration of China's commitment to the UN and its security functions as mandated by the UN Charter. It is not only useful for serving China's moral cause or fulfilling its international responsibility in the post–Cold War era. It also provides an arena in which China can learn to interact with the international community in ways commensurate with its status as a rising power" (Pang Zhongying, 2005: 87). Playing a role in Africa is particularly important for China, explains Elizabeth Economy from the Council on Foreign Relations, as it attempts to reassure the world that it is not motivated solely by its need for resources: "It has a number of reputational risks. Being seen as a force for peace and security is an important and good first step" (quoted in *Washington Post*, November 24, 2006).

As has been detailed elsewhere (see Chapter 4), China has been criticized for seeming inattention to the issue of human rights and for being seen to be impeding the resolution of conflicts in places such as Darfur. Sensitive to this criticism, Beijing is now steadily constructing a reputation for being at the forefront of conflict resolution in Africa—even if the numbers it actually contributes to various peace operations are small.[14] In fact, China has been relatively successful in projecting a positive diplomatic image vis-à-vis peace operations in Africa, earning the praise of various African commentators. Liberian president Ellen Johnson-Sirleaf, for instance, commended China for supporting Liberia in its peacekeeping, asserting that "Liberians will never forget the friendship of Chinese peacekeeping soldiers" (*People's Daily,* February

1, 2007). Similarly, in July 2007, President Isaias Afewerki of Eritrea called on China as a UNSC member to help implement the ruling on the Eritrea-Ethiopia border, clearly seeing it as an honest broker of sorts (*Xinhua*, July 23, 2007).

Interestingly, it was the Chinese who urged other nations to support the deployment of peacekeepers to Somalia during a UNSC mission to Addis Ababa in June 2006—"the first time [China] had taken the lead in the fifteen-nation council in promoting foreign intervention to resolve a conflict thousands of miles from its own borders" (*Washington Post,* November 24, 2006). According to Chinese reports, African governments pressed China to raise the issue with the Council. However, Princeton Lyman—a former US ambassador with expertise on Sino-African ties—has a more prosaic view, namely that China is seeking to score diplomatic points by supporting vital regional allies such as Ethiopia, which had itself sent thousands of troops to Somalia to protect the official interim government (*Washington Post,* November 24, 2006).

Whatever the real motives, it appears that an increasingly important aspect of China's African policy involves peacekeeping. Where it will lead remains open to question. The lack of strategic trust between China and many Western countries with regard to military involvement—including peacekeeping—around the world, not least in Africa, is problematic.[15] China is highly skeptical about the motives behind much Western interest in peace operations and understandably rejects US leadership at the UN and/or US interpretation of international relations.[16] China has always couched its concerns in terms of hegemony, and there is little evidence to suggest it will do otherwise in future. Indeed, following the NATO military strikes against Yugoslavia in the spring of 1999, one Chinese commentator wrote that "hegemonism and power politics are still developing, and there will be no peace under heaven in the twenty-first century" (Liaowang, May 17, 1999). And Wang Jincun, a senior researcher at CASS, asserted in an article titled "Global Democratization—Camouflage of US Hegemony" that "what deserves more attention is that the United States, not yet satisfied with its Cold War achievements, seeks to gain more advances through military means. . . . The military interference by the United States in Iraq, Somalia, Haiti, and Bosnia-Herzegovina, the bombing against Sudan and Afghanistan, and especially the ongoing air strikes against Yugoslavia serve as prominent examples" (*Xinhua,* May 27, 1999).

China remains resolute in its opposition to actions it perceives as interferences in the internal affairs of other states, and it will not assent to peace operations—let alone take part in them—without the agreement of the sovereign host government, however weak its rule may be.[17] Notes Tony Saich (2001: 275), China clings to an "outdated notion of sovereignty. . . . By and large, China is an empire with a Westphalian concept of the nation-state trying to operate in an increasingly multilateral world." This view of sovereignty has arguably often eclipsed China's perception of its responsibilities as a global power (Foot, 2001). Moreover, it has left China open to charges of hypocrisy on the subject of noninterference. For instance, in February 1999, China used its veto to prevent the continuation of the UN Preventive Deployment Force (UNPREDEP) because the host country, Macedonia, had recently established diplomatic relations with Taiwan. Yet in 2004, Beijing dispatched a large contingent of police officers to the UN Stabilization Mission in Haiti (MINUSTAH), which likewise maintained official ties with Taiwan. Such contradictions may be examples of the maturing of Chinese foreign policy. The Chinese share the prevalent suspicion among developing countries regarding the motives behind potential interventions by foreign powers, especially the United States and former colonial powers (Thakur, 2004). Thus they often take the position that, "in interventions carried out in the name of 'humanitarianism' . . . what the interveners themselves were concerned about [was] not humanitarianism per se but their own interests" (Qin Xiaocheng, 2003: 168). Interestingly, in so doing, they echo Peter Baehr's claim that "'humanitarian intervention' is a misnomer. It would be far better to speak of the use of military force for (allegedly) humanitarian purposes" (Baehr, 2004: 34). But such analyses—whether by Chinese or Western commentators—fail to generate insight into the rationale behind any given intervention. What is required in each case is an investigation into the claims that motivated the intervention and a methodical scrutiny of the endorsement of so-called humanitarianism. Both are sadly lacking.

A Chinese source, quoting a former deputy permanent representative to the UN, Shen Guofang, reminds us of Beijing's central tenet with respect to peacekeeping, namely that it should always observe "the principles of respect for state sovereignty, noninterference in internal affairs, fairness and neutrality, [and] nonuse of force except for self-defense [as well as obtain] prior consent from parties concerned" (*People's Daily,* October 21, 1999). Ambassador Zhang Yishan, at the 2006 Session of the Special Committee on Peacekeeping Operations, reiterated that any UN mission must "fully respect the views of the parties concerned and strictly preserve neutrality" (*Xinhua,* February 27, 2006). Let us remember that the Chinese government once described the Special Committee for Peacekeeping Operations as an attempt to create "a US-controlled headquarters of international gendarmes to suppress and stamp out the revolutionary struggles of the world's people" (quoted in Foot, 1995: 239). While such rhetoric has been muted in the postmillennium, the suspicion that Washington seeks to use the UN as a vehicle to project its interests and policies is still held by Beijing—and resonates in many African capitals as well—even though the United States under the Bush administration has not used the UN as much of a vehicle for anything.

Conceivably, the training and experience that is gained at very little cost and fully supported by an extensive logistical framework courtesy of the UN is a motivating factor in China's new willingness to undertake peace operations, as it is with South Asian nations who have traditionally provided peacekeepers.[18] Bonny Ling (2007: 48) describes the benefits thus: "The interpersonal aspect of international peacekeeping is most recognized in the form of technical training. For instance, participating in peacekeeping operation[s] provides a good opportunity for countries to test their equipment in harsh settings. It also trains troops for rapid combat deployment and provides key leadership experience to top military personnel while requiring them to work closely with top brass from other countries." What is more, the UN pays allowances directly to both the individual peacekeepers and to their government. As Drew Thompson (2005: 8) notes, "For middle- to lower-income countries, participating in UN operations is financially rewarding because the UN monthly reimbursement rate of approximately US$1,100 per person is higher than the monthly salary in many armies."

Yet while "participation in UNPKO may make some financial sense" for individuals, "the Chinese government does not enjoy financial gains from its participation in UNPKO" in any significant respect; UN peace operations are "not a source for generating revenue" (He Yin, 2007: 67). What China receives from the UN is merely compensation for the equipment it buys for its troops and police units. In fact, "the Chinese government has to invest a lot of money in peacekeeping" (He Yin, 2007: 68), particularly on the construction of peace-training facilities and the development of necessary equipment. Financial incentives thus can be discounted as a motive for Beijing's increasingly active role in peace missions.[19]

Thus much of the reward China receives takes the aforementioned form of training and experience for its peacekeepers, as well of a boost in reputation:

> The PLA and PAP [People's Armed Police] . . . directly benefit from involvement in UN peacekeeping operations. First, participation enhances training and skills that promote the modernization of the PLA and PAP. Second, deployment provides the opportunity to field-test equipment and methods, gain firsthand experience in the field, and assess the capabilities of other nations deploying or supporting the mission. Third, as China's gross domestic product rises, [its] share of UN contributions increases, arguing for greater involvement in operations and greater reimbursement for deployments from UN coffers. (Thompson, 2005: 9)

Indeed, speaking at the closing ceremony of the four-day PLA Peacekeeping Work Conference in Beijing in June 2007, Major-General Zhang Qinsheng, deputy chief of the general staff of the PLA, revealed that "active participation in the UN peacekeeping operations is . . . an important measure to display China's image of being a peace-loving and responsible big country and likewise an important avenue to get adapted to the needs of the revolution in military affairs in the world and enhance the quality construction of the army" (*PLA Daily*, June 22, 2007). Thus it happily meets a key criterion of Chinese political engagement with Africa—namely that China be seen as a friend of the continent—which means that China's visibility in African peace operations is only likely to grow.

In sum, China's stance on peace operations is intimately bound up with its position on state sovereignty—both of which have, however, evolved over time (Sutter, 2008: 117–118). China's membership in the WTO, for example, arguably reflects a noteworthy change in its conception of sovereignty and its increasing acceptance of global norms (Breslin, 2005b). Likewise, "China's attitudinal change to peacekeeping can be seen as part of the process of state socialization. . . . [P]articipation is an important learning or socializing process [for any] member of an international community. As this learning process continues, we should see a less passive and more active China that needs to craft its own strategies for participation in international affairs in the future" (Pang Zhongying, 2005: 98). According to Allen Carlson, "this process . . . aptly labeled 'norms diffusion' . . . led to the emergence within China of more open, flexible interpretations of sovereignty's role in international politics" (2006: 218; see also Johnston, 2008).

However, there are limits to Bejing's flexibility:

> Although China can be flexible in normative principles like state sovereignty and nonintervention. . . . [it] is aware that its flexibility regarding these norms may be a 'double-edged sword.' On the one hand, when properly used, flexibility can provide Beijing with more diplomatic options for dealing with international affairs, prevent unnecessary conflicts with other powers, and yield a favorable environment for its development strategy. On the other hand, when overexploited, it not only jeopardize[s] China's strategic interests regarding state sovereignty (especially the Taiwan Question) but also damages its image as a peace-loving power, especially in the eyes of the developing world. (He Yin, 2007: 57; see also Wang Hongying, 2000)

Paradoxically, the more Beijing becomes enmeshed in global activities, the more it perceives pressures that need to be managed (Shirk, 2007; Lampton, 2008). In fact, it could be argued that Chinese policy toward UN peace operations is largely decided by Beijing's evolving assessment of the global-security situation in relation to its national interests as much as by new thinking on sovereignty: "China's enhanced national strength and its improved status within the international environment provide [the] . . . resources and political currency that enable it to adopt an active policy on [UN peace operations]. The aims of such a policy are to sustain its core national interests—including the maintenance of its role as a responsible power, strengthening the UN regime, and sharing common concerns regarding peace and security" (He Yin, 2007: 14). International, institutional cooperation is thus now an important aspect of Chinese foreign policy (Lanteigne, 2005; Johnston, 2008).

Relatedly, we could argue that Beijing's increasing acceptance of international responsibility as defined by transnational actors like the UN and as reflected in Beijing's emerging status as a contributor to peace operations indicates broader changes in China's political economy. As the Chinese economy becomes more and more integrated into and influenced by the global capitalist system, the CPC is able to identify new, if indirect, sources of political legitimacy. This trend has spurred a "domestic hunger in China for global linkages [that has] brought down institutional impediments to transnational relations and weakened the state's control over its citizens, resources, and sovereignty" (Zweig, 2002: 268).

A peaceful international environment is attractive in this regard. Hu Jintao's concept of *hexie shijie* (*China Daily,* September 16, 2005) is grounded in the recognition that an interdependent, "harmonious world" is a precondition for China's peaceful development (see Yee Sienho, 2008). This new understanding of the international milieu, which relies on flexible definitions of state liability and legitimacy, reflects not only the transformation in Beijing's international relations (Zhao Quansheng, 1996) but also that of the Chinese state itself: "Such thinking serves as a guideline for China's active participation in international efforts and contribution to international peace and security," including UNPKOs (He Yin, 2007: 54). While the Chinese remain leery of intervention, they now also accept it as part of the post–Cold War world order. In this sense, "China is no longer so much of an outlier when compared with other states in the international system" (Carlson, 2006: 234).

However, this "cautious acceptance and incremental evolution" in Beijing's attitude toward UNPKOs (Carlson, 2006: 224) is a function of Chinese policymakers' attempts to control the terms of intervention, however imprecise they may be. If we state once and for all that Beijing's conditions for peace operations are that military force should be deployed only with the host government's consent, UNSC authorization, and the guarantee that Chinese core interests will not be jeopardized, we may then observe that Africa serves as "a 'bellwether' for Chinese attitudes on intervention" (*Washington Post,* November 24, 2006). This fact makes the study of Chinese contributions to peace operations on the continent particularly important. Beijing is resistant to processes whose definitions of sovereignty are out of its control—particularly if they are being shaped by Western powers.[20] As Foot (2001: 14) has pointed out, "The nature of the international regime in question, especially its level of intrusiveness and the extent to which it might erode strategic independence, threaten political control, or actually enhance China's power, has influenced Beijing's compliance and involvement for reasons that have become familiar in studies of Chinese foreign policy behavior." In short, Beijing is flexible on sovereignty so long as it is in a position to help define the terms of the debate but not so long as they are decided by Washington or by a General Assembly vote that it cannot veto. This stance has been clear with respect to the Darfur issue (Holslag, 2008). In other words, the PRC is strongly against the establishment of new norms on such issues. As for international humanitarian law,

"China complies as best it can when it is in its interest to do so but [otherwise] uses whatever techniques [are] at its disposal to resist intrusion into its domestic arena" (Lee, 2007: 452). On this score, "whether China is significantly different . . . from other countries is doubtful" (Peerenboom, 2005: n. 18).

The reality of Chinese self-interest has important implications not only for China's involvement in peace operations in Africa but also, sometimes unfortunately, for African peoples—Darfurians being the most recent and graphic example. Controlling the terms of the debate on sovereignty in ways that protect Chinese interests remains key to China's stance on intervention and, by extension, peacekeeping. Thus, while China has moved away from absolute repudiation of peace operations to a more responsible point of view that allows limited peace operations, it continues to insist on the express permission of the recipient state or host government. Given the instability of many African states, such insistence is highly problematic and in Sudan certainly delayed the sending of peacekeepers to Darfur long after they were needed.

But, as we have said, responsibility for Africa's domestic conflicts lie more with Africa than with China, a fact that may have an interesting impact on the development of Chinese policies toward sub-Saharan Africa in particular: "As China becomes involved in volatile regions in its peacekeeping, Beijing will be drawn into conflicts and postconflict situations and will be forced to think through a coherent policy regarding how such conflicts start and why. This will inevitably have implications for how Beijing regards the make-up of African states."[21] In sum, we might say that China's attitude toward peace operations has finally been normalized, such that "the contribution of personnel [to UNPKOs is] more of a routine action . . . than an exceptional policy move" (Carlson, 2006: 230). How Beijing navigates the African milieu as its involvement in peace operations in Africa deepens will be of great interest to observers of Sino-African relations.

▨   Notes

1. Interview with Shu Zhan, Chinese ambassador to Eritrea, Asmara, Eritrea, June 29, 2006.

2. Interview with He Wenping, CASS, Beijing, China, September 18, 2007.

3. Interview with Western diplomat, Asmara, Eritrea, June 29, 2006.

4. Interview with military attaché, Western embassy, Addis Ababa, Ethiopia, May 15, 2007.

5. Interview with Chinese diplomat, Abuja, Nigeria, September 5, 2007.

6. Interview with military attaché, Western embassy, Addis Ababa, Ethiopia, May 15, 2007.

7. Interview with Ethiopian academic, Addis Ababa, Ethiopia, November 22, 2005.

8. Interview with Pentagon official, Washington, DC, United States, April 5, 2007.

9. Interview with British diplomat, Addis Ababa, Ethiopia, May 15, 2007.

10. Interview with Pentagon official, Washington, DC, United States, April 5, 2007.

11. Interview with Chinese diplomat, Addis Ababa, Ethiopia, May 15, 2007.

12. Interview with Shu Zhan, Chinese ambassador, Asmara, Eritrea, June 29, 2006.

13. Interview with an official from the State Department, Washington, DC, United States, April 5, 2007.

14. Interview with military attaché, Western embassy, Addis Ababa, Ethiopia, May 15, 2007.

15. Interview with military attaché, Western embassy, Addis Ababa, Ethiopia, May 15, 2007.

16. Interview with Shu Zhan, Chinese ambassador to Eritrea, Asmara, Eritrea, June 29, 2006.

17. Interview with Shu Zhan, Chinese ambassador to Eritrea, Asmara, Eritrea, June 29, 2006.

18. Interview with military attaché, Western embassy, Addis Ababa, Ethiopia, May 15, 2007.

19. Interview with military attaché, Western embassy, Addis Ababa, Ethiopia, May 15, 2007.

20. Interview with Shu Zhan, Chinese ambassador to Eritrea, Asmara, Eritrea, June 29, 2006.

21. Interview with Naison Ngoma, African Union official, Addis Ababa, Ethiopia, May 15, 2007.

What Does It All Mean? | 7

In analyzing Sino-African relations and the policies that shape and are shaped by them, we must always keep in mind that there are many Chinas and equally, many Africas. Thus the allegation, leveled by Western and African commentators alike, that China is colonizing Africa is inherently misleading, based on the assumption that Chinese foreign policy in Africa follows an overarching grand strategy dictated by Beijing (Swaine and Tellis, 2000). Rather, it is at best acceptable to state that Beijing's policymakers have certain aspirations for specific facets of Sino-African ties. The most obvious example concerns China's state-owned oil corporations and their investments in African resource industries, which are clearly connected to the energy needs and domestic dynamics associated with China's rise. But even here, rivalries among energy companies point to the fact that the interests of one Chinese actor may not always coincide with those of another, be it state or private (Downs, 2008). Given the secrecy surrounding energy deals signed by Chinese corporations in Africa (which are by no means unique in this regard), untangling underlying impulses and motives can be extremely problematic.[1]

Beyond the energy sector, rivalries among Chinese provinces, cities, municipalities, and/or individuals play themselves out on a daily basis in Africa and lay bare the myth of a monolithic China relentlessly pushing forward on some sort of "trade safari" as per Jean-Christophe Servant (2005). Nuanced analyses of Sino-African relations transcend talk of a "Chinese strategy" for Africa, which encodes fears of conflict with Western interests; equally, they recognize that Sino-African relations are processes not of colonization but of globalization, involving the reintegration of China into the global economy— a project that has hitherto enjoyed the enthusiastic support of the capitalist West. It is ironic that, as the Chinese ambassador to Eritrea has put it, "the West taught [the Chinese] the market economy and now we are criticized for expanding into Africa using market principles."[2]

161

Where there is coherence in Sino-African relations (a contingency to which we soon will return), it is arguably based on several key aims of Chinese foreign policy. One is that Chinese corporations "go global" and help ensure regime security in the process, namely by gaining access to crucial resources.[3] A statement issued by the Chinese Ministry of Commerce explicitly posits Africa as "one of the most important regions for carrying out our 'go outward' strategy" (quoted in Gu Xuewu, 2005: 8). The resulting hike in commodity prices has in itself been good for many of Africa's economies, although it is obviously uneven and dependent upon resource attributes. The coincidence of higher prices and higher production levels propelled an increase in sub-Saharan Africa's real GDP by an average of 4.4 percent between 2001 and 2004, compared with a 2.6 percent in the previous three years. In 2007, Africa's economy grew by 5.8 percent, much of this linked to burgeoning Chinese demand. But the benefits are skewed toward select industries. South Africa provides iron ore and platinum, while the DRC and Zambia supply copper and cobalt. Timber is sourced from Gabon, Cameroon, Congo-Brazzaville, and Liberia, while various western and central African nations supply raw cotton to Chinese textile factories. It is, however, oil that remains China's biggest commercial interest in Africa, as Chapter 2 has shown.

Oil

China's growing dependence on foreign imported oil has become a major concern for Beijing, and it is within the context of oil security that we might identify a strategic element to Sino-African relations. The pressure on state-owned oil corporations to engage in international trade is predicated upon a single-minded interest in the accessibility and dependability of foreign oil supplies. It is apparent to scholars such as James Tang that some policy analysts in Beijing connect the global political milieu to domestic energy security and feel that China is vulnerable until and unless it can diversify its oil sources and secure greater access to the world's oil supplies. Africa is an intrinsic—and possibly central—target of this stratagem. Consider, for example, that the 1.8 million barrels per day the United States imported from Africa in 2005 made up only 18 percent of its total annual consumption, whereas China's African oil imports, although only 800,000 barrels a day, made up 31 percent of its total. In short, Africa is of much greater strategic importance to China than it is to the United States.

Thus Chinese policies regarding oil deals in Africa are driven by worries that there may one day be too little oil to meet worldwide demand and that the energy needs of foreign powers—in particular the United States—will eclipse those of China (*Washington Post,* July 13, 2005). Any reasonable state administration in Beijing's position would encourage its actors to do what Chinese state-owned oil corporations are doing, namely defending the national interest. We should, however, point out that Beijing also considers increased efficiency, greater exploitation of domestic supplies via prospecting and exploration, and the development of a strategic reserve to be vital parts of its energy policy.[4] Consequently, China cannot simply be accused of making a global "oil grab."[5]

Indeed, much Western concern about China's alleged "oil safari" across turf long held to be in the Western sphere of influence (for instance, West Africa) seems motivated by commercial rivalries (Carmody and Owusu, 2005) and is often tinged with nationalist sentiment (Taylor, 2007c; Zweig, 2007). Of course, as a Chinese diplomat wryly pointed out, Western corporations investing in China in the 1980s never consulted with China's Asian neighbors or asked them for permission.[6]

In fact, Chinese companies may simply, if vigorously, be seizing opportunities long overlooked by more established actors.[7] Granted, SOEs have an advantage over their private, commercial competitors, which they can, unbeholden to shareholders, outbid for major contracts by paying over the odds as has been alleged.[8] In addition, because they are state-owned, China's national oil companies can work with the government in a neomercantilist fashion, making sweetener deals involving generous loans and/or infrastructure-development projects in return for oil. Lubricating commercial deals with extras was, of course, precisely what Western powers were doing in Africa long before China arrived on the scene, and prior to the ascendancy of neoliberalism. Is it the case that, having enthusiastically adopted and promoted neoliberalism, Western policymakers are now uneasy over the potential disadvantage it creates for Western corporations competing overseas with companies from nations such as China, where the state is still involved in the economy?[9]

Overall, however, Western corporations long established in Africa have so many economic advantages that it is hardly surprising that Chinese competitors use whatever tools they do have at their disposal to secure their goals. That is the nature of capitalism, surely. And, from a Chinese point of view, the hypocrisy of Washington's opposition to the 2005 attempt of a Chinese oil company to buy Unocal on the grounds of defending American national interests exposes the motives beneath Western rhetoric regarding free markets and open and fair competition for the world's oil resources.[10] In fact, the 2005 controversy undoubtedly hastened the entry of Chinese oil companies into Africa's oil markets and further stimulated their pursuit of state-backed oil deals as a means to guarantee supplies. In Chinese minds, there is doubt as to whether the United States is willing to play fair when it comes to energy competition, especially after both the conflict in Iraq and the Unocal-CNOOC debacle.[11] Besides, China has had much less time than has the West to get used to the often brutal world of energy politics, essentially playing catch-up since 1993. Thus, in blocking the Unocal deal, Washington may have been partly if inadvertently responsible for China's increased presence in the continent's oil industries. Certainly, Beijing's backing lowers the political risks of investment for Chinese energy corporations—which, compounded by the availability of cheap loans from state-owned banks, means that Chinese companies enjoy a lower cost of capital than Western competitors.[12] However, because of the obscurity of many Sino-African oil deals, it remains largely unclear whether alleged overbidding on certain oil deals by Chinese NOCs reflects a conscious strategy or, on the contrary, a naïveté respecting the international oil trade.[13] Either way, it could be argued that Africa wins; if Chinese companies want to pay African governments over the odds for their oil, that is China's problem.[14] At one level that might even be true. But at another it might not; by committing themselves to oil contracts that preclude open bids—even when the asking price is artificially high—African leaders may be selling their countries short.[15]

Criticism of Chinese oil companies for engaging in such practices is often linked to the potential for corruption, which can be addressed in two ways. First, it is reasonable to charge Western oil corporations that complain about the Chinese making shady oil deals in the Gulf of Guinea with hypocrisy, since allegations that Western companies, with the tacit approval of their home governments, have used graft to secure deals are nothing new (Shaxson, 2007; Soares De Oliveira, 2007); in some cases, they are even confirmed.[16] For instance, the Elf scandal in France revealed that "annual cash transfers totaling about £10 million [US$5 million] were made to Omar Bongo, Gabon's president, while other huge sums were paid to leaders in Angola, Cameroon, and Congo-Brazzaville. The multimillion dollar payments were partly aimed at guaranteeing that it was Elf and not US or British firms that pumped the oil but also [at] ensur[ing] the African leaders' continued allegiance to France" (*Guardian*, November 13, 2003). Damning indictments against British agents of Shell for their activities in Nigeria are well documented (Okonta and Douglas, 2003), and US Secretary of State Condoleezza Rice publicly called Equatorial Guinea's notorious president, Teodoro Obiang Nguema, a "good friend" of the United States (*Washington Post*, April 18, 2006), even though many characterize his government as "criminal" (Wood, 2004). So condemning China's oil diplomacy while glossing over the duplicity of Western governments and corporations toward Africa's energy industries is somewhat unpalatable, smacking of a new, simplistic "two-whateverism" *(liangge fanshi)*: whatever China does is wrong and whatever the West does is right.

However, if we agree that China shouldn't follow in the West's hypocritical footsteps, we come to the second point concerning the potential for corruption in Sino-African oil trade. One of Beijing's key talking points is that China's ties with Africa are based on mutual benefit and that China will not exploit Africa as the colonial powers did. Replicating the objectionable activities and patterns of Western oil companies in Africa would neither reflect well on China nor square with the official rhetoric.[17] It is true that national interests shape policy considerations in Beijing as elsewhere; Condoleezza Rice herself has admitted that "nothing has really taken me aback more as secretary of state than the way that the politics of energy [are]—I will use the word 'warping'— diplomacy around the world" (*New York Times,* April 5, 2006). But if China wishes to be seen as a benevolent actor in Africa, its noninterference policy needs a rethink so as not to give succor to oppressive and corrupt regimes such as those in Angola and Sudan.[18] After all, the explicitly hands-off approach effectively privileges the principles (or lack thereof) of a host country's elites, who determine where the receipts from increased oil revenues go. Given that Chinese leaders predicate much of their domestic legitimacy on economic growth and development for the Chinese people, it is a bit galling that they do not extend the same courtesy to the people of Africa's resource-rich nations.[19] As soon as Chinese enterprises invest in Africa, they become stakeholders on the continent, like it or not (Downs, 2008); by the same token, Beijing is learning that as soon as it gets diplomatically involved in a country, it must take a stand on the nature of government there.[20] But this necessity is an opportunity rather than a danger, opening up space for policymakers to cement China's reputation as a responsible power in accordance with their diplomatic rhetoric:

> Because respect for [the] United States' foreign policy is declining worldwide, China has a golden opportunity to chart out its own roadmap of global responsibility. While several governments across Asia, Africa, the Middle East, and Latin America are comfortable with China's policy of noninterference in another country's affairs, citizens in these same countries do not necessarily welcome the emergence of another big power pursuing energy security in their homeland at any cost. (Jakobson and Zha Daojiong, 2006: 68)

However, to return to a theme that has been constant in this book, the behavior of Africa's elites—whether they will use oil receipts for development or squander them—is ultimately up to them.[21] It is the host that establishes the rules on foreign investment and it is the host country's responsibility to take advantage of China's increased interest in Africa's oil resources. In short, and we shall return to this point later, only Africans can develop their continent and its natural resources, not China or any other state, for that matter.[22] Admittedly, there are aspects of Sino-African energy policy that do not facilitate the types of development that would be welcomed by most, but they are not uniquely Chinese, and it is far too easy to make China a scapegoat for the very real structural problems facing Africa's oil industry, which the continent's leaders have generally neglected to address.[23]

However, it is important that China at least do no harm when engaging with Africa's oil-rich nations; otherwise, the clear oceans of difference that Beijing likes to portray between itself and the "traditional exploiters" of Africa becomes muddied. Granted, liberalization—encouraged by the West—has stimulated conditions whereby "the government and the NOCs sometimes hold different perceptions of market risks. As a matter of fact, the NOCs have the propensity to let the government take the dangerous consequences engendered by their foreign-oil and -gas quest" (Chen Shaofeng, 2008: 96). In other words, government control over the actions of Chinese national oil companies in places such as Africa may not be as easy as many commentators seem to think.

■   Trade with Africa

Although not explicitly raising concerns about human rights, the Chinese export trade is another aspect of Sino-African relations that has generated a fair bit of hyperbole, with critics often castigating "China" for its alleged encroachment on Africa's manufacturing industry—particularly the textile and clothing sector. Yet much of this criticism is unfair and incorrect in its portrayal of Chinese exports as the collective work of a unitary actor able to fully control processes and able to turn on or off the flow of Sino-African trade. Rather, Chinese clothing and textile exports come from factories that are either collectively owned or wholly foreign owned and—as is quite obvious to most observers of China's political economy—the capacity of the Chinese state to control the activities of entrepreneurs in the provinces and overseas is weakening. Though Maria Edin (2003) argues that the weakening process has been exaggerated, it is beyond doubt that Beijing's ability and/or willingness to expend energies on controlling the export of cheap clothes is conditional at best.

Indeed, we must remember two key points when evaluating Chinese business activities in Africa: first, Chinese actors do not do anything in Africa they do not do at home; second, Sino-African relations are not part of a centrally directed and controlled plan. In fact, according to one informant, the Ministry of Commerce is often unaware of the presence, never mind the behavior, of various Chinese actors in Africa.[24] To the extent that these actors face and even perpetuate rivalries, misunderstandings, and a general chaotic feeling to much Chinese activity in Africa can be explained by such a scenario. This milieu in Africa is often a reflection of China's own problems and do not necessarily suggest a lack of respect for Africa, Africans, or African conditions.

A good example comes from Zambia, where forty-nine Zambian workers died in 2005 following an explosion in a Chinese-owned explosives factory in Chambishi. In July 2006, six Zambian workers were shot dead while protesting against low wages and poor conditions in a Chinese-run mine. The outrage was such that on a visit to Zambia in early 2007, Hu Jintao was forced to cancel a trip to Copperbelt Province to lay the foundation stone for a Chinese-built national stadium for fear of anti-Chinese protests. At the time, Emily Sikazwe of the Zambian NGO Women for Change—a local gender and human-rights advocacy organization—asserted that "we expect China to make [its] investment in our country more meaningful by observing human rights, especially the right to livelihood and dignity" (*UN Integrated Regional Information Net-*

works, February 5, 2007). Guy Scott, secretary-general of Zambia's Patriotic Front, likewise stated that "people are very angry with China's investment in Zambia: they are paid poor salaries, they work under risky conditions—in some cases without protective clothes—and this is why no one seems to be supporting [the Chinese]" (*UN Integrated Regional Information Networks,* February 5, 2007).

But what Sikazwe and Scott may not have realized is that Chinese workers in China also work under often dangerous conditions for little pay.[25] China's reform process and the attendant turn to capitalism (widely applauded by the West) have arguably set the stage for such conditions in China itself; it can thus be no surprise that sharp practices, such as cutting corners even when it comes to employee safety and welfare, abound among some Chinese-owned business enterprises in Africa. This is not to let Chinese employers off the hook for such behavior but merely to put their activities in their proper context—and also to avoid the ontological separation between the domestic and the international, a common error in much international relations theory.

Unfortunately, as we have seen, even if Beijing's policymakers earnestly seek to regulate Chinese business practices in Africa, their ability to do so is extremely limited. Indeed, the more China liberalizes, the less easy it is to control private businesses domestically, let alone in far-off Africa.[26] This is a major conundrum for the Chinese government, striving as it does to safeguard Beijing's image as a responsible power—but it is not unique to Sino-African relations.[27] Chinese actors engaging in illegal behavior[28] are no more representative of Beijing's African policies than bad practices by a British or US company reflect London's or Washington's diplomatic objectives in Africa—or elsewhere, for that matter.

Compounding the problem for Beijing's rulers, however, is the fact that—as one Chinese political scientist put it—the world community still erroneously sees China as a centrally controlled, monolithic actor.[29] This perception is arguably informed not only by long-standing tradition, predating 1949, but by "Westerners frustrated by their inability to impose their will on China" (Waley-Cohen, 1999: 283):

> The Chinese state is often viewed as a machine whose parts all mesh smoothly. In fact, the system of central control and coordination is largely a sham. Closer to the mark is Kenneth Lieberthal's use of the term "fragmented authoritarianism" to characterize the regime. The problems of fraud and workplace fatalities—which persist despite what must in all fairness be acknowledged as serious central-government campaigns against them—expose . . . the Chinese state's inability [not only] to regulate society but also . . . to get its own agents to do their jobs. Some officials are simply corrupt and wink at dishonest or dangerous enterprises in return for bribes. Other officials, particularly at the local level, see millions of people looking for work and want to help generate jobs even if it means tolerating unsafe or unsavory businesses. Besides, cash-strapped local governments rely on such activities

for tax income, while central decrees often appear as nothing but unfunded mandates. (Wang Shaoguang, 2003: 39)

This problem is only growing as China reengages with the global economy under the conditions of de facto liberal capitalism and domestic trends spread overseas. For instance, if Shell engages in unsavory activities in Nigeria's Delta region, no one blames Gordon Brown or the British; no one makes a direct link between Shell and 10 Downing Street. Yet if a Chinese corporation acts in an unscrupulous fashion in Africa, "the Chinese" are instantly castigated, and Hu Jintao is almost personally implicated. State-ownership, as we have seen, is often nominal. Even the largest Chinese companies, which remain under direct government control, may be spurred on by the competition to behave autonomously.

In fact, just as Beijing has long had difficulty controlling what companies, domestic or foreign, do in China, its own call to "go global" *(zouchuqu)* has undermined its formerly strong control over Chinese companies acting overseas. Control over external investment has already been relaxed, and ongoing reforms will only make it easier for companies to act alone. Although Beijing has made both concerted efforts to educate Chinese traders operating in Africa about local labor laws and safety standards and patriotic appeals to protect the image of China abroad,[30] there is the distinct possibility it has failed on both counts: "The conception of a rich and powerful China that can . . . have a significant impact on policymakers across the world sits rather uneasily with analyses of serious domestic problems" (Breslin, 2007: 27) unleashed in part by the post-1978 Socialist Modernization project. Developments associated with marketization, combined with deepening corruption at many levels of the Chinese polity, compound any coherent attempts at control from Beijing. In short, the more Beijing loosens its grip, the harder it will be to restore it, a fact that impacts all levels of society as well as actors overseas (Clissold, 2004). Thus unpacking the loaded term "China" becomes increasingly urgent.

Complicating this scenario is the fact that many of the Chinese-made products sold in African markets are brought to the continent not by Chinese but by African traders.[31] There are now quite elaborate trading networks linking China and Africa, many centered in the southern province of Guandong, where a relatively large population of African entrepreneurs live and make deals.[32] Indeed, in the city of Guangzhou, an estimated 20,000 Nigerians alone live and work (*This Day,* September 13, 2007). A 2006 *China Daily* article on African traders conducting deals in the Tianxiu Building (the center of the African enclave in Guangzhou) profiled a Togolese entrepreneur who shipped about eight forty-foot containers of shoes to Togo a year and an Egyptian who, every two months, shipped twenty containers of goods from all over China. His routine was to visit a factory near Shanghai that had long been his supplier and then stay a couple of weeks in Guangzhou to make sure his shipments were sent to his warehouses in Egypt and Dubai (*China Daily,* May 23, 2006). Indeed, most Chinese-made products come via Dubai to both Eritrea and Guinea-Bissau.[33] Actually, African traders have long been established in Hong Kong, primarily at Chungking Mansions in Tsim Sha Tsui, where products from China are sold in large quantities to traders from across Africa, who ship their products via Chinese-owned cargo companies directly to Angola, Ghana, Ethiopia, Nigeria, Togo, Uganda, and Tanzania where Africans make up the vast majority of customers.[34] However, many of these traders are making the move to Guangzhou, as prices in mainland China are far cheaper than in Hong Kong.[35]

But the point is that Chinese traders are not simply flooding the African market with cheap Chinese goods; African actors are actively facilitating the inundation. We do not have estimates of the respective proportion of goods sold in Africa's markets by Chinese entrepreneurs to those sold by African traders, but information gleaned from various interviews and observations made in a variety of African marketplaces suggests that a large percentage was sourced and shipped by Africans. This is somewhat ironic given that many African trade unions and civil-society organizations lay the blame for the "Asian tsunami" of cheap products squarely on "the Chinese." Even those who argue that trade between Africa and China is becoming colonial in character must admit it is with the active cooperation of many Africans themselves, some of whose activities in Hong Kong and Guangzhou demonstrate how "processes of globalization generate both localized and internationalized networks . . . that need to be considered alongside the bilateral [ones] to gain a full understanding of how best to theorize contemporary Chinese international relations" (Breslin, 2007: 25).

Concerns aside, the accessibility of cheap Chinese-made products has not only radically enhanced the average African consumer's choices but given even poor Africans the opportunity to purchase clothing and other material goods that were formerly well beyond their means. Things that people in the West take for granted—primarily electronic goods but even the most basic domestic commodities—are now within reach of many Africans.[36] This is surely a good thing.

In addition, some historical context is needed for allegations that Africa's manufacturing base is collapsing due to Chinese imports. As detailed in Chapter 3, Africa's manufacturing sector began deteriorating long before cheap Chinese products arrived on the scene. Both Ghana's and Zambia's textile output has shrunk considerably over the years, for instance. Although the surge in Chinese-made products has obviously not helped matters, it remains the case that the decline of Africa's textile industries has been all but unavoidable; even their turn-of-the-millennium revitalization depended on the very generous provisions of the AGOA and the MFA, lasting only between 2001 and 2004. Moreover, a huge percentage of the supposedly African cloth being exported under such provisions was actually Chinese made. When the agreements expired,

Africa suffered as its apparel exports to the US market fell significantly. Low productivity levels, high transport and energy costs, and infrastructural inefficiency all combined to make African industry vulnerable to imports from abroad—and not only from China.

That said, there are two facets of Chinese business in Africa that are blameworthy. One is the apparently widespread intellectual theft of African clothing designs by Chinese manufacturers. But this problem is as much domestic as it is bilateral, as any visitor to Beijing's Silk Market will tell you. Moreover, Chinese diplomats appear embarrassed by, if largely powerless to address, the phenomenon.[37] The other concern, although not related to textiles, involves what one informant in Nigeria pinpointed as the safety and quality of Chinese products. During the 2007 scandals over the discovery of lead in children's toys and poison in dog food, African countries were deemed "sitting ducks" for unscrupulous importers of inferior or even dangerous products due to poor if existent customs controls.[38]

Given China's sensitivity to its image abroad, the PRC would be well advised to tackle the problem of counterfeit goods, as it is detrimental to China's reputation in Africa. Of course, if the counterfeit goods are being manufactured illicitly in China and brought in by African traders (a distinct possibility), Beijing's ability to do anything is limited.[39] As has been pointed out, economic liberalization, encouraged by the West, is making it ever harder for Chinese authorities to supervise what Chinese companies and traders are doing at home and abroad.[40] The activities of the main state-owned oil corporations are one thing, but the explosion of small-scale, often private, Chinese operations in Africa is another matter entirely. We must reemphasize that regarding the activities of private Chinese shopkeepers, or even those of ventures backed by municipalities or provinces, as strategic or even stereotypical is deeply inaccurate. How much more so when non-Chinese traders are flooding Africa's markets with cheap and poorly made products? Regardless of the liberalization that is reconfiguring China's political economy and the increasing diversity of Chinese actors and interests abroad, the conflation of "China" into a single entity with a single set of goals is untenable.

Still, it is important to note that where troublesome behavior by Chinese actors in Africa does occur, it is very often a function of poor regulatory oversight; the perpetrators can simply get away with it.[41] A tighter legal framework that would ensure enforcement of serious customs and excise policies and hence block cheap copies at the port of entry—particularly for clear examples of intellectual theft—is surely not beyond the remit of a state. African leaders have the indisputable prerogative to put in place rules to which imports from abroad may be subjected. Whether they have the political will is, of course, another matter, and the danger that "China" will continue to be blamed for their failings is very real.

Human Rights

One aspect of Sino-African relations for which the Chinese state is fairly held responsible concerns its historically troubling stance on human rights. Granted, its relations with some of the more notorious regimes in Africa are atypical; if we focus solely on the cases of Sudan or Zimbabwe, we might miss the bigger picture. Then again, the negative attention such cases have generated due to the very real dangers they pose itself warrants examination. So do the notions that it is not China's business or duty to promote good governance and/or broad human rights and that China's noninterference principle is valid in all cases, in contrast to the norms of international accountability.[42]

As noted in Chapter 4, the concept of human rights is essentially a contested concept, so the Chinese state and its critics invariably speak past one another when engaging it. Rather, observers of Sino-African relations and/or China's human-rights must be very careful to take the Chinese position into account, as it is in fact long-standing and reflects serious concerns. It is also important to note that rallying cries over human rights have long preceded power plays between countries that adhere to different political or economic models.[43] After all, the vote in May 2001 to remove the United States from the UN Human Rights Commission was a clear reflection of widespread resentment of Washington's unilateralism and perceived abuse of power with respect to human rights. There is no doubt that Beijing actively exploits this resentment to consolidate a support constituency, much of which is African. Thus the persistent call by Western leaders to universalize "international human rights"—which implicitly boil down to Western capitalist values—can be countered by Beijing and its African allies as reflecting neocolonial impulses. Conversely, however, China's leaders may be seeking to rationalize their policies on human rights in ways that universalize China's post-Mao developmental trajectories (Sullivan, 1999: 24). This goal arguably underpins the so-called Beijing Consensus, which is also a product of antihegemonism, the Five Principles, and statist-developmental thinking.

But as Robert Weatherley (1999) notes—and as we saw in Chapter 4—some of the most egregious violations of human rights in Africa in which China is held complicit cannot be justified even in terms of the Chinese discourse on human rights, particularly insofar as it depends on social development and welfare. This could be a perfectly respectable position to take, but its theoretical coherence is undermined by its practice, if Beijing supports some regimes that are antidevelopment—such as those in Sudan and Zimbabwe, which not only crush the civil and political rights of their citizens but also threaten the economic and social rights of the population. (Myanmar provides yet another example of China's failed attempt to maintain the sharp separation between trade and human rights.)

Given that economic and social rights are central to Beijing's discourse on human rights, such support is surely problematic. As Chapter 4 argued, Beijing attempts to skirt the contradiction by deploying the mantra of state sovereignty, namely that sovereignty is the ultimate guarantor of human rights and therefore that each sovereign state may abide by its own understanding of the rights of its people. This is all very well; state sovereignty is the cornerstone of the international system, without which anarchy might reign. Yet the reification of the state, compounded by the amalgamation of sovereignty and rights into a single principle of noninterference, loses much of its meaning in a continent dominated by quasi states, neopatrimonial regimes, and even warlords.

Yet, to paraphrase Li Xing (1996: 40), the difficulty facing Beijing is that on the one hand it has sought independence from Western political influence and on the other hand it has sought to catch up with the West and modernize its economy through ever-closer integration with the capitalist world market. Analyses that are spellbound by Beijing's phenomenal growth rates ignore these realities and their implications for development in China (Breslin, 2008). This contradiction often plays out around human-rights issues; in fact, it might be argued that some human-rights violations—poor domestic labor conditions, for instance—are *preconditions* for Beijing's reintegration into the global political economy, a move that is actively encouraged by the West and its profit-seeking corporations: "Human rights abuses under the banner of 'preserving order' are aimed at maintaining the position of the ruling elements [in China]. . . . [but also at] maintain[ing] long-term stability and predictability of the system in order to attract much-needed foreign investment and technology" (Li Xing, 1996: 34). In this light, it appears hypocritical to critique China for its stance on human rights in Africa while selectively overlooking the abuses that underpin much of the consumer boom in the developed world—where there is a market for cheap Chinese imports (Harney and Alexandra, 2008). Ignoring the West's own continued support for assorted dictators and corrupt regimes across Africa is equally disagreeable.

However, such analysis does not help the average African laboring under autocratic rule and casting a weary eye at Chinese support for his or her oppressor. We can pontificate about hypocrisy and selectivity, but Zimbabwe is still (at the time of writing) collapsing and women are still being raped in Darfur. Here, Beijing needs to modify its hands-off approach to human rights if it is to avoid being cast by critics as a friend of despots. Beijing must recognize that by dealing with some regimes in Africa it risks tarnishing its whole African enterprise. Fortunately, there is some evidence that Chinese thinking on human rights and sovereignty is not fixed but fluctuating: "Beijing's recent handling of the situation in Sudan shows that it is learning the limitations of noninterference, however much that principle remains part of its official rhetoric. The concept may have been useful when China was relatively weak and trying to protect itself from foreign interference. But China has found noninterference increasingly unhelpful as it learns the perils of tacitly entrusting its business interests to repressive governments" (Kleine-Ahlbrandt and Small, 2008: 47; see also Gill and Reilly, 2000: 42).

It is true that as long as there is divergence between liberal-democratic and Chinese policies regarding good governance, there is arguable convergence between Beijing and certain African autocrats. But this must prove temporary if China wishes to have a long-running and stable relationship with Africa as a whole.[44] China, like all other actors in Africa, needs stability and security in order for its investments to flourish and its connections to remain cohesive. Western nations have had to learn the hard way that propping up dictators willy-nilly is neither sustainable nor desirable, and China will learn likewise as its relations unfold. To quote Ndubisi Obiorah (2007: 40), "After an initial phase of snapping up resource-extraction concessions, it is almost conceivable that China will be compelled by instability and conflict . . . to realize that its long-term economic interests are best served by promoting peace in Africa and that this is most likely to come about by encouraging representative government . . . rather than supporting dictators." This has started to happen: "With its increased investments in pariah countries over the past decade, China has had to devise a more sophisticated approach to protecting its assets and its citizens abroad. It no longer sees providing uncritical and unconditional support to unpopular, and in some cases fragile, regimes as the most effective strategy" (Kleine-Ahlbrandt and Small, 2008: 38–39).

Thus, while in the late 2000s there is still some divergence, there can ultimately only be growing convergence between Chinese and Western policy aims—maybe not with regard to democracy (though even in this respect China is evolving in interesting directions; see Cheng Li, 2008), but certainly with regard to governance, security, and the problem of supporting regimes that undermine development and China's own notions of human rights.[45]

Furthermore, China's integration into the global economy and its acceptance of the responsibilities thereof, necessitate systemic reforms, particularly through increasing membership in multilateral bodies. In the long term, these could incorporate increased respect for the rule of international law and universal human rights. For instance, Beijing's membership in the WTO entails commitment to advancing the transparency and standardization of China's legal system. And since 1990 or so, Beijing has ratified a growing number of international instruments pertaining to human rights and labor as it signs on to various multilateral regimes (Lanteigne, 2005). Recognizing that different interpretations of human rights exist while working to ensure that the abuses perpetrated in Sudan and Zimbabwe are not repeated is in the interests of both Beijing and the West if they desire stability for and long-term roles in Africa's economies. On evidence, it appears that the Chinese leadership is beginning to realize this; the task for Western policymakers will be to encourage rather than perpetually criticize Beijing: "Western countries should accept that they are not any longer in a position to prevent the rise of China and other actors of global change. The objective should be to design a strategy toward China that does not only constrain competition but develop[s] common commitments [to confront] pressing global challenges" (Jing Gu, Humphrey, and Messner, 2007: 288).

■ Arms Sales

Another troubling aspect of Sino-African relations concerns China's arms sales to Africa. The issue is complex, as not all Chinese-made weaponry finds its way to Africa via Beijing. Granted, Beijing clearly regards the arms industry as too critical to China's national security to be privatized and keeps it under much tighter supervision than other reformed SOEs. But supervision of arms exports is another matter.[46] In fact, it is likely that a high percentage of weaponry makes its way to Africa via middlemen on the global arms market. China's small arms are among many being funneled illegally from all over the world into combat zones. This is why the UN is pushing—so far unsuccessfully—for an international registry.

When we consider as well the high levels of corruption in China and the ineffectiveness of state regulations on exports, despite best intentions, we see that the picture of a "China" supplying all and sundry with arms and ammunition willy-nilly is less credible than a more complicated one. In this picture, it seems apparent that the level of state control over exports—particularly of small arms—varies depending on the type of weapon being exported; the location of the arms exporter (there is generally less supervision over factories in the interior than those on the coast); and, as mentioned, the extent to which corruption facilitated the export process. Estimating the revenue generated by such sales is extremely difficult, particularly in the frequent event of creative accountancy: "Chinese arms-export companies tend to keep whatever profits they can and probably obfuscate account books to conceal money made" (Shambaugh, 2002b: 221). These practices spring from changes within China's political economy whereby "encouragement given to many organs to become increasingly self-supporting through bureaucratic entrepreneurship" has "strengthened the[ir] tendency . . . to work vigorously to promote and protect their own interests in the policymaking process" (Lieberthal, 1992: 9).

What is clear in this complex picture, then, is that Chinese arms sales reflect domestic trends, including the ongoing reform process, as much as or more than international issues (Mulvenon, 2007). For instance, profit, not politics, determines most sales of Chinese-made weaponry (with the exception of strategic weaponry sold as part of broader diplomatic packages). During the 1980s and the first half of the 1990s, Chinese arms sales abroad were an important source of funding for the PLA and the central government (Mulvenon, 2000). However, reforms aimed at taking the military out of business have diminished the importance of arms sales for the central government in Beijing (Cheung, 2001).

Referring specifically to China's defense industry, David Goodman has averred that in the reform era, the transition from a command economy to a market economy has presented considerable opportunities for corruption (1996: 38). As we saw in Chapter 5, export regulations do not include a catalog of the military items they cover. This omission has produced a degree of uncertainty regarding what sorts of weaponry are covered and what is not—and no doubt facilitates circumvention. So does the downsizing and restructuring of the Chinese government, processes that have been ongoing since 1998.

Yet overall, China's arms sales to Africa need global contextualization. As Chapter 5 detailed, China is a relatively small player in Africa's arms market. Although arms sales are an integral part of Beijing's trade links with a number of African states, the same can be said for most other external actors. In fact, Chinese arms exports are insignificant compared with those of the United States, Britain, France, or Russia.

Following the Soviet Union's collapse, China has been singled out by some US commentators (e.g., Timperlake and Triplett, 2002) as a threat bent on proliferating nonconventional nuclear and chemical weapons of mass destruction, as well as the materials and equipment necessary for their development. Based on the long-term strategic-global aspirations Chinese arms sales allegedly reveal, Beijing has also been criticized for compromising various international agreements (Shichor, 2000: 1). There are legitimate concerns about sales to regimes in places like Harare and Khartoum, but a close assessment of the quantity and quality of Chinese arms transfers to Africa shows that their military impact is largely inconsequential.[47] As David Shambaugh (2002: 224) puts it, "Chinese weapons are a last resort for most developing nations, and Beijing's failure to compete at all in the international arms market is further testimony to the pathetic state of [its] defense industries." Still, since its obscurantist policies have prevented clear, objective accounts of China's arms exports (as they did for SIPRI), China could work harder to make its export policies more transparent and thereby curtail suspicions and accusations (Bitzinger, 2003). And if, once again, Beijing does not want to be accused of replicating the mistakes of the West in Africa, a more hands-on approach to the sale and distribution of Chinese-made weaponry is needed. The Beijing Declaration, adopted at the 2006 FOCAC, calls for cooperation in halting the illegal production, circulation, and trafficking of small arms and light weapons to Africa. Time will tell as to whether it will be effective. However, as China wishes to be taken as a responsible power and to set itself apart from the West and its neocolonialist patterns of engagement with Africa, the impetus for achieving results is evident.

■ Peacekeeping

One way in which China is indeed showing itself to be a responsible great power *(fuzeren de daguo)* and playing a positive role on the continent involves its contribution to peace operations. As Chapter 6 has shown, Beijing was once highly skeptical of UN peace efforts and of the UN in general—from which the Chinese were excluded and over which they therefore had no influence for many years—primarily because it served to legitimize what was seen as aggressive military intervention during the Korean War. After all, given a history of invasion by the Great Powers—especially throughout the nineteenth century, when such interference ostensibly retarded its development and denied it its "rightful place" in the community of nations—China views intervention in any form with deep distrust. Consequently, even after Beijing took its seat on the UNSC, it remained guarded and refused to contribute to peacekeeping budgets for many years, even though as a permanent member it had a responsibility to do so.

But in recent years there has been a sea change in China's attitude toward peace operations, to which Beijing has emerged as a significant contributor. Measured against more traditional contributors such as Pakistan or Bangladesh, China's deployments remain thus far somewhat limited. But China puts many more blue helmets on the ground than do most of the other Security Council members. This is a major development in China's diplomacy and has positive implications for its relations with Africa, which is often beset with conflict.[48] That China is taking its responsibilities as a peacekeeper seriously puts the other great powers to shame, though their reluctance to get involved militarily is somewhat offset by their financial contributions to peace operations.

There are certain limitations to these developments however. China still resolutely opposes actions it perceives as interference in the domestic affairs of other states and will only agree to a peace operation if the host government concurs. It continues to suspect that interventions carried out in the name of humanitarianism are motivated by interests other than charity or international solidarity and that the United States in particular attempts to use the UN as a springboard for its own interests and policies. Thus China remains likely to closely investigate the grounds on which calls for intervention are made—which it is, of course, perfectly free to do.

That said, China also increasingly acknowledges the benefits of engaging in UN peace operations. As Chapter 6 notes, by taking part in such operations, Chinese troops gain training and experience without significant outlay from the annual military budget. This helps facilitate—albeit in a small way—the modernization of the PLA, as does the opportunity to test equipment and techniques in the field.[49] Furthermore, as China's role in global affairs increases, participation in UN peace operations allays its leaders' "fears about a backlash and the potential damage to [their] strategic and economic relationships with the United States and Europe" and supports their claims to be a responsible power (Kleine-Ahlbrandt and Small, 2008: 39).

Taking a more hands-on approach to conflict resolution and peacekeeping also helps lessen the concern Africans have expressed about Chinese actors on the continent, allowing China to cast itself as an "all-weather friend" that is deeply concerned about peace and the welfare of Africa, to the point that it is—unlike the United States—willing to put its troops on the frontline.[50] Consequently, Beijing is likely to increase its involvement in peace operations in Africa as its comfort with such missions vis-à-vis state sovereignty increases. As Bates Gill and James Reilly (2000: 41) note, "the nexus where defense of Chinese sovereignty meets the imperative of engaging the outside world defines both the limits and the possibilities [for] China['s negotiation of] the norms and institutions of international society." Beijing will increasingly have to contend with global expectations for its role in international affairs and its own need to shape the definition of sovereignty. Managing the debate and delimiting discussions of what sovereignty is and how it might be redefined is central to Beijing's position on intervention and peacekeeping.

Beijing has clearly shifted its foreign policy to one that is arguably more mature insofar as it permits limited peace operations: "Its policies have evolved from staking out a position of reluctant participation to one of expanded involvement in peacekeeping and humanitarian intervention" (Carlson, 2006: 218). What remains problematic is its insistence that the consent of the host state be obtained on each and every occasion. However, Beijing's policies are constantly evolving; China's emergence as a peacekeeper appears part of a pragmatic reorientation by policymakers, who are now more concerned with maintaining the image of a responsible great power than with protecting state sovereignty at all costs. Chinese blue helmets are here to stay on the continent.

■ Conclusion

Overall, the balance sheet on Sino-African ties is positive and the recent upsurge in Chinese activity holds a great deal of opportunity for the continent. Not least, it has spurred other external actors to take the continent's potential more seriously. Take France's new attitude toward Africa: "Thanks to the Chinese," an Élysée official commented, "we also rediscovered that Africa is not a continent of crises and misery but one of 800 million consumers" (*Business Day,* October 19, 2007).

Clearly, China is not the new imperialist in Africa. Although there are facets of Sino-African trade that fit the pattern usually described as neocolonial—for instance, the fact that Africa exports raw material and imports finished products—they are by no means unique. Rather, they characterize virtually all of Africa's bilateral trade relations and, according to many influential analysts (Rodney, 1973; Krieckhaus, 2006), have their roots in the colonial period—when China was wholly absent from Africa. Viewed in this light, the notion that China's economic engagement with Africa should be totally different from that of other external actors seems unrealistic.

Furthermore, Chinese economic policies, if at times arguably neomercantilist (Holslag, 2007b), are fundamentally capitalist. The post-Mao Chinese leadership is thus doing precisely what the West wants it to do and yet is, on occasion, castigated for doing so in areas formerly held to be in the West's sphere of influence. Here, the growing concern about global energy supplies is particularly apposite for explaining negative reactions to China's rise in Africa and elsewhere in the developing world, suggesting its emergence as a superpower: "China may not be a direct threat to the existing powers in the global political economy, but its growing importance for Latin America and Africa could provide an important indirect challenge" (Breslin, 2007: 19).

This challenge is most often flagged in debates over governance, whereby Chinese engagement with Africa is arguably less positive, relating as it does to Beijing's noninterference policies and de facto hands-off approach to issues of human rights. It is of course true that such policies are long-standing and shape relations beyond Africa. What is more, they have a certain cachet when the alternative is presented by overweening powers bent on promoting particular economic and political agendas as universal truths. However, a middle ground—one that respects international society and recognizes that borders cannot be used to shield miscreants from censure if and when they infringe upon basic rights to life, self-realization, and social development—is more appropriate. There is growing evidence that the Chinese leadership is approaching this middle ground, arguably spurred on by the damage to its reputation done by its relations with regimes such as those in Sudan and Zimbabwe. Certainly, Beijing is making a more proactive search for solutions to some of the problems facing these (and other) countries. This is quite a remarkable turnaround and reflects the reality that Chinese policies in Africa are in a complex process of evolution. It also reflects Beijing policymakers' realization that Chinese operations need security just as much as Western ones do and that if they wish to facilitate the extraction of Africa's resources in order to keep China's economy going, they must ensure a safe operating environment and the protection of investments. Oppressive regimes that stimulate uncertainty and instability appear, in this light, poor long-term partners.

If Sino-African relations could be reduced to their essence, three main points would stand out. First, China is not a unitary actor. This may seem elemental, but judging from a lot of the literature on Sino-African relations, it seems to have been overlooked. As the Chinese leadership has pursued its (admittedly uneven) post-Mao economic liberalization policies, they have encountered increasing difficulties in controlling—or even keeping abreast of—

the diverse activities in which various Chinese corporations and individual merchants are engaged overseas. Although major oil and other energy-based companies are probably under constant supervision (which rivalries may however complicate), the huge proliferation of small-scale traders operating in Africa, very often private individuals or families, is all but impossible to manage. Weak rule of law, endemic corruption, and bureaucratic tendencies at every level of government means that the central leadership is in a perpetual and losing struggle to keep up with a surging economy, whether domestic or when it is projected overseas. Furthermore, as has been repeatedly stressed, contention over foreign-policy aims and their implementation now defines debates within Beijing. For instance, "the Chinese Foreign Ministry is generally the most supportive of China's evolving . . . diplomacy [i.e., in dealing with pariah states] but it is rarely able to assert its position over the Ministry of Commerce or the military" (Kleine-Ahlbrandt and Small, 2008: 54). Thus demands that "China" should do *x, y,* or *z* in "Africa" miss the subtleties and realities of contemporary Chinese foreign policy. We should also always recognize that "because personalities differ, because politics [are] a highly contingent affair, and because ideologies are not uniform, policy is never neat and predictable. Shifts in outlook, contention over goals, and misapprehension of the situation quite predictably produce a messy and disjointed policy process. These features apply as much to the [CPC] as other policymaking bodies" (Hunt, 1996: 231).

Chinese trade with Africa has become, in many ways, normalized, which is to say diverse and involving multiple actors, rather than state directed and controlled. Tracing production networks—the processes by which things are made and/or finished and delivered to markets—is increasingly complicated (Breslin, 2004). This may be why so many analyses reduce relations between "China" and "Africa" to an almost bilateral level. To return to a point we have made, the concept of a China Inc., complete with master plan, either domestic or global, is intrinsically flawed. As Thomas Christensen (2001: 27) says of Chinese foreign policy in general, "many of the means to reach the regime's domestic and international security goals are so fraught with complexity, and sometimes contradiction, that a single, integrated grand plan is almost certainly lacking, even in the innermost circles of the Chinese leadership compound." How much more so as China continues to liberalize?

The second key point about Sino-African relations is that there has been a fair degree of scapegoating of China for its alleged negative impacts upon Africa. Upon close inspection, these allegations appear much less salient and accurate and are often balanced out in any case by positive impacts. For instance, Chinese construction companies are criticized for hiring only Chinese workers—even unskilled ones—so that infrastructure-development projects do not generate much local employment or promote skill acquisition. Yet a recent report on Chinese activities in the infrastructure sectors of Angola, Sierra

Leone, Tanzania, and Zambia found that, except in Angola, local people accounted for between 85 and 95 percent of the total workforce employed by Chinese construction companies (Centre for Chinese Studies, 2007). While many Chinese are employed as unskilled casual laborers, local Africans do attain management and administration positions. Given the low skills base in much of Africa though, it is unreasonable to expect a high proportion of the skilled jobs to be held by Africans in any case; Western corporations operating in Africa likewise tend to install expatriates at the management level, even after many years in country.

In observing the way Chinese workers work alongside African nationals, one may aver that the Chinese seem to have integrated well, at least in the construction industry.[51] Furthermore, the expansion of Chinese construction companies into Africa has lowered costs. For example, in Namibia, local Namibian and South African construction companies once monopolized the industry, inflating prices. But as Chinese construction companies entered Namibia, costs dramatically lowered, saving the average Namibian taxpayer a great deal of money.[52] Competition also forced local companies to improve productivity and service delivery.[53] Besides, Africa is in desperate need of infrastructure development that no other external actor appears prepared to deliver.

Another complaint about the Chinese is that their manufactured goods are flooding African countries, wiping out small and medium producers as well as local traders. However, as has been detailed, African consumers are benefiting—particularly those with limited incomes. And much of Africa's manufacturing industry collapsed long ago, well before Chinese imports appeared on the scene. Besides, it is not only African producers who have had to adjust to competition—between 1995 and 2002, more than 15 million factory jobs, representing 15 percent of the total manufacturing workforce, were lost in China (*Guardian,* March 2, 2004). Africa is not unique. It is possible that some Chinese exports may block avenues for Africa's diversification away from its traditional exports. Certainly, if Africa is to escape its dependent relationship on the global economy and move on from being simply an exporter of primary commodities, it needs to start manufacturing. But it needs to be argued that domestic problems figure more significantly in African manufacturers' plight. For one thing, Africans themselves import a huge amount of Chinese-made products; those that are shoddy or counterfeit should be regulated and controlled by African governments—some of which instead prefer simply to blame "China."

It is true that health and safety standards, as well as workers' rights and environmental issues, do not appear to be priorities for some Chinese companies. This is unfortunate and indefensible. But it reflects what is happening back home in China, where the leadership resolutely pursues the capitalist road to development (as any perusal of the *China Labour Bulletin* will reveal). And, again, it is up to African states to regulate the activities of foreign companies and ensure that extractive operations do not destroy the local environment or deny African workers their labor rights. Unfortunately, many of Africa's elites post-independence have shown scant regard for their citizens' constitutional rights in general; it is doubtful that they will suddenly spring into action where Chinese investment is concerned.[54] As a Kenyan newspaper put it, "the reasons why Africa continues to do badly . . . have to do mostly with internal conditions. . . . If things don't improve in Africa . . . China will leave us with huge holes in the ground, land polluted by oil spills, and wastelands where once lush forests stood. We shall be vilifying [China] the way we do the West today and waiting for a 'better deal'" (*East African,* August 21, 2007).

To reiterate, many of the criticisms of Sino-African ties point to Africa's domestic problems and then extrapolate to place the blame on "China." This is unreasonable. The Chinese leadership may, however, be culpable for a non-interference policy that has negative implications for the human rights of Africans. But, as mentioned, Chinese policy is evolving. Although the Chinese have considered their approach to Africa to be benign, they are beginning to feel exposed by the intricacies of Africa's politics.[55] Kidnappings in Nigeria, the murders of Chinese workers in Ethiopia, anti-Chinese riots in Zambia, a high-profile campaign against the Beijing Olympics over China's role in Darfur, and a threat by Darfurian rebels to target Chinese citizens—all these have provided a steep learning curve. As recently as 2005, Deputy Foreign Minister Zhou Wenzhong was quoted as saying of Sino-Sudan relations, "Business is business. We try to separate politics from business" (*New York Times,* August 22, 2005). Such a statement is now unthinkable.

Clearly, many of the complexities of diplomacy on the continent stem from the social and economic inequalities caused by malfunctioning political systems. But Beijing's complacency with respect to its African policies has not helped. Its attitude seemed to be that third-party criticism (or even African condemnation) amounted to China-bashing and could be safely disregarded. However, a flurry of extremely negative articles in the international media about Sino-African ties, as well as incidents on the ground in Africa, stimulated a rethink.[56] Furthermore, although Beijing bristles at being singled out for criticism, the fact that it is a rising and potentially great power means it can no longer hide behind the curtain of the developing world; it must accept that its policies will be placed much more directly under the microscope, especially by other great powers jockeying for influence.[57] The United States and the Soviet Union had to learn such lessons during the twentieth century and China will learn them, albeit reluctantly, in this one. In fact, now that Beijing acknowledges the need to promote the positive results of Chinese diplomacy in Africa, it will be interesting to see how Beijing accommodates Africa's idiosyncracies as its involvement with Africa broadens and deepens.[58]

This leads us to the third and final key point in our summary of Sino-African ties. It is up to African leaders to manage their relations with China to benefit their own economies and citizens: "It is not China's responsibility to 'look out' for African self-interest. This is the job of Africa's self-appointed and elected leaders. The idea that China's historical 'friendship' with Africa relieves Africans of the responsibility to forge a mutually beneficial relationship is dangerous" (*Christian Science Monitor,* February 1, 2007). Obviously, the internal structure of any given African state is all-important and varies widely across the continent. The fact that, for example, South Africa is a consolidated democracy by African standards accounts for the huge difference between the way Pretoria and, say, Sierra Leone deal with China. One walks away from interviews with government personnel in Mauritius and Nigeria with different degrees of confidence in their approaches to managing relations with Beijing.[59] Meanwhile, one leaves Ethiopia convinced that the government in Addis Ababa is competent to manage its relationship with Beijing and that its political leaders are more astute and savvy than many African elites who seem to think that anything non-Western is intrinsically good.[60] The same goes for the government in Cape Verde.

However, as a Kenyan report put it, "China has an Africa policy. Africa doesn't have a China policy" (*The Nation,* June 12, 2006). Informants within the African Union assert that there is in fact no official AU view on Sino-African ties, whether positive with regard to their benefits or negative with respect to their downsides.[61] This is partly because the PRC prefers bilateral dealings, which makes constructing a single "China policy" difficult. Furthermore, Beijing has warm relations with Morocco, a non-AU member, but not with the four African states that recognize Taiwan. Consequently, as a collective unit, Africa has little actual negotiating power over China.[62]

Fundamentally, Beijing's engagement with Africa is grounded in pragmatism, and so it is up to each African state to negotiate how and where it takes shape. China's abandonment of ideology for economic growth actually affords Africa greater room to maneuver—but Africa's elites must do so wisely, with an eye toward mutual benefit.[63] In some countries, they will. In others, however, predatory elites at the apex of neopatrimonial regimes, unconcerned with promoting development, will forfeit the chance to make the most of renewed Chinese interest in Africa. For instance, the DRC stood to benefit when cobalt "had suddenly become commercially attractive because the world price had been driven upwards by a surge in demand from China's fast-growing economy. The cobalt price had grown by 300 percent in less than a year" (Butcher, 2007: 64). Instead,

> The cobalt rock is simply bagged and driven out of the country. . . . That way ensures the smallest amount of benefit to the local economy—just the few dollars to each miner. If the local authorities were interested in helping the local economy, then they would have a processing plant here in Lubumbashi that converts the cobalt-rich rock into concentrated cobalt salts. It is not a complex process but it multiplies the value of the cobalt product by fifty

times, maybe a hundred times. . . . But the reality is this. The authorities in the Congo are not interested in how cobalt mining benefits the local economy. They are only interested in what they can take in bribes. And it is easier to count sacks of rock at the border and work out how many dollars you can cream off per bag. Until that fundamental attitude changes, then the cobalt boom driven by China will not benefit more than a few members of the Congo elite. (Butcher, 2007: 67–68)

Depending upon the elites in such states to do the right thing is risky. That is why African civil society must play a crucial role in the new engagement with China. It is up to Africans to organize, connect, and ensure that their leaders enter into relationships with Beijing with open eyes for the sake of mutual benefit. After all, "time and again, African governments [have] complain[ed] that they cannot deliver development due either to a lack of support or to interference from the West. The resources . . . now come with 'no strings attached.' Any failure to share growth and strengthen the whole economy will not be China's fault but that of the African recipient government" (Amosu, 2007). Ordinary Africans can play a crucial role in a true win-win situation by holding their leaders to account and critically examining the deals done with Beijing in their name. In short, Chinese involvement in Africa offers up a wealth of opportunities for the continent, but only if it approaches them prudently. How Sino-African relations will play out in the years to come, which Africans and which Chinese will benefit or lose, in which states and economic sectors, are questions for future studies on the multifarious nature of Chinese engagement with the continent.

▓ Notes

1. Interview with Chinese academic, School of International Studies, Peking University, Beijing, China, September 20, 2007.
2. Interview with Shu Zhan, Chinese ambassador, Asmara, Eritrea, June 29, 2006.
3. Interview with Chinese academic, School of International Studies, Peking University, Beijing, China, September 20, 2007.
4. Interview with Chinese academic, School of International Studies, Renmin University, Beijing, China, February 21, 2008.
5. Interview with African Union official, Addis Ababa, Ethiopia, May 16, 2007.
6. Interview with Shu Zhan, Chinese ambassador to Eritrea, Asmara, Eritrea, June 29, 2006.
7. Interview with government official, Gaborone, Botswana, September 25, 2004.
8. Interview with Western diplomat, Abuja, Nigeria, September 3, 2007.
9. Interview with Ethiopian academic, Addis Ababa, Ethiopia, November 22, 2005.
10. Interview with Chinese academic, School of International Studies, Peking University, Beijing, China, September 20, 2007.

11. Interview with British diplomat, Addis Ababa, Ethiopia, May 15, 2007.

12. Interview with oil company executive, London, United Kingdom, November 22, 2007.

13. Interview with Chinese academic, School of International Studies, Peking University, Beijing, China, September 20, 2007.

14. Interview with a representative from the House of Representatives, Abuja, Nigeria, September 3, 2007.

15. Interview with oil company executive, London, United Kingdom, November 22, 2007.

16. Interview with a journalist from the *Abuja Inquirer,* Abuja, Nigeria, September 3, 2007.

17. Interview with a journalist from the *Abuja Inquirer,* Abuja, Nigeria, September 3, 2007.

18. Interview with Western diplomat, Abuja, Nigeria, September 4, 2007.

19. Interview with a journalist from the *Abuja Inquirer,* Abuja, Nigeria, September 3, 2007.

20. Interview with He Wenping, CASS, Beijing, China, September 18, 2007.

21. Interview with African Union official, Addis Ababa, Ethiopia, May 15, 2007.

22. Interview with Henning Melber, Namibian political economist, Windhoek, Namibia, August 14, 2006.

23. Interview with DFID official, Beijing, China, September 20, 2007.

24. Interview with He Wenping, CASS, Beijing, China, September 18, 2007.

25. Interview with Chinese diplomat, Abuja, Nigeria, September 5, 2007.

26. Interview with Chinese trader, Praia, Cape Verde, November 5, 2007.

27. Interview with the acting head of the Political Affairs Section, Chinese Embassy, Windhoek, Namibia, August 13, 2006.

28. Interview with Shu Zhan, Chinese ambassador, Asmara, Eritrea, June 29, 2006.

29. Interview with Chinese academic, Center for International Political Economy, Peking University, Beijing, China, September 20, 2007.

30. Interview with He Wenping, CASS, Beijing, China, September 18, 2007.

31. Interview with market trader, Assomada, Cape Verde, November 5, 2007.

32. Interview with market trader, Kampala, Uganda, November 4, 2006.

33. Interview with Eritrean shopkeeper, Massawa, Eritrea, July 1, 2006; interview with Guinea-Bissaun worker in Santa Maria, Cape Verde, November 7, 2007.

34. Interview with employee of Chungking Mansions–based cargo company, Hong Kong, November 13, 2006.

35. Interview with African trader, Chungking Mansions, Hong Kong, November 13, 2006.

36. Interview with Cape Verdean hotel owner, Praia, Cape Verde, November 5, 2007.

37. Interview with Chinese diplomat, Abuja, Nigeria, September 5, 2007.

38. Interview with a journalist from the *Guardian,* Abuja, Nigeria, September 5, 2007.

39. Interview with Chinese diplomat, Abuja, Nigeria, September 5, 2007.

40. The revelation in early 2008 that a factory in Guangdong was manufacturing the flag of the Tibetan government-in-exile, to fulfill an overseas order, is emblematic of this reality.

41. Interview with African Union official, Addis Ababa, Ethiopia, May 16, 2007.

42. Interview with Western diplomat, Asmara, Eritrea, June 29, 2006.

43. Interview with Shu Zhan, Chinese ambassador to Eritrea, Asmara, Eritrea, June 29, 2006.

44. Interview with Pentagon official, Washington, DC, United States, April 5, 2007.

45. Interview with British diplomat, Addis Ababa, Ethiopia, May 15, 2007.

46. Interview with military attaché, Western embassy, Addis Ababa, Ethiopia, May 15, 2007.

47. Interview with military attaché, Western embassy, Addis Ababa, Ethiopia, May 15, 2007.

48. Interview with African Union official, Addis Ababa, Ethiopia, May 16, 2007.

49. Interview with military attaché, Western embassy, Addis Ababa, Ethiopia, May 15, 2007.

50. Interview with Chinese diplomat, Addis Ababa, Ethiopia, May 15, 2007.

51. Observations by the author in Addis Ababa, Abuja, Freetown, Gaborone, Lusaka, Massawa, and Windhoek.

52. Interview with Moses Pakote, deputy director of Investor Services, Namibia Investment Centre, Ministry of Trade and Industry, Windhoek, Namibia, August 11, 2006.

53. Interview with Robin Sherborne, editor of *Insight,* Windhoek Namibia, August 14, 2006.

54. Interview with Western diplomat, Abuja, Nigeria, September 3, 2007.

55. Interview with British diplomat, Addis Ababa, Ethiopia, May 14, 2007.

56. I look forward to the day that *some* Chinese academics equally abandon their immediate hostility to the slightest analytical comment on Sino-African relations.

57. Interview with Chinese academic, School of International Studies, Renmin University, Beijing, China, February 21, 2008.

58. Interview with He Wenping, CASS, Beijing, China, September 18, 2007.

59. Interviews with officials in Port Louis and Abuja, October 2003 and September 2007, respectively.

60. Interview with British diplomat, Addis Ababa, Ethiopia, May 15, 2007.

61. Interview with African Union official, Addis Ababa, Ethiopia, May 15, 2007.

62. Interview with African Union official, Addis Ababa, Ethiopia, May 16, 2007.

63. Interview with Ethiopian academic, Addis Ababa, Ethiopia, November 22, 2005.

Acronyms

ADB	African Development Bank
AGOA	African Growth and Opportunity Act
AU	African Union
CASS	Chinese Academy of Social Sciences
CATIC	National Aero-Technology Import and Export Corporation
CCP/ID	International Department of the Chinese Communist Party
CICIR	China Institutes of Contemporary International Relations
CIIS	China Institute of International Studies
CIISS	China Institute of International Strategic Studies
CITES	Convention on International Trade in Wild Species of Fauna and Flora
CIWEC	China International Water and Electric Corporation
CNOOC	China National Offshore Oil Corporation
CNPC	China National Petroleum Corporation
COMESA	Common Market for Eastern and Southern Africa
CPA	Comprehensive Peace Agreement
CPC	Communist Party of China
DDR	Disarmament, Demobilization, and Reintegration
DDRRR	Disarmament, Demobilization, Repatriation, Resettlement, and Reintegration
DFID	Department for International Development
DPKO	UN Department of Peacekeeping Operations
DRC	Democratic Republic of Congo
ECOSOC	UN Economic and Social Council
ECOWAS	Economic Community of West African States
EITI	Extractive Industries Transparency Initiative
ESI	Export Similarity Index
EU	European Union

FDI	foreign direct investment
FOCAC	Forum on China-Africa Cooperation
GDP	gross domestic product
GNP	gross national product
GNPOC	Greater Nile Petroleum Operating Company
IFI	international financial institution
IMF	International Monetary Fund
ISAF	International Security Assistance Force (Afghanistan)
JEM	Justice and Equality Movement
LDC	least developed country
MDC	Movement for Democratic Change
MEND	Movement for the Emancipation of the Niger Delta
MFA	Multi-Fiber Agreement
MFA	Ministry of Foreign Affairs (PRC)
MINUCI	UN Mission in Côte d'Ivoire
MINURCA	UN Mission in the Central African Republic
MINURSO	UN Mission for the Referendum in Western Sahara
MINUSTAH	UN Stabilization Mission in Haiti
MOFTEC	Ministry of Foreign Trade and Economic Cooperation
MONUA	UN Observer Mission in Angola
MONUC	UN Organization Mission in Democratic Republic of Congo
MOU	Memorandum of Understanding
NATO	North Atlantic Treaty Organization
NEPAD	New Partnership for Africa's Development
NGO	nongovernmental organization
NNPC	Nigerian National Petroleum Corporation
Norinco	China North Industries Corporation
NPDC	Nigerian Petroleum Development Company
OML	Oil Mining Lease
ONLF	Ogaden National Liberation Front
ONUMOZ	UN Operation in Mozambique
ONUSAL	UN Observer Mission in El Salvador
PAP	People's Armed Police
PLA	People's Liberation Army
PRC	People's Republic of China
PRSP	Poverty Reduction Strategy Paper
PSC	production-sharing contract
ROC	Republic of China on Taiwan
RUF	Revolutionary United Front
SASAC	State-owned Assets Supervision and Administration Commission
SATUC	Southern African Trade Union Council
Sinopec	China Petroleum and Chemical Corporation

SIPRI	Stockholm International Peace Research Institute
SLA	Sudanese Liberation Army
SLM	Sudanese Liberation Movement
SOE	state-owned enterprise
TIV	trend indicator value
UN	United Nations
UNAMID	United Nations–African Union Mission in Darfur
UNAMIR	UN Assistance Mission for Rwanda
UNAMSIL	UN Mission in Sierra Leone
UNFICYP	UN Peacekeeping Force in Cyprus
UNITAF	Unified Task Force (Somalia)
UNMEE	UN Mission in Ethiopia and Eritrea
UNMIL	UN Mission in Liberia
UNMIS	UN Mission in Sudan
UNOCI	UN Operation in Côte d'Ivoire
UNOSOM	UN Operation in Somalia
UNPKO	United Nations peacekeeping operation
UNPREDEP	UN Preventive Deployment Force (Macedonia)
UNPROFOR	UN Protection Force (Yugoslavia)
UNSC	UN Security Council
UNSCPO	UN Special Committee on Peacekeeping Operations
UNTAC	UN Transitional Authority in Cambodia
UNTAET	UN Transitional Administration in East Timor
UNTSO	United Nations Truce Supervision Organization
VAT	value-added tax
WTO	World Trade Organization
ZANU	Zimbabwe African National Union
ZANU-PF	Zimbabwe African National Union–Patriotic Front

Bibliography

Afeikhena, J., S. Adjibolosoo, and D. Busari (2005). "Addressing Oil Related Corruption in Africa: Is the Push for Transparency Enough?" *Review of Human Factor Studies,* vol. 11, no. 1, pp. 7–32.

Africa-China-US Dialogue (2006). *Report of the First Meeting of the Trilateral Dialogue, Tswalu Kalahari Reserve, South Africa, August 4–6.* Brenthurst Discussion Papers 6/2006, Johannesburg: Brenthurst Foundation.

Ahmad, M. (2005). "Textiles and Clothing," paper presented to the United Nations Conference on Trade and Development (UNCTAD) meeting, "Strengthening the Participation of Developing Countries in Dynamic Sectors in World Trade: Trends, Issues and Policies," Geneva, February 9.

Ake, C. (1991). "How Politics Underdevelops Africa," in A. Adedeji, O. Teriba, and P. Bugembe (eds.), *The Challenge of African Economic Recovery and Development.* London: Frank Cass, pp. 316–329.

Aluko, M. (2002). "The Institutionalization of Corruption and Its Impact on Political Culture in Nigeria," *Nordic Journal of African Studies,* vol. 11, no. 3, pp. 393–402.

Amnesty International (2006a). *People's Republic of China: Sustaining Conflict and Human Rights Abuses: The Flow of Arms Accelerates.* New York: Amnesty International.

——— (2006b). "China: Secretive Arms Exports Stoking Conflict and Repression," press release, June 11.

——— (2007). *Sudan: Arms Continuing to Fuel Serious Human Rights Violations in Darfur.* London: Amnesty International.

Amosu, A. (2007). "China in Africa: It's (Still) the Governance, Stupid," *Foreign Policy in Focus,* March 9, pp. 1–6.

Andrews-Speed, P., S. Dow, and Gao Zhiguo (2000). "The Ongoing Reforms to China's Government and State Sector: The Case of the Energy Industry," *Journal of Contemporary China,* vol. 9, no. 23, pp. 5–20.

Angle, S. (2002). *Human Rights and Chinese Thought: A Cross-Cultural Inquiry.* New York: Cambridge University Press.

Annan, K. (1999). "Two Concepts of Sovereignty," *The Economist,* September 18, p. 8.

Askouri, A. (2007). "China's Investment in the Sudan: Displacing Villages and Destroying Communities" in F. Manji and S. Marks (eds.), *African Perspectives on China in Africa.* Cape Town, South Africa: Fahamu, pp. 71–86.

Badescu, C. (2007). "Authorizing Humanitarian Intervention: Hard Choices in Saving Strangers," *Canadian Journal of Political Science,* vol. 40, no. 1, pp. 51–78.

Badie, B. (2000). *The Imported State: The Westernization of the Political Order.* Stanford, CA: Stanford University Press.

Baehr, P. (2004). "Humanitarian Intervention: A Misnomer," in M. Davis, W. Dietrich, B. Scholdan, and D. Sepp (eds.), *International Intervention in the Post–Cold War World: Moral Responsibility and Power Politics.* Armonk, NY: M. E. Sharpe, pp. 23–39.

Barabantseva, E. (2005). "Trans-nationalizing Chineseness: Overseas Chinese Policies of the PRC's Central Government," *ASIEN: Journal for Politics, Economy and Culture,* no. 96, pp. 7–28.

Barnes, S. (1986). *Patrons and Power: Creating a Political Community in Metropolitan Lagos.* Manchester, UK: Manchester University Press.

Barnouin and Changgen Yu (1998). *Chinese Foreign Policy During the Cultural Revolution.* New York: Kegan Paul.

Bartholomew, C. (2005). "Statement of Ms. Carolyn Bartholomew, Commissioner, U.S.-China Economic and Security Review Commission," in the *Hearing Before the Subcommittee on Africa, Global Human Rights and International Operations of the Committee on International Relations,* House of Representatives, One Hundred Ninth Congress, first session, July 28, 2005, Serial No. 109–174. Washington, DC: Government Printer, pp. 17–21.

Baum, R. (1994). *Burying Mao: Chinese Politics in the Age of Deng Xiaoping.* Princeton, NJ: Princeton University Press.

Bellamy, A. (2005). "Responsibility to Protect or Trojan Horse? The Crisis in Darfur and Humanitarian Intervention after Iraq," *Ethics and International Affairs,* vol. 19, no. 2, pp. 31–54.

Bellamy, A., and P. Williams (2004). "What Future for Peace Operations? Brahimi and Beyond," *International Peacekeeping,* vol. 11, no. 1, pp. 183–212.

Bellamy, A., P. Williams, and S. Griffin (2004). *Understanding Peacekeeping.* Cambridge, UK: Polity Press.

Berman, E. (2000). *Re-Armament in Sierra Leone: One Year After the Lomé Peace Agreement.* Geneva: Small Arms Survey.

Bermingham, J., and E. Clausen (1981). *Sino-African Relations 1949–1976.* Pasadena, CA: California Institute of Technology Press.

Besha, P. (2008). *Village Democracy and Social Unrest in China.* Saarbrücken, Germany: VDM Verlag Dr. Mueller.

Bitzinger, R. (2003). "Just the Facts, Ma'am: The Challenge of Analysing and Assessing Chinese Military Expenditures," *China Quarterly,* no. 173, pp. 164–175.

Blasko, D. (2006). *The Chinese Army Today: Tradition and Transformation for the 21st Century.* London: Routledge.

Blum, S. (2003). "Chinese Views of US Hegemony," *Journal of Contemporary China,* vol. 12, no. 35, pp. 239–264.

Bonga-Bonga, L. (2006). "Can China Help Revive the African Textile Industry?" *Univers: Foreign Affairs,* December 7, p. 2.

Boone, C. (2004). "China in the 'Easy Phase' of Opening," *Issues and Studies,* vol. 40, no.1, pp. 226–231.

Boutros-Ghali, B. (1992). *An Agenda for Peace: Preventive Diplomacy, Peacemaking and Peacekeeping.* New York: United Nations.

Brahm, L. (2002). *Zhu Rongji and the Transformation of Modern China.* Chichester, UK: John Wiley and Sons.

Bratton, M., and N. van de Walle (1994). "Neopatrimonial Regimes and Political Transitions in Africa," *World Politics,* vol. 46, no. 4, pp. 453–489.

————— (1997). *Democratic Experiments in Africa: Regime Transitions in Comparative Perspective.* Cambridge: Cambridge University Press.

Brautigam, D. (1998). *Chinese Aid and African Development: Exporting the Green Revolution.* New York: St. Martin's Press.

————— (2007). *"Flying Geese" or "Hidden Dragon"? Chinese Business and African Industrial Development.* Los Angeles: Globalization Research Center–Africa.

Breslin, S. (1996a). *China in the 1980s: Centre-Province Relations in a Reforming Socialist State.* Basingstoke, UK: Macmillan.

————— (1996b). "China: Developmental State or Dysfunctional Development?" *Third World Quarterly,* vol. 17, no. 4, pp. 689–706.

————— (2003). "Reforming China's Embedded Socialist Compromise: China and the WTO," *Global Change,* vol. 15, no. 3, pp. 213–229.

————— (2004). "China in the Asian Economy," in B. Buzan and R. Foot (eds.), *Does China Matter? A Reassessment.* London: Routledge, pp. 107–123.

————— (2005a). "Power and Production: Rethinking China's Global Economic Role," *Review of International Studies,* vol. 31, no. 4, pp. 735–753.

————— (2005b). "China and the Political Economy of Global Engagement," in R. Stubbs and G. Underhill (eds.), *Political Economy and the Changing Global Order.* Ontario: Oxford University Press, pp. 465–477.

————— (2006). "Globalization, International Coalitions and Domestic Reform in China," *Critical Asian Studies,* vol. 36, no. 4, pp. 657–675.

————— (2007). *China and the Global Political Economy.* Basingstoke, UK: Palgrave.

————— (2008). "Why Growth Equals Power—And Why It Shouldn't: Constructing Visions of China," *Journal of Asian Public Policy,* vol. 1, issue 1, pp. 3–17.

Brookes, P., and Shin Ji Hye (2006). "China's Influence in Africa: Implications for the United States," *Heritage Foundation Backgrounder,* no. 1916, February 22, pp. 1–9.

Brown, K. (2007). *Struggling Giant: China in the 21st Century.* London: Anthem Press.

Burstein, D. (1988). *Yen! Japan's New Financial Empire and Its Threat to America.* New York: Simon and Schuster.

Burstein, D., and A. De Keijzer (1999). *Big Dragon: Future of China—What It Means for Business, the Economy and the Global Order.* New York: Touchstone.

Butcher, T. (2007). *Blood River: A Journey to Africa's Broken Heart.* London: Chatto and Windus.

Byers, M. (2002). "Terrorism, the Use of Force and International Law After 11 September," *International and Comparative Law Quarterly,* vol. 51, no. 2, pp. 401–414.

————— (2003). "Letting the Exception Prove the Rule," *Ethics and International Affairs,* vol. 17, no. 1, pp. 9–16.

Byman, D., and R. Cliff (2000). *China's Arms Sales: Motivations and Implications.* Santa Monica, CA: RAND.

Calabrese, J. (2006). "China's Global Economic Reach and US Primacy in China's Role in the World: Is China a Responsible Stakeholder?" in the *Hearing Before the US-China Economic Security Review Commission,* House of Representatives, One Hundred Ninth Congress, second session, August 3–4, Washington, DC: Government Printer, pp. 12–25.

Canadian Security Intelligence Service (2003). *Weapons Proliferation and the Military-Industrial Complex of the PRC.* Commentary No. 84. Ottawa: Canadian Security Intelligence Service.

Carlson, A. (2004). "Helping to Keep the Peace (Albeit Reluctantly): China's Recent Stance on Sovereignty and Multilateral Intervention," *Pacific Affairs,* vol. 77, no. 1, pp. 1–14.

——— (2006). "More than Just Saying No: China's Evolving Approach to Sovereignty and Intervention," in A. Johnston and R. Ross (eds.), *New Directions in the Study of China's Foreign Policy.* Stanford, CA: Stanford University Press, pp. 217–241.

Carmody, P. (2007). *Neoliberalism, Civil Society and Security in Africa.* London: Palgrave.

Carmody, P., and F. Owusu (2005). "Competing Hegemons? Chinese versus American Geo-Economic Strategies in Africa," *Political Geography,* vol. 8, no. 2, pp. 504–524.

Catholic Relief Services (2003). *Bottom of the Barrel: Africa's Oil Boom and the Poor.* Baltimore: Catholic Relief Services.

Centre for Chinese Studies (2007). "China's Interest and Activity in Africa's Construction and Infrastructure Sectors: A Research Undertaking Evaluating China's Involvement in Africa's Construction and Infrastructure Sector Prepared for DFID China." Stellenbosch, South Africa: Centre for Chinese Studies.

Cesarz, E., S. Morrison, and J. Cooke (2003). *Alienation and Militancy in Nigeria's Niger Delta.* Washington, DC: Center for Strategic and International Studies.

Chan, A. (2001). *China's Workers Under Assault: Exploitation and Abuse in a Globalizing Economy.* Armonk, NY: M. E. Sharpe.

Chandler, G. (1998). "Oil Companies and Human Rights," *Business Ethics: A European Review,* vol. 7, no. 2, pp. 69–72.

Chang, G. (2002). *The Coming Collapse of China.* London: Random House.

Chen, A. (2000). "Chinese Cultural Tradition and Modern Human Rights," *Perspectives,* vol. 1, no. 5, pp. 1–12.

Chen Jie (2002). *Foreign Policy of the New Taiwan: Pragmatic Diplomacy in Southeast Asia.* Aldershot, UK: Elgar.

Chen Shaofeng (2008). "Motivations Behind China's Foreign Oil Quest: A Perspective from the Chinese Government and the Oil Companies," *Journal of Chinese Political Science,* vol. 13, no. 1, pp. 79–104.

Chen Zhimin (2005). "Nationalism, Internationalism and Chinese Foreign Policy," *Journal of Contemporary China,* vol. 14, no. 42, pp. 35–53.

Cheng Li (ed.) (2008). *China's Changing Political Landscape: Prospects for Democracy.* Washington, DC: Brookings Institution.

Cheng Xiaoxia (2003). "Interference vs. 'International Intervention': Change and Constancy in International Law," in *International Intervention and State Sovereignty.* Beijing: China Reform Forum, pp. 137–152.

Cheru, F. (2007). *Love at First Sight! Or Confused Priorities? Decoding the Evolving China-Africa Relations,* Los Angeles: Globalization Research Center–Africa.

Cheung, G. (1998). *Market Liberalism: American Foreign Policy Toward China.* New Brunswick, NJ: Transaction Publishers.

Cheung, T. (2001). *China's Entrepreneurial Army.* Oxford: Oxford University Press.

China Reform Forum (2003). *International Intervention and State Sovereignty.* Beijing: China Reform Forum.

Choedon, Y. (2005). "China's Stand on UN Peacekeeping Operations: Changing Priorities of Foreign Policy," *China Report,* vol. 41, no. 1, pp. 39–57.

Chong, D. (2002). "Relief and Reconstruction—UNTAC in Cambodia: A New Model for Humanitarian Aid in Failed States?" *Development and Change,* vol. 33, no. 5, pp. 957–978.

Chossudovsky, M. (1986). *Towards Capitalist Restoration? Chinese Socialism After Mao.* New York: St. Martin's Press.

Christensen, T. (2001). "China," in R. Ellings and A. Friedberg (eds.), *Strategic Asia 2001–02: Power and Purpose.* Seattle: National Bureau of Asian Research, pp. 27–69.

Christian Aid (2004). *Rags to Riches to Rags*. London: Christian Aid.

Christoffersen, G. (1999). *China's Intentions for Russian and Central Asian Oil and Gas*. Washington, DC: National Bureau of Asian Research.

Chu Shulong (2002). "China and Human Security." Program on Canada-Asia Policy Studies, North Pacific Policy Papers no. 8, Vancouver: University of British Columbia.

———— (2003). "China, Asia and Issues of Sovereignty and Intervention," in *International Intervention and State Sovereignty*. Beijing: China Reform Forum, pp. 176–199.

Clapham, C. (1985). *Third World Politics: An Introduction*. London: Croom Helm.

———— (1996). "The Developmental State: Governance, Comparison and Culture in the 'Third World,'" in L. Imbeau and R. McKinlay (eds.), *Comparing Government Activity*. Basingstoke, UK: Macmillan, pp. 159–178.

Clark, P. (2008). *The Chinese Cultural Revolution: A History*. Cambridge, UK: Cambridge University Press.

Clissold, T. (2004). *Mr. China*. London: Constable and Robinson.

Cohen, J. (1973). "China and Intervention: Theory and Practice," *University of Pennsylvania Law Review*, vol. 121, no. 3, pp. 471–505.

Constantin, C. (2007). "Understanding China's Energy Security," *World Political Science Review*, vol. 3, no. 3, pp. 16–32.

Cooper, J. (1994). "Peking's Post-Tiananmen Foreign Policy: The Human Rights Factor," *Issues and Studies*, vol. 30, no. 10, pp. 65–78.

Corporate Council on Africa (2006). "AGOA Apparel Imports Fall During 2005 as Imports from China Surge with the End of the MFA," *Africa Journal*, Spring, pp. 19–21.

Council on Foreign Relations (2006). *More Than Humanitarianism: A Strategic US Approach Toward Africa*. Washington, DC: Council on Foreign Relations.

Curran, L. (2007)."Clothing's Big Bang: The Impact of the End of the ATC on Developing Country Clothing Suppliers," *Journal of Fashion Marketing and Management*, vol. 11, no. 1, pp. 32–47.

Davies, G., and G. Ramia (2008). "Governance Reform Towards 'Serving Migrant Workers': The Local Implementation of Central Government Regulations," *China Quarterly*, vol. 193, pp. 140–149.

Davis, J. (2005). *Export Controls in the People's Republic of China, 2005*. Athens, GA: Center for International Trade and Security.

De Burgh, H. (2006). *China: Friend or Foe?* London: Icon Books.

Deng, F., S. Kimaro, T. Lyons, D. Rothchild, and I. Zartman (1996). *Sovereignty as Responsibility: Conflict Management in Africa*. Washington, DC: Brookings Institution Press.

Deng Xiaoping (1985). *Build Socialism with Chinese Characteristics*. Beijing: Foreign Languages Press.

———— (1994). *Selected Works 1982–1992*, vol. 3. Beijing: Foreign Languages Press.

Deng Yong (2008). *China's Struggle for Status: The Realignment of International Relations*. New York: Cambridge University Press.

De Sardan, O. (1999). "A Moral Economy of Corruption in Africa?" *Journal of Modern African Studies*, vol. 37, no.1, pp. 25–52.

Deutsche Bank Research (2006). *China's Commodity Hunger: Implications for Africa and Latin America*. Frankfurt am Main, Germany: Deutsche Bank.

Dickson, B. (2003). *Red Capitalists in China: The Party, Private Entrepreneurs, and Prospects for Political Change*. Cambridge, UK: Cambridge University Press.

——— (2007). "Integrating Wealth and Power in China: The Communist Party's Embrace of the Private Sector," *China Quarterly*, vol. 192, pp. 827–854.

——— (2008). *Wealth into Power: The Communist Party's Embrace of China's Private Sector.* Cambridge, UK: Cambridge University Press.

Dikötter, F. (1992). *The Discourse of Race in Modern China.* London: Hurst and Company.

Dirlik, A. (2006). "Beijing Consensus: Beijing 'Gongshi'—Who Recognizes Whom and to What End?" mimeo.

Downs, E. (2007). "The Fact and Fiction of Sino-African Energy Relations," *China Security*, vol. 3, no. 3, pp. 42–68.

——— (2008). "Business Interest Groups in Chinese Politics: The Case of the Oil Companies," in Cheng Li (ed.), *China's Changing Political Landscape: Prospects for Democracy.* Washington DC: Brookings Institute, pp. 121–141.

Dreyer, J. (2000). *The PLA and the Kosovo Conflict.* Carlisle, PA: Strategic Studies Institute.

——— (2007). "Sino-American Energy Cooperation," *Journal of Contemporary China*, vol. 16, no. 52, pp. 461–476.

Duckett, J. (1998). *The Entrepreneurial State in China: Real Estate and Commerce Departments in Reform-Era Tianjin.* London: Routledge.

Duyvendak, J. (1949). *China's Discovery of Africa.* London: Probsthain.

Ebel, R. (2005). *China's Energy Future: The Middle Kingdom Seeks Its Place in the Sun.* Washington, DC: Center for Strategic and International Studies.

Edin, M. (2003). "State Capacity and Local Agent Control in China: CCP Cadre Management from a Township Perspective," *China Quarterly*, no. 173, pp. 35–52.

Eisenman, J. (2005). "Zimbabwe: China's African Ally," *China Brief*, vol. 5, July 15, pp. 8–11.

Elegant, R. (1963). *The Centre of the World: Communism and the Mind of China.* London: Methuen.

Embassy of Angola (2004). "Angola-China: An Example of South-South Cooperation," Angola Press Agency report, March 26, mimeo.

Embassy of the People's Republic of China in the Republic of Zimbabwe (2000a). "Strengthen Solidarity, Enhance Co-operation and Pursue Common Development by Zhu Rongji," mimeo.

——— (2000b). "The Beijing Declaration of the Forum on China-Africa Co-operation," mimeo.

Energy Information Administration (1999). *China Country Analysis Brief,* http://www.eia.doe.gov/emeu/cabs/china.html.

Evans, P. (1995). *Embedded Autonomy: States and Industrial Transformation.* Princeton: Princeton University Press.

Fatton, R. (1988). "Bringing the Ruling Class Back In: Class, State, and Hegemony in Africa," *Comparative Politics*, vol. 20, no. 3, pp. 253–264.

——— (1990), "Liberal Democracy in Africa," *Political Science Quarterly*, vol. 105, no. 3, pp. 455–473.

——— (1999). "Civil Society Revisited: Africa in the New Millennium," *West Africa Review*, vol. 1, no. 1, pp. 1–18.

Fewsmith, J. (2001). *China Since Tiananmen: The Politics of Transition.* Cambridge, UK: Cambridge University Press.

Filesi, T. (1972). *China and Africa in the Middle Ages.* London: Frank Cass.

Fine, B., C. Lapavitsas, and J. Pincus (eds.), (2001). *Development Policy in the Twenty-First Century: Beyond the Post-Washington Consensus.* London: Routledge.

Fingleton, E. (2008). *In the Jaws of the Dragon: America's Fate in the Coming Era of Chinese Hegemony.* New York: Thomas Dunne Books.

Fishman, T. (2006). *China, Inc.: How the Rise of the Next Superpower Challenges America and the World.* New York: Scribner.

Flanary, R. (1998). "The State in Africa: Implications for Democratic Reform," *Crime, Law and Social Change,* vol. 29, nos. 2–3, pp. 179–196.

Foot, R. (1995). *The Practice of Power.* Oxford: Oxford University Press.

————— (2001). "Chinese Power and the Idea of a Responsible State," *China Journal,* no. 45, pp. 1–19.

————— (2006). "Chinese Strategies in a US-Hegemonic Global Order: Accommodating and Hedging," *International Affairs,* vol. 82, no. 1, pp. 77–94.

Frankenstein, J. (1999). "China's Defense Industries: A New Course?" in J. Mulvenon and R. Yang (eds.), *The People's Liberation Army in the Information Age.* Santa Monica, CA: RAND, pp. 187–216.

Fraser, A., and J. Lungu (2007). *For Whom the Windfalls? Winners and Losers in the Privatisation of Zambia's Copper Mines.* London: Christian Aid.

French, P. (2007). *North Korea: The Paranoid Peninsula—A Modern History.* London: Zed Books.

Friedman, E., and M. Lebard (1991). *The Coming War with Japan.* London: St. Martin's Press.

Friedrich-Ebert-Stiftung (2004). *The "Look East Policy" of Zimbabwe Now Focuses on China.* Harare, Zimbabwe: Friedrich-Ebert-Stiftung.

Fundira, T. (2008). "Africa-China Trading Relationship," Stellenbosch, South Africa: Trade Law Centre for Southern Africa.

Gao Jinyuan (1984). "China and Africa: The Development of Relations over Many Centuries," *African Affairs,* vol. 83, no. 331, pp. 241–250.

Gao Mobo (2008). *The Battle for China's Past: Mao and the Cultural Revolution.* London: Pluto Press.

Garfinkle, A. (2003). "Humanitarian Intervention and State Sovereignty: A Realist View," in *International Intervention and State Sovereignty.* Beijing: China Reform Forum, pp. 237–266.

Gary, I., and T. Karl (2003). *Bottom of the Barrel: Africa's Oil Boom and the Poor.* Baltimore, MD: Catholic Relief Services.

Geldenhuys, D. (1990). *Isolated States: A Comparative Analysis.* Cambridge, UK: Cambridge University Press.

Gereffi, G. (1999). "International Trade and Industrial Upgrading in the Apparel Commodity Chain," *Journal of International Economics,* vol. 48, no. 1, pp. 38–70.

Gertz, B., and C. Menges (2005). *China: The Gathering Threat.* Nashville, TN: Nelson Current.

Ghazvinian, J. (2007). *Untapped: The Scramble for Africa's Oil.* Orlando, FL: Harcourt.

Gill, B. (2007). *Rising Star: China's New Security Diplomacy.* Washington, DC: Brookings Institution Press.

Gill, B., and E. Medeiros (2000). "Foreign and Domestic Influences on China's Arms Control and Nonproliferation Policy," *China Quarterly,* no. 161, pp. 66–94.

Gill, B., and J. Reilly (2000). "Sovereignty, Intervention and Peacekeeping: The View from Beijing," *Survival,* vol. 42, no. 3, pp. 41–60.

————— (2007). "The Tenuous Hold of China Inc. in Africa," *Washington Quarterly,* vol. 30, no. 3, pp. 37–52.

Gilley, B. (1998). *Tiger on the Brink: Jiang Zemin and China's New Elite.* Berkeley: University of California Press.

Glaser, B. (2007). "Ensuring the 'Go Abroad' Policy Serves China's Domestic Priorities," *China Brief,* vol. 7, no. 5, pp. 2–5.

Glaser, B., and E. Medeiros (2007). "The Changing Ecology of Foreign Policy-Making in China: The Ascension and Demise of the Theory of 'Peaceful Rise,'" *China Quarterly,* no. 190, pp. 291–310.

Glaser, B., and P. Saunders (2002). "Chinese Civilian Foreign Policy Research Institutes: Evolving Roles and Increasing Influence," *China Quarterly,* vol. 171, pp. 601–620.

Goodman, D. (1996). "Corruption in the PLA," in G. Segal and R. Yang (eds.), *Chinese Economic Reform: The Impact on Security.* London: Routledge, pp. 35–52.

——— (1997). *China's Provinces in Reform: Class, Community and Political Culture.* London: Routledge.

——— (2008). *The New Rich in China: Future Rulers, Present Lives.* London: Routledge.

Goodman, D., and G. Segal (eds.), (1994). *China Deconstructs: Politics, Trade and Regionalism.* London: Routledge.

Gries, P. (2001). "Tears of Rage: Chinese Nationalist Reactions to the Belgrade Embassy Bombing," *China Journal,* no. 46, pp. 25–43.

——— (2005). *China's New Nationalism: Pride, Politics, and Diplomacy.* Los Angeles: University of California Press.

Grimmett, R. (1994). *Conventional Arms Transfers to the Third World, 1986–1993.* Washington, DC: Library of Congress.

——— (2006). *Conventional Arms Transfers to Developing Nations, 1998–2005.* Washington, DC: Library of Congress.

Gu, G. (2006). *China's Global Reach: Markets, Multinationals, and Globalization.* Palo Alto, CA: Fultus.

Gu Weiqun (1995). *Politics of Divided Nations: The Case of China and Korea.* Boulder, CO: Westview Press.

Gu Xuewu (2005). "China Returns to Africa," *Trends East Asia,* no. 9, pp. 1–14.

Guo Sujian (ed.), (2006). *China's "Peaceful Rise" in the 21st Century: Domestic and International Conditions.* Aldershot, UK: Ashgate.

Hagan, J., and A. Palloni (2006). "Death in Darfur," *Science,* no. 313, pp. 817–818.

Han Nianlong (1990). *Diplomacy of Contemporary China.* Beijing: New Horizon Press.

Harney, A. (2008). *The China Price: The True Cost of Chinese Competitive Advantage.* London: Penguin.

Hart-Landsberg, M., and P. Burkett (2005). *China and Socialism: Market Reforms and Class Struggle.* New York: Monthly Review Press.

——— (eds.), (2007). *Critical Perspectives on China's Economic Transformation: A "Critical Asian Studies" Roundtable on the Book* China and Socialism. Delhi: Daanish Books.

Hartzenberg, T. (2007). *The Competitiveness of the South African Clothing Industry.* Stellenbosch, South Africa: Trade Law Centre for Southern Africa.

Haugen, H., and J. Carling (2005). "On the Edge of the Chinese Diaspora: The Surge of Baihuo Business in an African City," *Ethnic and Racial Studies,* vol. 28, no. 4, pp. 639–662.

Hayes, S. (2003). "Testimony by Mr. Stephen Hayes, President, Corporate Council on Africa to the United States Senate Committee on Foreign Relations," Dirksen Senate Office Building, Room SD-419, June 25. Washington, DC: Senate Committee on Foreign Relations.

He Wenping (2007). "The Balancing Act of China's Africa Policy," *China Security,* vol. 3, no. 3, pp. 23–40.

He Yin (2007). *China's Changing Policy on UN Peacekeeping Operations*. Stockholm: Institute for Security and Development Policy.

Hickey, D. (2007). *Foreign Policy Making in Taiwan: From Principle to Pragmatism*. London: Routledge.

Hinton, W. (1991). *The Great Reversal: The Privatization of China, 1978–1989*. London: Earthscan.

——— (1993). "Can the Chinese Dragon Match Pearls with the Dragon God of the Sea? A Response to Zongli Tang," *Monthly Review*, vol. 45, no. 3, pp. 87–104.

Holslag, J. (2007a). *Friendly Giant? China's Evolving Africa Policy*. Brussels: Brussels Institute of Contemporary China Studies.

——— (2007b). "China's New Mercantilism in Central Africa," *African and Asian Studies*, vol. 5, no. 2, pp. 133–169.

——— (2008). "China's Diplomatic Manoeuvring on the Question of Darfur," *Journal of Contemporary China*, vol. 17, issue 54, pp. 71–84.

Holstrom, N., and R. Smith (2000). "The Necessity of Gangster Capitalism: Primitive Accumulation in Russia and China," *Monthly Review*, vol. 51, no. 9, pp. 1–15.

Hong Eunsuk and Sun Laixiang (2006). "Dynamics of Internationalization and Outward Investment: Chinese Corporations' Strategies," *China Quarterly*, vol. 187, pp. 610–634.

House of Commons (2007). *Written Answers to Questions, Monday, January 22, 2007*. London: Hansard.

Huang Zu'an (2007). *Theory of Stress on Peace in Chinese Military Strategy*. Beijing: Foreign Languages Press.

Hughes, N. (2002). *China's Economic Challenge: Smashing the Iron Rice Bowl*. Armonk, NY: M. E. Sharpe.

Hu Jintao (2007), "Hold High the Great Banner of Socialism with Chinese Characteristics and Strive for New Victories in Building a Moderately Prosperous Society in All Respects," in *Report to the Seventeenth National Congress of the Communist Party of China on October 15, 2007*. Beijing: Foreign Languages Press, pp. 1–73.

Human Rights Watch (1998). "Sudan: Global Trade, Local Impact: Arms Transfers to All Sides in the Civil War in Sudan," press release, August 2.

——— (2006). "China-Africa Summit: Focus on Human Rights, Not Just Trade: Chinese Leadership Should Pressure Sudan, Zimbabwe on Human Rights," press release, November 2.

Hunt, M. (1996). *The Genesis of Chinese Communist Foreign Policy*. New York: Columbia University Press.

Hutchison, A. (1975). *China's African Revolution*. London: Hutchinson.

Hutton, W. (2007). *The Writing on the Wall: China and the West in the 21st Century*. London: Little, Brown.

Hyer, E. (1992). "China's Arms Merchants: Profits in Command," *China Quarterly*, vol. 132, pp. 1101–1118.

Ikenberry, G. J. (2008). "The Rise of China and the Future of the West: Can the Liberal System Survive?" *Foreign Affairs*, January–February, pp. 23–37.

Information Office of the State Council (2002). *White Paper on China's National Defence*. Beijing: Information Office of the State Council.

Institute of Development and Education for Africa (2005). "The Tragedy of African Textile Industries," press release, February 14.

International Monetary Fund (2005). *Direction of Trade Statistics*. Washington, DC: IMF.

Ismael, T. (1971). "The People's Republic of China and Africa," *Journal of Modern African Studies*, vol. 9, no. 4, pp. 507–529.

Israel, C. (2006). *Testimony of Chris Israel, US Coordinator for International Intellectual Property Enforcement before the US-China Economic and Security Review Commission on Piracy and Counterfeiting in China.* Washington, DC: Office of the US IPR Coordinator.

Jackson, R. (1993). "Armed Humanitarianism," *International Journal,* vol. 48, no. 4, pp. 579–606.

———— (1993). *Quasi-States: Sovereignty, International Relations and the Third World.* Cambridge, UK: Cambridge University Press.

Jackson, R., and C. Rosberg (1994). "The Political Economy of African Personal Rule," in D. Apter and C. Rosberg (eds.), *Political Development and the New Realism in Sub-Saharan Africa.* Charlottesville: University of Virginia Press, pp. 300–314.

Jacob, H. (2004). "India-Sudan Energy Ties: Implications," *Observer Research Foundation,* August 31.

Jaffe, A., and S. Lewis (2002). "Beijing's Oil Diplomacy," *Survival,* vol. 44, no. 1, pp. 115–134.

Jakobson, L., and Zha Daojiong (2006). "China and the Worldwide Search for Oil Security," *Asia-Pacific Review,* vol. 13, no. 2, pp. 60–73.

James, A. (1993). "Internal Peace-Keeping: A Dead End for the U.N.?" *Security Dialogue,* vol. 24, no. 4, pp. 359–368.

Jauch, H., and R. Traub-Merz (eds.), (2006). *The Future of the Textile and Clothing Industry in Sub-Saharan Africa.* Bonn, Germany: Friedrich-Ebert-Stiftung.

Jenkins, R., and C. Edwards (2006). "The Economic Impacts of China and India on Sub-Saharan Africa: Trends and Prospects," *Journal of Asian Economics,* vol. 17, no. 2, pp. 207–225.

Jiang Wenran (2005). *Fueling the Dragon. China's Quest for Energy Security and Canada's Opportunities.* Vancouver: Asia Pacific Foundation of Canada.

Jing Gu, J. Humphrey, and D. Messner (2007). "Global Governance and Developing Countries: The Implications of the Rise of China," *World Development,* vol. 36, no. 2, pp. 274–292.

Johnson, D. (2003). *The Root Causes of Sudan's Civil Wars.* London: International African Institute.

Johnston, A. (1996). "Learning Versus Adaptation: Explaining Change in Chinese Arms Control Policy," *China Journal,* no. 35, pp. 27–61.

———— (2003). "Is China a Status Quo Power?" *International Security,* vol. 27, no. 4, pp. 5–56.

———— (2008). *Social States: China in International Institutions, 1980–2000.* Princeton, NJ: Princeton University Press.

Joseph, R. (1984). "Affluence and Underdevelopment: The Nigerian Experience," *Journal of Modern African Studies,* vol. 16, no. 2, pp. 221–239.

Kang, D. (2008). *China Rising: Peace, Power, and Order in East Asia.* New York: Columbia University Press.

Kaplinsky, R. (2004). *The Role of FDI in Reviving the Kenyan Manufacturing Sector.* Brighton, UK: Institute of Development Studies.

Kaplinsky, R., and M. Morris (2006). *Dangling by a Thread: How Sharp Are the Chinese Scissors?* Brighton, UK: Institute of Development Studies.

———— (2007), "Do the Asian Drivers Undermine Export-Oriented Industrialization in SSA?" *World Development,* vol. 36, no. 2, pp. 254–273.

Kaplinsky, R., D. McCormick, and M. Morris (2006). *The Impact of China on Sub-Saharan Africa.* Brighton, UK: Institute of Development Studies.

Kapur, H. (ed.) (1985). *The End of an Isolation: China After Mao*. Dordrecht, Netherlands: Martinus Nijhoff.

Karumbidza, J. (2007). "Win-win Economic Co-operation: Can China Save Zimbabwe's Economy?" in F. Manji and S. Marks (eds.), *African Perspectives on China in Africa*. Cape Town, South Africa: Fahamu, pp. 87–106.

Kavalski, E. (2005). "Coercing Order in the Balkans: Coming to Terms with NATO's Enforcement Capabilities," *Croatian International Relations Review*, vol. 11, nos. 38–39, pp. 36–47.

Keidel, A. (2006). "China's Social Unrest: The Story Behind the Stories," in Carnegie Endowment for International Peace Policy Brief no. 48, September.

Kim, S. (1994). "China's International Organizational Behavior," in T. Robinson and D. Shambaugh (eds.), *Chinese Foreign Policy: Theory and Practice*. Oxford: Oxford University Press, pp. 401–434.

——— (2003). "China's Path to Great Power Status in the Globalization Era," *Asian Perspective*, vol. 27, no. 1, pp. 35–75.

Kitissou, M. (2007). *Africa in China's Global Strategy*. London: Adonis and Abbey.

Kleine-Ahlbrandt, S., and A. Small (2008). "China's New Dictatorship Diplomacy: Is Beijing Parting with Pariahs?" *Foreign Affairs*, January–February, pp. 38–76.

Kornberg, K., and J. Faust (2005). *China in World Politics: Policies, Processes, Prospects*. Boulder, CO: Lynne Rienner Publishers.

Krieckhaus, J. (2006). *Dictating Development: How Europe Shaped the Global Periphery*. Pittsburgh: University of Pittsburgh Press.

Krilla, J. (2005). Regional Program Director for Africa, International Republican Institute, in the *Hearing Before the Subcommittee on Africa, Global Human Rights and International Operations of the Committee on International Relations*, House of Representatives, One Hundred Ninth Congress, first session, July 28, 2005, Serial No. 109–174. Washington, DC: Government Printer.

Kurlantzick, J. (2006). "China's Charm: Implications of Chinese Soft Power," Carnegie Endowment for International Peace Policy Brief no 47, June.

——— (2007). *Charm Offensive: How China's Soft Power Is Transforming the World*. New Haven, CT: Yale University Press.

Lado, C. (2000). "The Political Economy of Oil Discovery and Mining in the Sudan: Constraints and Prospects on Development," paper presented at the Fifth International Conference on Sudan Studies, University of Durham, England, August 30–September 1.

Lam, W. (2006). *Chinese Politics in the Hu Jintao Era: New Leaders, New Challenges*. Armonk, NY: M. E. Sharpe.

Lampton, D. (ed.), (1987). *Policy Implementation in Post-Mao China*. Berkeley: University of California Press.

——— (ed.), (2001). *The Making of Chinese Foreign and Security Policy in the Era of Reform*. Stanford, CA: Stanford University.

——— (2007). "The China Fantasy," *China Quarterly*, vol. 191, pp. 745–749.

——— (2008). *The Three Faces of Chinese Power: Might, Money, and Minds*. Berkeley: University of California Press.

Lande, S., M. Gale, R. Arora, and N. Sodhi (2005). *Impact of the End of MFA Quotas on COMESA's Textiles and Apparel Exports Under AGOA: Can the Sub-Saharan African Textile and Apparel Industry Survive and Grow in the Post-MFA World?* Nairobi: East and Central Africa Global Competitiveness Hub.

Landry, P. (2008). *Decentralized Authoritarianism in China: The Communist Party's Control of Local Elites in the Post-Mao Era*. Cambridge, UK: Cambridge University Press.

Lanteigne, M. (2005). *China and International Institutions: Alternate Paths to Global Power.* London: Routledge.

———— (2008). "The Developmentalism/Globalization Conundrum in Chinese Governance," in A. Laliberté and M. Lanteigne (eds.), *The Chinese Party-State in the 21st Century: Adaptation and the Reinvention of Legitimacy.* London: Routledge, pp. 162–184.

Larkin, B. (1971). *China and Africa 1949–1970.* Berkeley: University of California.

Larus, E. (2006). "Taiwan's Quest for International Recognition," *Issues and Studies,* vol. 42, no. 2, pp. 23–52.

———— (2008). "China's New Security Concept and Peaceful Rise: Trustful Cooperation or Deceptive Diplomacy?" *American Journal of Chinese Studies,* vol. 12, no. 2, pp. 16–29.

Lee, K. (2007). "China and the International Covenant on Civil and Political Rights: Prospects and Challenges," *Chinese Journal of International Law,* vol. 6, no. 2, pp. 445–474.

Leftwich, A. (2000). *States of Development: On the Primacy of Politics in Development.* Cambridge, UK: Polity Press.

Legum, C. (1979). *The Western Crisis and Southern Africa.* London: Africana Publishing House.

Leonard, D., and S. Straus (2003). *Africa's Stalled Development: International Causes and Cures.* Boulder, CO: Lynne Rienner Publishers.

Leonard, M. (2008). *What Does China Think?* London: Fourth Estate.

Lewis, P. (1996). "Economic Reform and Political Transition in Africa: The Quest for a Politics of Development," *World Politics,* vol. 49, no. 1, pp. 92–129.

———— (2004). "Getting the Politics Right: Governance and Economic Failure in Nigeria," in R. Rotberg (ed.), *Crafting the New Nigeria: Confronting the Challenges.* Boulder, CO: Lynne Rienner Publishers, pp. 99–124.

———— (2006). "China in Africa," *Saisphere,* Winter, p. 1–5.

Li Xiaobing (2007). *A History of the Modern Chinese Army.* Lexington: University Press of Kentucky.

Li Xing (1996). "Democracy and Human Rights: China and the West," *Monthly Review,* vol. 48, no. 7, pp. 29–40.

———— (2001). "The Chinese Cultural Revolution Revisited," *China Review,* vol. 1, no. 1, pp. 137–165.

Liao Kuangsheng (1990). *Antiforeignism and Modernization in China.* Hong Kong: Chinese University Press.

Liao Xuanli (2006). *Chinese Foreign Policy Think Tanks and China's Policy Toward Japan.* Hong Kong: Chinese University Press.

Lieberthal, K. (1992). "Introduction: The 'Fragmented Authoritarianism' Model and Its Limitations," in K. Lieberthal and D. Lampton (eds.), *Bureaucracy, Politics and Decision Making in Post-Mao China.* Berkeley: University of California Press, pp. 1–20.

———— (1995). *Governing China: From Revolution Through Reform.* New York: W. W. Norton.

Lieberthal, K., and D. Lampton (eds.), (1992). *Bureaucracy, Politics and Decision Making in Post-Mao China.* Berkeley: University of California Press.

Lieberthal, K., and M. Oksenberg (1988). *Policy Making in China: Leaders, Structures, and Processes.* Princeton, NJ: Princeton University Press.

Ling, B. (2007). "China's Peacekeeping Diplomacy," *China Rights Forum,* no. 1, pp. 1–3.

Liu Guijin (2004). "China-Africa Relations: Equality, Cooperation and Mutual Development," speech to the Institute of Security Studies, Pretoria, South Africa, November 9.

Liu Guoli (ed.), (2004). *Chinese Foreign Policy in Transition.* Hawthorne, NY: Aldine de Gruyter.

―――― (2006). "The Dialectic Relationship Between Peaceful Development and China's Deep Reform," in Guo Sujian (ed.), *China's "Peaceful Rise" in the 21st Century: Domestic and International Conditions.* Aldershot, UK: Ashgate, pp. 17–38.

Liu Yong (2007). "China's Soft Power and the Development of China-Africa Relations," *China International Studies,* no. 7.

Lovell, J. (2007). *The Great Wall: China Against the World, 1000 BC–AD 2000.* London: Atlantic Books.

Lubman, S. (2004). "The Dragon as Demon: Images of China on Capitol Hill," *Journal of Contemporary China,* vol. 13, no. 40, pp. 541–565.

Lyman, P. (2005). "China's Rising Role in Africa," presentation to the US-China Commission, Washington, DC, July 21.

MacFarquhar, R., and M. Schoenhals (2006). *Mao's Last Revolution.* Cambridge, MA: Harvard University Press.

Manchester Trade Team (2005). "Impact of the End of MFA Quotas and COMESA's Textile and Apparel Exports under AGOA: Can the Sub-Saharan Africa Textile and Apparel Industry Survive and Grow in the Post-MFA World?" report prepared for USAID East and Central Africa Global Competitiveness Trade Hub.

Manji, F., and S. Marks (eds.), (2007). *African Perspectives on China in Africa.* Cape Town, South Africa: Fahamu.

Mann, J. (2007). *The China Fantasy: How Our Leaders Explain Away Chinese Repression.* New York: Viking Books.

Markman, J. (2006). "How China Is Winning the Oil Race," April 27. http://www.thestreet.com/story/10281893/1/how-china-is-winning-the-oil-race.html.

Markovitz, I. (ed.), (1987). *Studies in Power and Class in Africa.* Oxford: Oxford University Press.

Mattlin, M. (2007). "The Chinese Government's New Approach to Ownership and Financial Control of Strategic State-Owned Enterprises," BOFIT Discussion Paper no. 10. Helsinki: Bank of Finland.

McGregor, J. (2005). *One Billion Customers: Crucial Lessons from the Front Lines of Doing Business in China.* London: Nicholas Brealey Publishing.

Medecins Sans Frontieres (2002). "Violence, Health, and Access to Aid in Unity State/Western Upper Nile," press release.

Medeiros, E. (2004). *Analyzing China's Defense Industries and the Implications for Chinese Military Modernization.* Arlington, VA: RAND.

Medeiros, E., and B. Gill (2000). *Chinese Arms Exports: Policy, Players, and Process.* Carlisle, PA: Strategic Studies Institute.

Meidan, M. (2006). "China's Africa Policy: Business Now, Politics Later," *Asian Perspective,* vol. 30, no. 4, pp. 69–93.

Meisner, M. (1996). *The Deng Xiaoping Era: An Inquiry into the Fate of Chinese Socialism, 1978–1994.* New York: Hill and Wang.

―――― (1999). *Mao's China and After: A History of the People's Republic.* New York: Free Press.

Melvern, L. (2000) *A People Betrayed: The Role of the West in Rwanda's Genocide.* London: Zed Books.

Melville, C., and O. Owen (2005). "China and Africa: A New Era of 'South-South' Co-operation," *Open Democracy,* July 8, pp. 2–6.

Mertha, A. (2007). *The Politics of Piracy: Intellectual Property in Contemporary China.* Ithaca, NY: Cornell University Press.

Ming Xia (2000). *The Dual Developmental State: Development Strategy and Institutional Arrangements for China's Transition.* Aldershot, UK: Ashgate.

Ministry of Foreign Affairs (2000). "The Signing of the International Convention on Civil and Political Rights by the Chinese Government," Beijing: Ministry of Foreign Affairs.

———— (2006). *China's African Policy.* Beijing: Ministry of Foreign Affairs.

Misra, K. (1998). *From Post-Maoism to Post-Marxism: Erosion of Official Ideology in Deng's China.* London: Routledge.

Mooney, P. (2005). "China's African Safari," *YaleGlobal,* January 3, pp. 1–3.

Morphet, S. (2000). "China as a Permanent Member of the Security Council, October 1971–December 1999," *Security Dialogue,* vol. 31, no. 2, pp. 151–166.

Morrison, W. (2007). *China's Economic Conditions.* Washington, DC: Congressional Research Service, Library of Congress.

Mosher, S. (2000). *Hegemon: China's Plan to Dominate Asia and the World.* New York: Encounter.

Muekelia, D. (2004). "Africa and China's Strategic Partnership," *African Security Review,* vol. 13, no. 1, pp. 5–12.

Muggah, R., and P. Batchelor, (2002). *"Development Held Hostage": Assessing the Effects of Small Arms on Human Development: A Preliminary Study of the Socio-Economic Impacts and Development Linkages of Small Arms Proliferation, Availability and Use.* New York: United Nations Development Programme.

Mulvenon, J. (2000). *Soldiers of Fortune: The Rise and Fall of the Chinese Military-Business Complex, 1978—1998.* Armonk, NY: M. E. Sharpe.

———— (2007). "The PLA in the New Economy: Plus Ça Change, Plus C'est la Même Chose" in D. Finkelstein and K. Gunness (eds.), *Civil-Military Relations in Today's China: Swimming in a New Sea.* Armonk, NY: M. E. Sharpe, pp. 67–89.

Murtha, A. (2005). *The Politics of Piracy: Intellectual Property in Contemporary China.* Ithaca, NY: Cornell University Press.

Mutume, G. (2006). "Loss of Textile Market Costs African Jobs: Diversification, Efficiency Hold Key for Economic Recovery," *Africa Renewal,* vol. 20, no. 1, pp. 12–27.

Mwega, F. (2007). "China, India and Africa: Prospects and Challenges," revised version of a paper earlier presented at the AERC-AFDB International Conference "Accelerating Africa's Development Five Years into the Twenty-First Century," November 22–24, 2006, Tunis, Tunisia.

Naidu, S. (2006). "South Africa's Relations with the People's Republic of China: A South-South Relationship of Mutual Opportunities or Hidden Threats?" in S. Buhlungu, J. Daniel, R. Southall, and J. Lutchman (eds.), *State of the Nation: South Africa 2005–2006.* Pretoria: Human Science Research Council, pp. 457–483.

Naidu, S., and M. Davies (2006). "China Fuels Its Future with Africa's Riches," *South African Journal of International Affairs,* vol. 13, no. 2, pp. 69-83.

Narayanan, R. (2005). "Foreign Economic Policy-Making in China," *Strategic Analysis,* vol. 29, no. 3, pp. 448–469.

Nathan, A. (1994). "Human Rights in Chinese Foreign Policy," *China Quarterly,* no. 139, pp. 622–643.

Nathan, A., and R. Ross (1997). *The Great Wall and the Empty Fortress: China's Search for Security.* New York: W. W. Norton.

Naughton, B. (2007). *The Chinese Economy Transitions and Growth.* Cambridge, MA: MIT Press.

Navarro, P. (2006). *The Coming China Wars: Where They Will Be Fought and How They Can Be Won.* New York: Financial Times/Prentice Hall.

Ncube, P., R. Bate, and R. Tren (2005). *State in Fear: Zimbabwe's Tragedy Is Africa's Shame: A Report on Operation Murambatsvina—"Operation Drive Out the Filth"—and Its Implications.* Bulawayo, Zimbabwe: Catholic Archdiocese of Bulawayo.

Nealer, K. (2004). "The PLA, Trade and US Interests," in S. Flanagan and M. Marti (eds.), *The People's Liberation Army and China in Transition.* Honolulu, HI: University Press of the Pacific, pp. 239–246.

Nolan, P. (2004). *China at the Crossroads.* Cambridge, UK: Polity Press.

Nolan, P., and Zhang Jin (2002). *The Challenge of Globalization for Large Chinese Firms.* Geneva: UNCTAD.

Nordas, H. (2004). *Global Textiles and Clothing Industry Post the Agreement in Textiles and Clothing.* Geneva: WTO.

Obiorah, N. (2007). "Who's Afraid of China in Africa?" in F. Manji and S. Marks (eds.), *African Perspectives on China in Africa.* Cape Town, South Africa: Fahamu, pp. 35–56.

Ogden, S. (1995). *China's Unresolved Issues: Politics, Development and Culture.* Englewood Cliffs, NJ: Prentice Hall.

Ogunsanwo, A. (1974). *China's Policy in Africa, 1958–1971.* Cambridge, UK: Cambridge University.

Oi, J., and A. Walder (eds.), (1999). *Property Rights and Economic Reform in China.* Stanford, CA: Stanford University Press.

Okonta, I., and O. Douglas (2003). *Where Vultures Feast: Shell, Human Rights and Oil.* London: Verso.

Omolo, J. (2006). "The Textile and Clothing Industry in Kenya" in H. Jauch and R. Traub-Merz (eds.), *The Future of the Textile and Clothing Industry in Sub-Saharan Africa.* Bonn, Germany: Friedrich-Ebert-Stiftung, pp. 147–164.

Ong, R. (2007). "'Peaceful Evolution,' 'Regime Change' and China's Political Security," *Journal of Contemporary China,* vol. 16, no. 53, pp. 717–727.

Öniş, Z. (1991). "The Logic of the Developmental State," *Comparative Politics,* vol. 24, no. 1, pp. 109–126.

Overholt, W. (1993). *The Rise of China: How Economic Reform Is Creating a New Superpower.* New York: W. W. Norton.

Pan Chengxin (2008). "'Peaceful Rise' and China's New International Contract" in L. Li (ed.), *The State in Transition: Processes and Contests in Local China.* London: Routledge, pp. 127–144.

Pang Zhongying (2005). "China's Changing Attitude to UN Peacekeeping," *International Peacekeeping,* vol. 12, no. 1, pp. 87–104.

Patey, L. (2007). "State Rules: Oil Companies and Armed Conflict in Sudan," *Third World Quarterly,* vol. 28, no. 5, pp. 997–1016.

Payne, R., and C. Veney (2001). "Taiwan and Africa: Taipei's Continuing Search for International Recognition," *Journal of Asian and African Studies,* vol. 36, no. 4, pp. 437–450.

Pearson, M. (1999). *China's New Business Elite: The Political Consequences of Economic Reform.* Los Angeles: University of California Press.

Peerenboom, R. (2005). "Assessing Human Rights in China: Why the Double Standard?" *Cornell International Law Journal,* vol. 38, no. 1, pp. 71–172.

——— (2007). *China Modernizes: Threat to the West or Model for the Rest?* Oxford: Oxford University Press.

Pham, J. (2007). "Hu's Selling Guns to Africa," *World Defense Review,* June 28, pp. 1–3.

Puska, S. (2007). "Resources, Security and Influence: The Role of the Military in China's Africa," *Strategy China Brief,* vol. 7, no. 11, pp. 2–7.

Qian Qichen (2005). *Ten Episodes in China's Diplomacy.* New York: HarperCollins.

Qin Xiaocheng (2003). "Reflections on 'Globalization' and State Sovereignty," in *International Intervention and State Sovereignty.* Beijing: China Reform Forum, pp. 153–175.

Quartey, P. (2006). "The Textiles and Clothing Industry in Ghana," in H. Jauch and R. Traub-Merz (eds.), *The Future of the Textile and Clothing Industry in Sub-Saharan Africa.* Bonn, Germany: Friedrich-Ebert-Stiftung, pp. 134–146.

Ramo, J. (2004). *The Beijing Consensus: Notes on the New Physics of Chinese Power.* London: Foreign Affairs Policy Centre.

Ramsbotham, O. (1997). "Humanitarian Intervention, 1990–5: A Need to Reconceptualize?" *Review of International Studies,* vol. 23, no. 4, pp. 445–468.

Rawnsley, G. (2006). "May You Live in Interesting Times: China, Japan and Peacekeeping," in R. Utley (ed.), *Major Powers and Peacekeeping: Perspectives, Priorities and the Challenges of Military Intervention.* London: Ashgate, pp. 81–100.

Reeves, E. (2007). *China, Darfur, and the Olympics: Tarnishing the Torch?* New York: Dream for Darfur.

Refugees International (2006). "Sudan: Oil Exploration Fueling Displacement in the South," June 14, press release.

Reno, W. (1993). "Old Brigades, Money Bags, New Breeds, and the Ironies of Reform in Nigeria," *Canadian Journal of African Studies,* vol. 27, no. 1, pp. 66–87.

——— (1998). *Warlord Politics and African States.* Boulder, CO: Lynne Rienner Publishers.

Richardson, C. (2007). "How Much Did Droughts Matter? Linking Rainfall and GDP Growth in Zimbabwe," *African Affairs,* no. 106, pp. 463–478.

Rigger, S. (2005). "Party Politics and Taiwan's External Relations," *Orbis,* vol. 49, no. 3, pp. 413–428.

Riskin, C., Renwei Zhao, and Shi Li (eds.), (2001). *China's Retreat from Equality: Income Distribution and Economic Transition.* Armonk, NY: M. E. Sharpe.

Rodney, W. (1973). *How Europe Underdeveloped Africa.* Dar-es-Salaam: Tanzanian Publishing House.

Roughneen, S. (2006). "Influence Anxiety: China's Role in Africa," *ISN Security Watch,* May 15, pp. 1–4.

Roy, D. (1998). *China's Foreign Relations.* London: Macmillan Press.

Saich, T. (2001). *Governance and Politics of China.* Basingstoke, UK: Palgrave.

Sandrey, R., D. Maleleka, A. Matlanyane, and D. Van Seventer (2006). *Lesotho: Potential Export Diversification Study.* Stellenbosch, South Africa: Trade Law Centre for Southern Africa.

Saunders, P. (2006). *China's Global Activism: Strategy, Drivers, and Tools.* Institute for National Strategic Studies Occasional Paper 4. Washington, DC: National Defense University Press.

Sautman, B. (1994). "Anti-Black Racism in Post-Mao China," *China Quarterly,* no. 138, pp. 413–437.

——— (1997). "Racial Nationalism and China's External Behavior," *World Affairs,* vol. 160, no. 2, pp. 78–96.

Sautman, B., and Yan Hairong (2007). "Friends and Interests: China's Distinctive Links with Africa," *African Studies Review,* vol. 50, no. 3, pp. 75–114.

Schnabel, A. (2002). "Post-Conflict Peacebuilding and Second-Generation Preventive Action," *International Peacekeeping*, vol. 9, no. 2, pp. 7–31.

Scobell, A. (2003). *China's Use of Military Force: Beyond the Great Wall and the Long March.* Cambridge, UK: Cambridge University Press.

Scott, D. (2007). *China Stands Up: The PRC and the International System.* London: Routledge.

Servant, J.-C. (2005). "China's Trade Safari in Africa," *Le Monde Diplomatique* (English edition), May, pp. 3–5.

Shambaugh, D. (2002a). "China's International Relations Think Tanks: Evolving Structure and Process," *China Quarterly*, no. 171, pp. 575–586.

———— (2002b). *Modernizing China's Military: Progress, Problems and Prospects.* Berkeley: University of California Press.

———— (2007). "China's 'Quiet Diplomacy': The International Department of the Chinese Communist Party," *China: An International Journal*, vol. 5, no. 1, pp. 26–54.

———— (2008). *China's Communist Party: Atrophy and Adaptation.* Berkeley, CA: University of California Press.

Sharma, H. (ed.) (2007). *Critical Perspectives on China's Economic Transformation: A "Critical Asian Studies" Roundtable on the Book 'China and Socialism' by Martin Hart-Landsberg and Paul Burkett.* New Delhi: Daanish Books.

Shaxson, N. (2007). *Poisoned Wells: The Dirty Politics of African Oil.* London: Palgrave.

Shichor, Y. (2000). "Mountains out of Molehills: Arms Transfers in Sino–Middle Eastern Relations," *Middle East Review of International Affairs*, vol. 4, no. 3, pp. 68–79.

Shieh, S. (2005). "The Rise of Collective Corruption in China: The Xiamen Smuggling Case," *Journal of Contemporary China*, vol. 14, issue 42, pp. 67–91.

Shinn, D. (2006a). "The China Factor in African Ethics," *Policy Innovations,* December 21.

———— (2006b). "Africa and China's Global Activism," paper presented at the National Defense University Pacific Symposium, "China's Global Activism: Implications for U.S. Security Interests," Fort Lesley J. McNair, June 20.

Shirk, S. (2007). *China: Fragile Superpower: How China's Internal Politics Could Derail Its Peaceful Rise.* Oxford: Oxford University Press.

Smith, D. (2007). *The Dragon and the Elephant: China, India and the New World Order.* London: Profile Books.

Snow, P. (1988). *The Star Raft: China's Encounter with Africa.* London: Weidenfeld and Nicholson.

Soares De Oliveira, R. (2007). *Oil and Politics in the Gulf of Guinea.* London: Hurst.

Solidarity Peace Trust (2007). *A Difficult Dialogue: Zimbabwe–South Africa Economic Relations Since 2000.* Port Shepstone, South Africa: Solidarity Peace Trust.

Solinger, D. (2008). "The Political Implications of China's Social Future: Complacency, Scorn and the Forlorn," in Cheng Li (ed.), *China's Changing Political Landscape: Prospects for Democracy.* Washington, DC: Brookings Institution Press, pp. 251–266.

Soyinka, W. (1996). *The Open Sore of a Continent: A Personal Narrative of the Nigerian Crisis.* New York: Oxford University Press.

Srivastava, A. (2005). *China's Export Controls: Can Beijing's Actions Match Its Words?* Washington, DC: Arms Control Association.

Staehle, S. (2006). "China's Participation in the United Nations Peacekeeping Regime," MA thesis, Elliott School of International Affairs, George Washington University.

Stockholm International Peace Research Institute (2008). *SIPRI Arms Transfers Database.* Stockholm: SIPRI.

Strange, S. (1996). *The Retreat of the State: The Diffusion of Power in the World Economy.* Cambridge, UK: Cambridge University Press.

Sullivan, M. (1999). "Developmentalism and China's Human Rights Policy," in P. Van Ness (ed.), *Debating Human Rights: Critical Essays from the United States and Asia.* New York: Routledge, pp. 120–143.

Sun Yan (2004). *Corruption and the Market in Contemporary China.* Ithaca, NY: Cornell University Press.

Sutter, R. (2008). *Chinese Foreign Relations: Power and Policy Since the Cold War.* Lanham, MD: Rowman and Littlefield.

Swaine, M. (1995). *China: Domestic Change and Foreign Policy.* Santa Monica, CA: RAND.

Swaine, M., and A. Tellis (2000). *Interpreting China's Grand Strategy: Past, Present, and Future.* Santa Monica, CA: RAND.

Sylvanus, N. (2007). "'Chinese Devils'? Perceptions of the Chinese in Lomé's Central Market," Los Angeles, CA: Globalization Research Center–Africa.

Tang, J. (2006). *With the Grain or Against the Grain? Energy Security and Chinese Foreign Policy in the Hu Jintao Era.* CNAPS Working Paper Series, October, Washington, DC: Brookings Institution Press.

Tanner, M. (2002). "Changing Windows on a Changing China: The Evolving 'Think Tank' System and the Case of the Public Security Sector," *China Quarterly,* no. 171, pp. 559–574.

Taylor, I. (1997). *China's Foreign Policy Towards Southern Africa in the 'Socialist Modernisation' Period.* East Asia Project Working Paper 18, Department of International Relations, University of the Witwatersrand.

———— (1998a). "China's Foreign Policy Towards Africa in the 1990s," *Journal of Modern African Studies,* vol. 36, no. 3, pp. 443–460.

———— (1998b). "Africa's Place in the Diplomatic Competition Between Beijing and Taipei," *Issues and Studies,* vol. 34, no. 3, pp. 126–143.

———— (2000). "The Ambiguous Commitment: The People's Republic of China and the Anti-Apartheid Struggle in South Africa," *Journal of Contemporary African Studies,* vol. 18, no. 1, pp. 91–106.

———— (2002a). "Taiwan's Foreign Policy and Africa: The Limitations of Dollar Diplomacy," *Journal of Contemporary China,* vol. 11, no. 30, pp. 125–140.

———— (2002b). "The New Partnership for Africa's Development and the Zimbabwe Elections: Implications and Prospects for the Future," *African Affairs,* vol. 101, no. 404, pp. 403–412.

———— (2004a). "The 'All-Weather Friend?' Sino-African Interaction in the Twenty-first Century," in I. Taylor and P. Williams (eds.), *Africa in International Politics: External Involvement on the Continent.* London: Routledge, pp. 83–101.

———— (2004b). "Blind Spots in Analyzing Africa's Place in World Politics," *Global Governance,* vol. 10, no. 4, pp. 411–417.

———— (2005a). "The Developmental State in Africa: The Case of Botswana," in P. Mbabazi and I. Taylor (eds.), *The Potentiality of 'Developmental States' in Africa: Botswana and Uganda Compared.* Dakar, Senegal: Codesria, pp. 44–56.

———— (2005b). *NEPAD: Towards Africa's Development or Another False Start?* Boulder, CO: Lynne Rienner Publishers.

———— (2006a). *China and Africa: Engagement and Compromise.* London: Routledge.

———— (2006b). "Challenges Facing the Commonwealth and the Millennium Development Goals in Africa," *Round Table: Commonwealth Journal of International Affairs,* vol. 95, no. 385, pp. 365–382.

———— (2006c), "China's Oil Diplomacy in Africa," *International Affairs*, vol. 82, no. 5, pp. 937–960.

———— (2007a). "China's Growth into Sub-Saharan Africa," in L. Castellani, Pang Zhongying, and I. Taylor (eds.), *China Outside China: China in Africa*. Turin, Italy: Centro di Alti Studi Sulla Cina Contemporanea, pp. 7–22.

———— (2007b). "China and Africa: The Real Barriers to Win-Win," *Foreign Policy in Focus*, March 9, pp. 1–2.

———— (2007c). "Sino-African Relations in the Twenty-First Century: Time for Dialogue," *Chinese Cross Currents*, vol. 4, no. 2, pp. 8–21.

Taylor, I., and P. Williams (2002). "The Limits of Engagement: British Foreign Policy and the Crisis in Zimbabwe," *International Affairs*, vol. 78, no. 3, pp. 547–566.

Taylor Fravel, M. (1996). "China's Attitude Toward UN Peacekeeping Operations Since 1989," *Asian Survey*, vol. 36, no. 11, pp. 1102–1121.

Teather, D., and H. Yee (eds.), (1999). *China in Transition: Issues and Policies*. London: Macmillan.

Textiles and Clothing Core Team (2006). *Textiles and Clothing Sector*. Pretoria: Advanced Manufacturing Technology Strategy.

Thakur, R. (2004). "Developing Countries and the Intervention-Sovereignty Debate," in R. Price and M. Zacher (eds.), *The United Nations and Global Security*. London: Palgrave, pp. 193–208.

Thompson, D. (2005). "Beijing's Participation in UN Peacekeeping Operations," *Jamestown Foundation China Brief*, vol. 5, no. 11, pp. 41–55.

Thompson, J.-P. (2007). "China's Crucial Role in Africa," *At Issue*, vol. 6, no. 1, pp. 1–8.

Timperlake, E., and W. Triplett (2002). *Red Dragon Rising: Communist China's Military Threat to America*. Washington, DC: Regnery Publishing.

Tjønneland, E., with B. Brandtzæg, A. Kolås, and G. le Pere (2006). *China in Africa: Implications for Norwegian Foreign and Development Policies*. Bergen, Norway: Christian Michelsen Institute.

Transparency International (2006). *Bribe Payers Index (BPI) 2006: Analysis Report*. Berlin: Transparency International.

Traub-Merz, R. (2006). "The African Textile and Clothing Industry: From Import Substitution to Export Orientation," in H. Jauch and R. Traub-Merz (eds.), *The Future of the Textile and Clothing Industry in Sub-Saharan Africa*. Bonn, Germany: Friedrich-Ebert-Stiftung, pp. 9–35.

Troush, S. (1999). *China's Changing Oil Strategy and its Foreign Policy Implications*. CNAPS Working Paper, Washington, DC: Brookings Institution Press.

Tubilewicz, C. (ed.), (2006). *Critical Issues in Contemporary China*. London: Routledge.

Tull, D. (2006). "China's Engagement in Africa: Scope, Significance and Consequences," *Journal of Modern African Studies*, vol. 44, no. 3, pp. 459–479.

Unendoro, B. (2007). "A Sense of Impunity," Institute for War and Peace Reporting, *Zimbabwe Crisis Reports*, March 16.

United Nations Department of Peacekeeping Operations (2008). "Ranking of Military and Police Contributions to UN Operations," January 31. New York: United Nations.

United Nations Secretary-General (2000), "Identical Letters Dated 21 August 2000 from the Secretary-General to the President of the General Assembly and the President of the Security Council," Press Release A/55/305–S/2000/809. New York: United Nations.

United Nations Security Council (1997). "Security Council Establishes UN Observer Mission in Angola (MONUA) Mandated to Assist Angolan Parties to Consolidated Peace," Press Release SC/6390, June 30. New York: United Nations.

——— (1999). "Security Council Extends Central African Republic Mission Until 15 November," Press Release SC/6651, February 26. New York: United Nations.

US Department of Commerce (2007). *Summary of AGOA I.* Washington, DC: US Department of Commerce.

US State Department (2007). "Top U.S. Diplomat Cites Chinese Cooperation on Darfur," Washington, DC, April 11, press release.

Van der Westhuizen, C. (2007), "The Clothing and Textile Industries in Sub-Saharan Africa: An Overview with Policy Recommendations," in G. le Pere (ed.), *China in Africa: Mercantilist Predator or Partner in Development?* Johannesburg: Institute for Global Dialogue/South African Institute of International Affairs.

Van Eeden, J. (2007). *The South African Implemented Quotas on Chinese Clothing and Textile Imports.* Stellenbosch, South Africa: Trade Law Centre for Southern Africa.

Vlok, E. (2006). "The Textile and Clothing Industry in South Africa," in H. Jauch and R. Traub-Merz (eds.), *The Future of the Textile and Clothing Industry in Sub-Saharan Africa.* Bonn, Germany: Friedrich-Ebert-Stiftung, pp. 227–246.

Waging Peace (2008). *China in Africa: The Human Rights Impact.* London: Waging Peace.

Waley-Cohen, J. (2000). *The Sextants of Beijing: Global Currents in Chinese History.* New York: W. W. Norton.

Wan Ming (2001). *Human Rights in Chinese Foreign Relations: Defining and Defending National Interests.* Philadelphia: University of Pennsylvania Press.

——— (2005). "Democracy and Human Rights in Chinese Foreign Policy," in Deng Yong and Wang Fei-ling (eds.), *China Rising: Power and Motivation in Chinese Foreign Policy.* Lanham, MD: Rowman and Littlefield, pp. 279–304.

Wang, G., and J. Wong (eds.), (2007). *Interpreting China's Development.* Singapore: World Scientific.

Wang Chaohua (ed.), (2003). *One China, Many Paths.* London: Verso.

Wang Fei-ling (2005). "Preservation, Prosperity and Power: What Motivates China's Foreign Policy?" *Journal of Contemporary China,* vol. 14, no. 45, pp. 669–694.

Wang Hongying (2000). "Multilateralism in Chinese Foreign Policy: The Limits of Socialization," *Asian Survey,* vol. 40, no. 3, pp. 475–491.

——— (2003). *China's New Order: Society, Politics and Economy in Transition.* Cambridge, MA: Harvard University Press.

——— (2007). "'Linking Up with the International Track': What's in a Slogan?" *China Quarterly,* no. 189, pp. 1–23.

Wang Jianwei (1999). "Managing Conflict: Chinese Perspectives on Multilateral Diplomacy and Collective Security," in Deng Yong and Wang Fei-ling (eds.), *In the Eyes of the Dragon: China Views the World.* Lanham, MD: Rowman and Littlefield, pp. 73–96.

Wang Jian-ye (2007). *What Drives China's Growing Role in Africa?* IMF Working Paper WP/07/211. Washington, DC: International Monetary Fund.

Wang Jifu (2007). *Chinese State-owned Enterprises: Strategic Challenges and Strategic Responses.* Oxford, UK: Chandos.

Wang Shaoguang (2003). "The Problem of State Weakness," *Journal of Democracy,* vol. 14, no. 1, pp. 36–42.

Wang Shaoguang and Hu Angang (2000). *The Political Economy of Uneven Development: The Case of China.* Armonk, NY: M. E. Sharpe.

Wang Sheng-wei (2008). *China's Ascendancy: Opportunity or a Threat?* Washington, DC: International Publishing House for China's Culture.

Wang Yiwei (2005). "China's Role in Dealing with the North Korean Nuclear Issue," *Korea Observer,* vol. 36, no. 3, pp. 465–488.

Wang Zhengyi (2004). "Conceptualizing Economic Security and Governance: China Confronts Globalization," *Pacific Review*, vol. 17, no. 4, pp. 523–545.

Weatherley, R. (1999). *The Discourse of Human Rights in China: Historical and Ideological Perspectives*. London: Macmillan.

————— (2001). "The Evolution of Chinese Thinking on Human Rights in the Post-Mao Era," *Journal of Communist Studies and Transition*, vol. 17, no. 2, pp. 19–42.

Weil, R. (1994). "Of Human Rights and Wrongs: China and the United States," *Monthly Review*, vol. 46, no. 3, pp. 101–113.

————— (1996). *Red Cat, White Cat: China and the Contradictions of "Market Socialism."* New York: Monthly Review Press.

————— (2006). "'To Be Attacked by the Enemy is a Good Thing': The Struggle Over the Legacy of Mao Zedong and the Chinese Socialist Revolution," *Socialism and Democracy*, vol. 20, no. 2, pp. 1–12.

Weinstein, H. (ed.), (1975). *Chinese and Soviet Aid to Africa*. New York: Praeger.

Weiss, T. (2003). "Contemporary Views on Humanitarian Intervention and China: 'The Responsibility to Protect,'" in *International Intervention and State Sovereignty*. Beijing: China Reform Forum, pp. 267–290.

Wheeler, N. (2000). *Saving Strangers: Humanitarian Intervention in International Society*. New York: Oxford University Press.

Wilkinson, R. (2007). "Building Asymmetry: Concluding the Doha Development Agenda," in D. Lee and R. Wilkinson, (eds.), *The WTO After Hong Kong: Progress in and Prospects for the Doha Development Agenda*. London: Routledge, pp. 248–261.

Williams, M., Kong Yuk-Choi, and Yan Shen (2002). "Bonanza or Mirage? Textiles and China's Accession to the WTO," *Journal of World Trade*, vol. 36, no. 3, pp. 98–113.

Wilson, E. (2006). "Testimony to China's Role in the World: Is China a Responsible Stakeholder in Africa?" *Hearing Before the U.S.-China Economic and Security Review Commission*, August 3–4.

Woo-Cumings, M. (ed.), (1999). *The Developmental State*. Ithaca, NY: Cornell University.

Wood, G. (2004). "Business and Politics in a Criminal State: The Case of Equatorial Guinea," *African Affairs*, vol. 103, no. 413, pp. 547–567.

World Trade Organization (2005). *International Trade Statistics*. Geneva: WTO.

Wright, C. (1997). "Ethics in the Petrochemical Industry," *Business Ethics: A European Review*, vol. 6, no. 1, pp. 52–57.

Wright, L. (2001). "Seizing an Opportunity: The Changing Character of Chinese Arms Sales to Africa," *Armed Forces Journal International*, no. 139, pp. 92–95.

Wright, T. (2007). "State Capacity in Contemporary China: 'Closing the Pits and Reducing Coal Production,'" *Journal of Contemporary China*, vol. 16, no. 5, pp. 173–194.

Wu Guoguang (2005). *Anatomy of Political Power in China: Regime Operation, Political Transformation, and Foreign Relations*. Singapore: Times Academic Press.

Wu Yanrui (2003). *China's Economic Growth: A Miracle with Chinese Characteristics*. London: Routledge.

Xia Liping (2001). "China: A Responsible Great Power," *Journal of Contemporary China*, vol. 10, no. 26, pp. 17–25.

Xiao Gongqin (2003). "The Kosovo Crisis and the Nationalism of Twenty-First-Century China," *Contemporary Chinese Thought*, vol. 35, no. 1, pp. 21–48.

Xin Ma, and P. Andrews-Speed (2006). "The Overseas Activities of China's National Oil Companies: Rationale and Outlook," *Minerals and Energy*, vol. 1, pp. 1–8.

Yan Xuetong (2006). "The Rise of China and Its Power Status," *Chinese Journal of International Politics,* vol. 1, no. 1, pp. 5–33.

Yao Yuangming (2006). "China's Oil Strategy and Its Implications for US-China Relations," *Issues and Studies,* vol. 42, no. 3, pp. 165–201.

Yates, D. (1996). *The Rentier State in Africa: Oil, Rent Dependency and Neocolonialism in the Republic of Gabon.* Trenton, NJ: Africa World Press.

Yee Sienho (2008). "Towards a Harmonious World: The Roles of the International Law of Co-Progressiveness and Leader States," *Chinese Journal of International Law,* vol. 7, no. 1, pp. 99–105.

Youde, J. (2007). "Why Look East? Zimbabwean Foreign Policy and China," *Africa Today,* vol. 53, no. 3, pp. 3–19.

Young, O. (1967). *The Intermediaries: Third Parties in International Crises.* Princeton, NJ: Princeton University Press.

Yu, G. (1970). *China and Tanzania: A Study in Co-operation.* Berkeley: University of California.

——— (1975). *China's African Policy: A Study of Tanzania.* New York: Praeger.

Zafar, A. (2007). "The Growing Relationship Between China and Sub-Saharan Africa: Macroeconomic, Trade, Investment, and Aid Links," *World Bank Research Observer,* vol. 22, no. 1, pp. 103–130.

Zha Daojiong (1999). "Chinese Considerations of 'Economic Security,'" *Journal of Chinese Political Science,* vol. 5, no. 1, pp. 69–87.

——— (2005a). "Comment: Can China Rise?" *Review of International Studies,* vol. 31, no. 4, pp. 775–785.

——— (2005b). "China's Energy Security and Its International Relations," *China and Eurasia Forum Quarterly,* vol. 3, no. 3, pp. 39–54.

——— (2006). "China's Energy Security: Domestic and International Issues," *Survival,* vol. 48, no. 1, pp. 179-190.

Zha Daojiong, and W. Hu (2007). "Promoting Energy Partnership in Beijing and Washington," *Washington Quarterly,* vol. 30, no. 4, pp. 105–115.

Zhang Jianjun (2008). "State Power, Elite Relations, and the Politics of Privatization in China's Rural Industry: Different Approaches in Two Regions." *Asian Survey,* vol. 48, no. 2, pp. 215–238.

Zhang Li (2003). "Some Reflections on International Intervention," in *International Intervention and State Sovereignty.* Beijing: China Reform Forum, pp. 200–226.

Zhang Yongjin (1998). *China in International Society Since 1949: Alienation and Beyond.* Oxford: St. Martin's Press.

——— (2005). *China Goes Global.* London: Foreign Policy Centre.

Zhao Dingxin (2002). "An Angle on Nationalism in China Today: Attitudes Among Beijing Students After Belgrade 1999," *China Quarterly,* no. 172, pp. 885–905.

Zhao Quansheng (1996). *Interpreting Chinese Foreign Policy: The Micro-Macro Linkage Approach.* Oxford: Oxford University Press.

——— (2005). "Impact of Intellectuals and Think Tanks on Chinese Foreign Policy," in Hao Yufan and Su Lin (eds.), *China's Foreign Policy Making: Societal Force and Chinese American Policy.* Burlington, VT: Ashgate, pp. 123–139.

——— (2006). "Epistemic Community, Intellectuals, and Chinese Foreign Policy," *Policy and Society,* vol. 25, no. 1, pp. 39–59.

Zheng Bijian (2005). "China's 'Peaceful Rise' to Great Power Status," *Foreign Affairs,* vol. 84, no. 5, pp. 18–24.

Zheng Shiping (2003). "Leadership Change, Legitimacy, and Party Transition in China," *Journal of Chinese Political Science,* vol. 8, nos. 1–2, pp. 47–63.

Zheng Yongnian (1999). *Discovering Chinese Nationalism in China: Modernization, Identity, and International Relations.* Cambridge, UK: Cambridge University Press.

——— (2004). *Globalization and State Transformation in China.* Cambridge, UK: Cambridge University Press.

Zhong Lianyan (2007). *International Relations of the Communist Party of China.* Beijing: China Intercontinental Press.

Zweig, D. (2002). *Internationalizing China: Domestic Interests and Global Linkages.* Ithaca, NY: Cornell University Press.

——— (2007). *"Resource Diplomacy" Under Hegemony: The Sources of Sino-American Competition in the 21st Century?* Hong Kong: Center on China's Transnational Relations Working Paper No. 18, Hong Kong University of Science and Technology.

Zweig, D., and Bi Jianhai (2005). "China's Global Hunt for Energy," *Foreign Affairs,* vol. 84, no. 5, pp. 25–38.

Index

About the Book

Although China denies that it harbors ambitions to become a superpower, its leadership has made clear its intention that the country be a major player in the global arena. Against this backdrop, Ian Taylor explores the nature and implications of China's burgeoning role in Africa.

Taylor argues that Beijing is using Africa not only as a source of needed raw materials and potential new markets, but also to bolster its own position on the international stage. After tracing the history of Sino-African relations, he addresses key current issues: What will be the long-term consequences, for example, of China's successes in securing access to the continent's oil? How will cheap Chinese imports affect Africa's manufacturing base? What has been the impact of China's arms sales to Africa?

Based on extensive field research in both China and across Africa, *China's New Role in Africa* is a major contribution to illuminating a little-known, but increasingly important, relationship.

Ian Taylor is professor in the School of International Relations at the University of St. Andrews. His recent publications include *Nepad: Toward Africa's Development or Another False Start?*